The Theatre Book of the Year

1942 ❦ 1943

The Theatre Books of George Jean Nathan

The THEATRE Book

OF THE YEAR

1942 ✦ 1943

A Record and an Interpretation

B Y

GEORGE JEAN NATHAN

New Introduction by Charles Angoff

Rutherford • Madison • Teaneck
Fairleigh Dickinson University Press

Library of Congress Catalogue Card Number: 75-120099

Reprinted 1971

Associated University Presses, Inc.
Cranbury, New Jersey 08512

ISBN 0-8386-7946-3
Printed in the United States of America

Introduction
By CHARLES ANGOFF

With *The Theatre Book of the Year, 1942–1943*, George Jean Nathan inaugurated a series of volumes that continued for a decade and that will undoubtedly be invaluable to future historians of the American theatre. That Nathan was a superb critic needs no confirmation at this late date, but that, both wittingly and unwittingly, he was also a first-rate historian, is not so well known. His present volume is subtitled "A Record and an Interpretation." There were other such records in his day, as there are now. But Nathan's is different. His record is filled with trenchant, fearless commentary, and it is enriched with a scholarship that spanned the whole range of world dramatic history. Nathan never ceased to relate a play he was reviewing to other American plays dealing with the same theme, but he also related it to relevant plays in other lands at all times. A Nathan review was more than a mere report; it was an essay brimming with philosophy, vast knowledge, good humor, and extraordinarily alive writing.

The year, 1942–1943, in the United States, Nathan tells us, was far from an illustrious one. There was no new O'Neill play, no new Robert Sherwood play, and no new plays by Paul Green, Elmer Rice, Marc Connelly, Lillian Hellman, or George Kelly. What is probably more deplorable, there were no fresh talents on view. And some of the old hands, such as Maxwell Anderson and Philip Barry, and Thornton Wilder, had come forth with, to put it gently, inferior works. Says Nathan, "The year on the whole was . . . deficient in drama of real standing." Still, he does give an accolade of sorts to Sidney Kingsley's "The Patriots," William Saroyan's "Hello Out There," Elena Miramova and Eugenie Leontovitch's "Dark Eyes," and Irving Berlin's "This is the Army." It was also a year of no noteworthy foreign plays: "The foreign showing was dismal, consisting of English and Russian war plays that amounted to little more than propaganda self-handshakings."

Whether one agrees with Nathan is not of paramount importance. The man was always stimulating and fascinating to read. It was virtually impossible for him to be boring. He piles insight upon insight, he insults with such deftness that one cannot help admiring his rapier skill, and always he documents his judgements with an overwhelming display of learning. Of the numerous war plays at the time he said, "Let us be patriots all, surely, but let those of us whose job is dramatic criticism not confuse it with the job of flying a bomber over Berlin." He takes most of his colleagues to task for daring to offer extensive comments upon the Yiddish play, "Oy, is Dus a Leben," about Molly Picon. He begins by admitting he doesn't know a word of Yiddish, and then ridicules the silliness of those who wrote "knowingly" about the play: "Yiddish scholar Richard Lockridge . . . Yiddish authority Wilella Waldorf . . . Yiddish expert John Mason Brown . . . Yiddish humor scholar Burns Mantle . . . Yiddish solon Joseph Pihodna . . . Yiddish luminary Robert Coleman . . . Yiddish medallist Brooks Atkinson." Nathan's onslaught upon the *chutzpah* of these pretenders is so devastating as to be almost cruel.

Nathan had long been an admirer of the playwright S. N. Behrman and the actors Lynn Fontanne and Alfred Lunt, but when Behrman came up with a poor play, "The Pirate," he labeled it for what it was, and he took occasion to tell the whole truth, as he saw it, about the two actors: "That there may be more talented actors it is true; but when it comes to squirting bright color into a stage they have few peers."

In short, we have in *The Theatre Book of the Year, 1942–1943*, another work of enduring dramatic criticism by a man who knew the theatre as probably no other American to date has known it, yet who loved it so passionately that he had no hesitation in telling the truth, the whole truth, and nothing but the truth about it.

Fairleigh Dickinson University
Rutherford, New Jersey

Foreword

THE PRESENT VOLUME, should it prove acceptable to the public, is the first of a projected series whose aim is a statistical record and critical interpretation of the plays produced annually in the American theatre. In that critical interpretation, which in turn aims generally to relate the immediate exhibits to the theatre and drama past, present, and possibly immediate future, lies the project's difference from other current records.

It may be gathered by some that the book is constituted merely of reprints of its author's casual play reviews. This is not the case. There are included some such reviews, though all carefully checked, revised, and here and there considerably elaborated, but only in those instances where the opinion has seemed of some relative permanence, where there has been no call showily to express the same thought in different phrases, and where the point of view guarantees the underlying interpretative design of the book.

The plays are arranged in chronological order and provide a complete seasonal record. If perchance several contradictions may appear in the way of critical consideration, they are the contradictions less of criticism than those whimsically imposed upon it by the eccentricities of a changing theatre, ever the most cynical enemy of critical didacticism.

The outstanding characteristics of the year were the multiplicity of plays dealing with the war, the continued imitative production of plays dealing with adolescents, the attempt to revive vaudeville, the production of but a single Shakespearean play, and the noticeable great increase of popular interest in the theatre, both in New York and on the road. Of the established American playwrights, there was no representation by Eugene O'Neill, who, though he has completed several new plays, has preferred to withhold them until he personally can supervise their production; Robert Sherwood, who was in the service of the government; Paul Green, Elmer Rice, Marc Connelly, George Kaufman, Clifford Odets, Lillian Hellman, and George Kelly, among others. Of those who were in evidence, Sidney Kingsley distinguished himself with an historical-biographical play that had numerous points of merit; S. N. Behrman lazily contented himself with a paraphrase of an old German comedy; Maxwell Anderson appeared with a war play at least gratefully free from his usual self-indulgence in overstuffed verse; Saroyan, after two negligible little plays, demonstrated in his all too brief and excellent *Hello Out There* that he is as successful in the more conventional dramatic form as in the bizarre; and Philip Barry, manufacturing still another comedy vehicle for the box-office Katharine Hepburn, again got critically nowhere.

As for others, Thornton Wilder was represented by a fantasy that was proclaimed the acme of originality until it was discovered that he had borrowed heavily for his inspiration from a little-known work of James Joyce's; John Van Druten delivered a romantic comedy in collaboration with Lloyd Morris that, while smoothly written as is his wont, was fundamentally lacking; and the Messrs. Lindsay and Crouse, who were responsible for the large success of the dramatization of the Day family chronicles, *Life with Father,* earned no respect with a cheap mixture of burlesque and sentiment called *Strip for Action.*

Although the year on the whole was thus deficient in drama of real standing, it offered its share of happy rough humor. Such farce-comedies as *The Doughgirls, Dark Eyes,* and *Kiss and Tell* provided their own kind of light holiday and gratified a public surfeited with loud bombing effects masquerading as important war documents. This was also true in the instance of several above-the-average musical shows like *Star and Garter, Something for the Boys,* and *Oklahoma!*

Foreword

The foreign showing was dismal, consisting chiefly of English and Russian war plays that amounted to little more than propaganda self-handshakings.

One item in conclusion. The season witnessed again the threat of theatrical censorship in the suppression by court action — following moralist hounding — of the show called *Wine, Women and Song*. Only the quick resolve of certain other producers to modify elements in several of their exhibits forestalled additional forced closings. The producers of *Native Son*, aided by sympathetic and resolute colleagues, alone refused to be frightened, fought it out on the line, and drove the censors to ignominious cover.

In the pages that follow, these and all other aspects of the year duly unfold themselves.

Contents

The Theatre Book of the Year

1942 ❧ 1943

Honor List

THE BEST FULL-LENGTH AMERICAN PLAY:
  THE PATRIOTS, by Sidney Kingsley

THE BEST SHORT AMERICAN PLAY:
  HELLO OUT THERE, by William Saroyan

THE BEST FOREIGN PLAY:
  None worthy of even relative record

THE BEST FARCE-COMEDY:
  DARK EYES, by Elena Miramova and
                    Eugenie Leontovitch

THE BEST MUSICAL SHOW:
  THIS IS THE ARMY, by Irving Berlin

THE BEST DRAMATIC REVIVAL:
  Chekhov's THE THREE SISTERS, by the
  Guthrie McClintic-Katharine Cornell company

THE BEST MALE ACTING PERFORMANCE:
  CECIL HUMPHREYS, in *The Patriots*

THE BEST FEMALE ACTING PERFORMANCE:
  HELEN HAYES, in *Harriet*

THE BEST STAGE DIRECTOR:
  ELIA KAZAN (*The Skin of Our Teeth*)

THE BEST SCENE DESIGNER:
  LEMUEL AYRES (*The Pirate*)

THE BEST COSTUME DESIGNER:
  MILES WHITE (*The Pirate*)

THE BEST STAGE LIGHTING:
  FREDERICK FOX (*Men in Shadow*)

The Year's Productions

BY JUPITER. JUNE 3, 1942.

A musical comedy by Richard Rodgers and Lorenz Hart based on Julian F. Thompson's comedy, The Warrior's Husband, *remembered chiefly for its revelation of the young Katharine Hepburn in approximate puris naturalibus and, figuratively speaking, sensational. Produced by Dwight Deere Wiman and Richard Rodgers in association with Richard Kollmar.*

PROGRAM

ACHILLES	*Bob Douglas*	ANTIOPE	*Constance Moore*
AGAMEMNON	*Robert Hightower*	A HUNTRESS	*Helen Bennett*
BURIA	*Jayne Manners*	AN AMAZON DANCER	*Flower Hujer*
SERGEANT	*Monica Moore*	THESEUS	*Ronald Graham*
CAUSTICA	*Maidel Turner*	HOMER	*Berni Gould*
HEROICA	*Margaret Bannerman*	MINERVA	*Vera-Ellen*
POMPOSIA	*Bertha Belmore*	HERCULES	*Ralph Dumke*
HIPPOLYTA	*Benay Venuta*	PENELOPE	*Irene Corlett*
SAPIENS	*Ray Bolger*		

SYNOPSIS: Act I. Scene 1. A Greek camp, a week's march from Pontus. Scene 2. A terrace of Hippolyta's palace in Pontus, two days later. Act II. Scene 1. Before Hippolyta's tent, afternoon, a week later. Scene 2. The Greek camp, the same night. Scene 3. Inside Theseus' tent, immediately thereafter.

FOR FORTY YEARS one of the standbys of the burlesque shows was the episode involving a statuesque blonde and an effeminate comedian. It usually ran about ten minutes. In this case we engaged it again, the only difference being that it ran about two hours and a quarter and that the scene, instead of being the familiar beach at Monte Carlo, was ancient Greece. In place of Mrs. Gotrox it was Hippolyta the Amazon, and in place of Percy it was Sapiens. The joke, after the old ten minutes, became increasingly feebler dur-

ing the additional one hundred and twenty-five. A few of
Rodgers' tunes helped periodically to ease the acuteness of
the situation, which is more than could be said for the ladies
of the ensemble. A less attractive congress had not been
assembled on one stage since the occasion of *Broadway
Nights,* on July 15, 1929.

The success of the exhibit, however, indicated a still further collapse of the legend that a good-looking chorus is
one of the principal assets of a musical show. Of all the
many such prosperous entertainments produced in the New
York theatre during the last half-dozen years, three and only
three have disclosed any girls with anything at all in the
way of looks above the average: *Louisiana Purchase, Boys
and Girls Together* and *Let's Face It,* and the second-
named, at that, having recourse to some especially hired
professional models to provide relief from the chorus-line
puttyfaces and steinwaylegs. The girls in one of the outstanding successes, *Best Foot Forward,* though youngsters,
were, with a single exception, of a pulchritude level hardly
higher than that encountered among Childs waitresses or
society débutantes. *Hellzapoppin,* the biggest success in
American musical-show history, offered not so much as one
girl who wouldn't have frightened a rookie policeman. And
the same with its sequel, *Sons o' Fun. Panama Hattie,* a
gold mine, had a pair in the chorus who could get by if
the shade on the parlor lamp were thick enough; *Cabin in
the Sky* vouchsafed two chocolates who were not half-bad;
Pal Joey hadn't even one maiden to fluster the connoisseur. In the season before the one directly under consideration, in point of fact only the before mentioned *Let's Face
It,* among all the successes, presented a chorus that could
be surveyed on the whole without the acquisition of puru-
lent conjunctivitis.

The truth seems to be that the simon-pure girl-show is
largely a thing of the past and that its place in the public
affection has been taken either by the comedian show or by
the plot song-and-dance show like *Oklahoma!,* irrespective
of the personal attractiveness of the girls in it. The girls in
themselves are no longer enough, as Earl Carroll some time

ago discovered when he returned to town with enough peachblossoms to have satisfied two or three old Ziegfeld *Follies* but with, unfortunately, nothing else. A single Bobby Clark or Ray Bolger or Ethel Merman today draws more trade than any returned-to-earth enchanting George Lederer chorus possibly could, and Ethel Waters singing "Taking a Chance on Love," the while a quorum of spindle-shanked pickaninnies kick themselves into a frenzy, galvanizes a house to an even greater degree than the Bonnie Maginns, Edna Chases, Vera Maxwells, and Kay Laurells used to.

A second, subsidiary critical delusion in regard to musical shows is that there is something exceptionally stimulating and overwhelmingly engaging about youth. (*Vide* all save two of the reviewers' testimonials to *Best Foot Forward,* with its cast made up almost entirely of girls and boys who had not yet reached the age of twenty.) While I am perfectly willing to agree that youth is in some cases refreshing and in some others even more, it can nevertheless be swallowed only in homeopathic doses. A lot of youth in one big dose is pretty trying as, at the other extreme, a lot of old age in single assembly is. A whole stageful of it conducting itself for two uninterrupted hours after the forbiddingly effervescent pattern is rather more than one can calmly take. One's feeling under the circumstances is inclined to be much of a piece with that induced by being compelled to bounce up and down for a couple of hours on a gymnasium electric horse the while an attendant ceaselessly keeps shouting the "Maine Stein Song" into one's ear.

Too much youth, in short, is a bore, since youth lacks variety and has little to fall back upon but animal spirits, which are an even greater bore. In all the musical shows of the last ten years there has been only one youngster in her teens whose youth was a critical asset rather than a liability: Grace McDonald in *Babes in Arms.* And only one boy in his teens: Gil Stratton, Jr., in this *Best Foot Forward.* And it is the same with the dramatic stage. The only young girl who in the same period of time has combined her seventeen years with comfortable charm was Betsy Blair in *The Beautiful People*. And the only boy, Eddie Bracken in *So Proudly We Hail*. As for me, in the case of all the others, I generally much prefer my stage youth to be played in musicals by girls of twenty-three or twenty-four like Marcy Wescott or Nanette Fabray and in drama by girls of twenty-five or twenty-six like Dorothy McGuire. And so with the boys.

A third supplementary delusion, and one that has persisted longer than the oldest sitter around the stove can remember, is that the girls in the front line of a chorus are always and invariably better-looking than those in the second line. It may have been true once upon a time, but if it is true any longer someone has deceived me on the quality of my opera-glasses. It has come to be the practice of producers and their directors to fill the first line with the better dancers and singers and it is often the regrettable case that the better dancers and singers are not blessed with the looks of the girls somewhat less skillful. These latter are accordingly relegated to the second or third row and it is thus that in these rear rows the alert eye detects the real or at least approximate dandies, if any. The only even remotely attractive girl in the entire youthful chorus of *Best Foot Forward* was a slim, dark little thing hidden away in the second line behind the front line of agile polypi.

But if the girls in *By Jupiter* were hardly of the species to make one oblivious of the weakness of the book, the humor was correspondingly successful in making one conscious of it. Such inversions as references to the ribald stories of traveling salesladies, swearing like a longshorewoman, and conducting oneself like a man of the streets, not to mention such lines as "What do the Greeks do?" — "I hear they run restaurants," would surely require the combined accessory efforts of Arthur Sullivan, Flagstad, Mordkin, Pavlova, and once again Katharine Hepburn in her birthday clothes to preserve one in one's seat.

THE CAT SCREAMS. JUNE 16, 1942

A mystery melodrama by Basil Beyea based on a novel of the same beaux-arts title by Todd Downing, apparently sold mainly in drugstores and hence unknown to this fit commentator. Produced by Martha Hodge.

PROGRAM

CONSUELO	*Cecilia Callejo*	MADAME	*Lea Penman*
PROFESSOR PARKHAM		CARL PARKHAM	*Gordon Oliver*
	Herbert Yost	MICAELA	*Osceola Archer*
GWEN REID	*Doris Nolan*	OLIVER REID	*Harry Sheppard*
MISS GIDDON	*Mildred Dunnock*	DOCTOR OTERO	*Martin Wolfson*
STEVEN TYBALT	*Lloyd Gough*		

SYNOPSIS: Act I. Scene 1. *Night.* Scene 2. *Two weeks later, noon.* Act. II. Scene 1. *The following night.* Scene 2. *The same, a few hours before dawn.* Act III. *A short time later.*

The action takes place in the lounge of a pension in La Jorta, Mexico.

THE MAJORITY of these mystery plays with their disappointing last-minute solutions are like sitting nervously around for two hours waiting for a telephone call from one's best girl and then at long length suddenly hearing the bell ring, jumping up eagerly to answer it, and finding that it is her mother. This was no exception. After an evening complexly devoted to exotic suicides and murders and involving everything from cats sinisterly whispered to be the reincarnations of Eli Shonbrun and Madeline Webb to Mexicans even more forebodingly hinted to be possessed of the diabolical powers of Aztec bloodsuckers, the explanation of the criminal secret suggested that the author had written two plays simultaneously and had accidentally tacked it onto the wrong one.

As with a number of such plays, a frankly farcical treatment of the materials might have been much more successful, since it is difficult legitimately to persuade an audience that more than two corpses in a single play are not funny and since in this one there were almost as many on and off stage as in *Arsenic and Old Lace*. The truth of this was attested to when one of the female characters soberly remarked: "I'm glad it's almost over with; the strain is too great!" and when the audience thereupon rewarded her with loud sardonic applause. The play was further invalidated by the author's periodic attempt to intellectualize it and thus give it a surface air of being more important than it was or even in the hands of Immanuel Kant possibly could have been. Several of the other lines, as, for example, the old professor's reply to a sneering criticism of one of the characters: "He doesn't like children and dogs: he can't really be so bad," were fair enough. Several of the devices, as, for example, the suspensive opening of a murdered man's last note, which was expected to provide the clue to the murders and which read in effect: "I know who has done all this and more. I have known for some time, but if you think you are going to learn from me, to hell with you!" — several of such tricks were also acceptable enough. But when it was all over, the heavily calculated chills were found to have been induced considerably less by the mystery melodrama itself than by the over-zealous summer cooling system in the Martin Beck Theatre. And the exhibit lasted, accordingly, for just seven performances, to an estimated financial loss of fifteen thousand dollars.

One of the playwright's dramaturgical errors, it may be profitably noted, was his exaggerated solicitude in abiding by the old principle that if you stimulate an audience's curiosity you must invariably satisfy it. One of these plays' most successful devices consists, on the contrary, in arousing an audience's keen expectation that something is going to happen and then never allowing it to happen. The opposite, as suggested, is unanimously held to be true and has been held to be true since the theatre's very beginning; to wit, as the parroted phrase goes: a playwright must above all never under any circumstances disappoint an audience. Yet, like so many other things confidently announced by the pundits, it isn't so. The audiences at the exceptionally successful thriller *Angel Street* were led by the dramatist throughout the evening to expect someone imminently to appear on the eerily lighted staircase in the house of murder, yet at the end of the play no one had appeared and the resident impression was twice as thrilling and dramatically twice as satisfying. In *Family Portrait,* the drama about the family of Christ, the audiences were made to anticipate the entrance of Jesus at various points during the course of the play, but He never appeared, and again the effect was perfect. There are any number of other such cases and they prove once again that the more the professors insist you cannot do a certain thing in drama, the more you may be sure you not only can do it but can get away with it handsomely.

Another point: In the reviews of the exhibit, one observed again the critics' adherence to the irrational punctilio in elaborately refusing to give away the solution to the plot. It is the frequent custom of authors of this species of play to insert in the program a request that the reviewers not tip off the explanation of the murder mystery "lest the enjoyment of future audiences be impaired." Aside from seeming to take the enjoyment of such future audiences, along with the audiences themselves, for granted, any such request is unwarranted and quite presumptuous, particularly when the murder-mystery play in point is a poor one, which four times out of five it is. If the play is really ingenious and in its field meritorious, I am perfectly willing to string along with the playwright or producer and keep the secret for him, but when the play is neither and largely fraudulent it amounts to a critical swindling of future audiences to conceal the silly plot hocus from them.

Just why the writers of murder-mystery plays consider themselves apart from and above the writers of other kinds of plays in this respect I can't make out. No other playwright requests of a critic that he not tell the how and why of his plot solution, whether the play be tricky in its nature or not or whether it be a good play or a poor one. It is the uniform custom of the great majority of reviewers, as every theatregoer knows, to describe all the ins and outs of play plots, and it has always been their custom. Thus a bad play will be ridiculed out of future audiences' respect and patronage not only by a literal recital of its plot and its plot's final maneuverings but by a lot of very relevant and appropriate twitting of that plot. We accordingly get the critical beans spilled in waggish loads when inferior playwrights seek a thematic out for their characters in dubious suicides, equally dubious marriages, even more dubious self-exiles to ranches, and other such bald subterfuges. Let us reserve the same treatment for the writers of inferior mystery plays.

When a playwright laboriously builds up a mystery murder and then cheats audiences with an explanation far from logical and swallowable, why keep the news from future audiences and why, by keeping it from them, imagine that their hypothetical enjoyment will be less hypothetical? If O'Neill, Behrman, Sherwood, and other such dramatists do not complain when criticism may now and again betray the fact that their solutions of their characters' problems are faulty and when it duly sets forth those solutions in cold print, why should the writers of childish puzzle shows? Yet if a reviewer lets the frowziest cat out of the bag in the instance of the latter's exhibits, they in turn let out an injured yell that can be heard as far away as Baker Street and the Rue Morgue.

LAUGH, TOWN, LAUGH. June 22, 1942

Another in the series of hopeful vaudeville pulmotors, this one sponsored by the eminent funny-hat virtuoso Ed Wynn. Produced by M. Wynn.

PROGRAM

MASTER OF CEREMONIES *Ed Wynn*	GYPSY FLAMENCO DANCER *Carmen Amaya*
TRAPEZE PERFORMERS *The Herzogs*	ACROBATS *Hermanos Williams Trio*
VOLGA SINGERS *Nicholas Vasilieff and Co.*	BADMINTON EXHIBITION PLAYERS *Davidson and Forgie*
VENTRILOQUIST *Señor Wences*	COMEDY ACT *Smith and Dale*
BLUES SINGER *Jane Froman*	DOG ACT *Hector and Pals*

THE PROGRAM COMBINES sufficient information with automatic criticism. For such persons as still relish female trapeze performers, including the inevitable one who esteems herself a comedy scream; glue-faced Russians moaning the "Volga Boatmen's Song"; ventriloquists who twirl plates on long rods the while their dummies squealingly profess to be fearful that the plates will fall off and hit them; female blues singers so vain of their vocal gifts that they render Broadway juke-box songs as if they were operas by Wagner; flamenco dancers, however good, with ferocious scowls, clattering heels that give off the din of a bombing raid on Barcelona, and cataracts of brunette perspiration; equilibrists who indicate their versatility by breaking periodically into what they imagine is song; and any kind of dog act if only it contains a cute puppy that can stand on its hind legs — for these the show was undoubtedly everything that could be desired. For others, only the expertly droll Wynn and the rare old team of Smith and Dale in their celebrated *Dr. Kronkheit* skit made amends.

The aforesaid skit remains, after countless years, one of the low-comedy masterpieces of the American stage. Revolving about a doctor's consulting-room, it presents one of the comedians as the medico in charge and the other as a patient. The latter enters, inquires if this is the doctor's insulting-room, and forthwith demands to know of the doc what is the matter with him. The doc, vouchsafing a quick glance at him, promptly launches into a lengthy description of his various horrendous ailments. "I'm dubious," allows the patient. The doc grabs his hand and shakes it cordially. "Glad to meet you, Mr. Dubious," he beams. He thereupon seizes a stethoscope and applies it to the visitor's bosom. "What are you doing?" demands the latter. "I'm making a Diogenes," replies the doc. The patient takes a deep breath and discharges it so violently that the doc is knocked off his feet. "What are your other symptoms?" the doc subsequently inquires. "I don't know," doubtfully responds the patient, "but every time I eat a heavy meal I don't feel so hungry."

And so on. It's wonderful! Not only audiences but even the sourest professional critics have been unable to resist it after all of twenty-five years. And it persists as one of the champion laugh exhibits in American show business.

The history of that eccentric business discloses various other comedy acts whose longevity remains the wonder and awe — and the acute envy — of present-day showmen. For example:

The curtain went up and disclosed a couple of dilapidated old shanties. An Irish comedian entered, looked around him quizzically, and said he thought he "smelled a mushrat," whereupon issued forth a Dutch comedian. They sat down at a table and the Irish comedian put his feet on it, whereat the Dutch comedian commanded him to take them off and "give the Limburger a chance." Followed a colloquy on the Dutch comedian's newborn son, during which the Irish comedian idly passed a remark that the baby resembled *him*. This brought on a gala rough-and-tumble fight, the star feature of which was a fifteen-minute throwing of dozens of dead cats at each other.

The name of the sketch was *Krausmeyer's Alley;* it brought Billy Watson, the burlesque comic, to fame; it played all over America to audiences who laughed their heads off at it; and it ran not merely for twenty-five but for all of thirty-one years. It never failed, and it ranks as one of the top all-time laugh-getters in the record of the native stage.

More than twenty-five years ago a man in the tattered clothes of a hobo one night came out on a vaudeville stage trundling a hand-me-down bicycle. He mounted it and the handlebars fell off, dejecting him on his rear. Gathering himself together, the tramp drew a whiskbroom from his pocket and, with the elaborate meticulousness of a Brummell's valet, flicked the dust from his already filthy rags. The audience yelled.

The bum remounted his bicycle and the pedals and one wheel fell off, again landing him on his posterior. And again came forth the whiskbroom and again delicately he brushed off his shredded vestments. The audience yelled louder.

This business was repeated until all that was left of the bicycle was half its frame and the pedestrian-warning little bell and all that was left of the bum's clothes was his underwear, and throughout it the audience's mirth continued apace. The act played to roaring customers all over the country — incidentally, all over Europe too — for more than a quarter of a century; it was, indeed, until recently still playing to customers who could hardly restrain themselves from falling into the aisles; and it made all kinds of money for the late illustrious Mr. Joe Jackson.

The most prosperous laugh-getter of all times is, of course, the farce *Charley's Aunt,* which has now been running successfully all over the world for fifty years and which will in all probability go on running for at least another fifty. Its chief comic asset is a comedian who dons woman's dress in order to help out a couple of college chums who are in trouble and whose masquerade brings on a succession of uproarious embarrassments, among them the conviction of the girls that he is really a sweet old lady and their consequent confiding to him of their intimate problems. Apparently so irresistible are the humors of the exhibit that

when it was shown in New York again season before last
— it has been shown in New York time and again — it ran
for no less than two hundred and thirty-three performances.

Produced originally in 1892 in London, where it played
for years, it came to America in the following year and ran
for three successive years. It was subsequently revived and
ran for another two years. And since then, as noted, it has
had audiences here and in other parts of the globe in
stitches.

Long years ago there came into the field of entertainment a couple of blackface comedians who billed themselves as *The Georgia Minstrels*. Their main comedy act
was based on a consuming hunger. Always stranded in a
livery stable without a cent to assuage their enormous ap-
petites, the one would tell the other of a geographical locality not far away to which they would one day make a
pilgrimage and richly satisfy their palates, gratis. The locality, it appeared, had vines on which pretzels grew in pro-
fusion, trees blooming with luscious Virginia hams, swamps
full of fried sweet potatoes, and streams running with un-
believably delicious schnapps. As for watermelons, they
were so thick on the ground that one had to walk half a
mile around the spot not to tumble over them and break
a leg; and as for fried chicken — but by this time the
smaller blackface comedian had fainted.

McIntyre and Heath were the boys who became famous
in that one and who enchanted audiences with it season
after long season.

Not less auspicious in gathering in audiences' money in
return for guffaws has been the act known as *Withers' Op'ry
House,* presided over for more years than one can remember by Charles Withers in the makeup of an old 'way-down-
east Yankee. For æsthetes given to an admiration of slapstick humors, Charlie's act is what is described in the higher
artistic circles as the nuts. When it comes to slapstick,
Charlie has left out nothing. If a shower of flour isn't de-
scending upon him and making him look like the entire
cast of *Men in White,* it's a paper snowstorm that buries

him under it, and if it isn't a paper snowstorm it's a half ton of coal or a bucket of paste. The act is a one-man *Hellzapoppin*, and how Charlie has outlived its rigors all these many years is one of the phenomena of the trade.

For twenty-five years a burlesque trio composed of Watson (not the aforementioned Billy), Bickel, and Wrothe delighted the nation with a number called *Me, Him and I*. Bickel was the Dutch comedian, Watson the tramp, and Wrothe the stooge who stood at a distance silently admiring the twain in wide-eyed wonder. Bickel had a miniature fiddle which he would laboriously tune up for fully ten minutes and which he would then painstakingly adjust to his third chin and instruct his colleagues to give close heed to his imminent display of virtuosity. He would thereupon play one or two notes on the fiddle, which, to the despair of his friends, would again require another full ten minutes of tuning up. These were embellished by divers gratuitous prattfalls on the part of Watson and incidental loud cheers of encouragement on the part of the frowzy Wrothe, and would culminate in Bickel's playing one or two more notes and wholesale enraptured prattfalls on the part of the entire trio.

It knocked audiences, including your present historian, for a loop. And when the trio ultimately recovered their feet again and rubbed their bottoms with tragicomic assiduity, it knocked them for a loop all over again.

There was another item in the act that similarly never failed to floor an audience. Bickel, in his thick German accent filtered through pursed lips, would observe that the notes that had emanated from his fiddle were so beautiful that they were immortal and would persist in the circumambient ether through time unending. Watson would pantomimically express some skepticism, naturally including another prattfall. Whereupon Bickel, to prove his assertion, would approach the footlights, would with finical delicacy reach out with thumb and forefinger for one of the deathless notes, would put it back onto his fiddle, and — to the conviction of Watson — would play it again. Whereupon, in turn, Watson would be so overcome that there was nothing for him to do to indicate his entrancement but to negotiate still another prattfall.

Weber and Fields' Meyer and Mike act, in which Fields periodically exclaimed: "My Gott, how I luff you!" and poked his finger into Weber's eye, was enough to agitate audiences so immoderately that pedestrians three blocks away ran for cover under the impression that there was an earthquake in the neighborhood. But for real audience belly-busting even Weber and Fields never quite equaled the puissance of the old burlesque show act, hereinbefore alluded to, called *At Monte Carlo*. For at least a quarter of a century it had the customers reduced to jocose tears and, forsooth, in its various slight paraphrases is still, as also noted, going big today.

A red-nosed, floppy-pants comedian, a Hebrew comedian, and a straight man in the conventional excessive blue are seated at a table on the beach at Monte Carlo, customarily depicted on the backdrop as bearing a strong resemblance to Coney Island. Enter a stately, bejeweled blonde, by name Mrs. Astorbilt. "Won't you join we gentlemen, madamoosl?" bows the courtly straight man, and the elegant lady promptly and naturally obliges, which so impresses the parsimonious Hebrew comedian that he "opens wine," the waiter popping the cork with the explosion of a howitzer and so scaring the red-nosed comedian that he absentmindedly seizes the bottle and drains it. The lady, haughtily oblivious of the Hebrew comedian, who has now stood on his chair the better to peer into her décolletage, suggests a little food might be in order. "What would you prefer?" bids the courtly straight man. Mrs. Astorbilt allows she isn't at all hungry and desires only a mere snack consisting of some horace dovers, a thick Porterhouse steak with onions and French fried potatoes, lobster à la Newburk, pâté de phew gras, apple pie — and a cup of corfee. The two comedians have meanwhile crawled under the table the better to survey the lady's ankles. "Make it a bowl of noodle soup!" the erst courtly straight man instructs the waiter, and when the bowl is served — the two comiques have meantime emerged from beneath the table and have again retrieved their seats — the red-nosed one claps it, noodles and all, over the lady's head.

Upon the beauty's indignant exit, followed by the ex-postulating straight man, the two comedians are left alone. "So you are a member of the union," observes one to the other, apropos of nothing. "Don't you call me a onion!" says the other and swats him over the head with a stalk of celery. "You have grocery insulted me!" proclaims the victim.

Enter a great swell in a full swallowtail evening full-dress suit and silk hat. The two comedians contemplate him in awe as he nonchalantly fingers an enormous roll of green-backs, one of which he lets drop and which the Hebrew comedian precipitantly falls upon. "What!" shouts the swell one, "would you demean yourself for a paltry one-thousand-dollar bill?" The Hebrew comedian gets up, properly ashamed of himself. "I didn't know it was a poul-try bill," he abjectly apologizes. "Anyway," drawls the high-toned one, "it has been contaminatered from contract with the germs on the floor" — and he hails a page boy in the person of a chorus girl with a minimum of clothes on to take the bill and quickly deposit it in the garbage can. The two comedians dash after the girl. The nabob asks them where they are going. "If you want to find us, you can have us paged in the garbage can!" they shout over their shoul-ders.

Low stuff maybe, but nevertheless there you have in es-sence one of the recorded greatest howl marathons in the American theatre. It has beaten by countless miles De Wolf Hopper's memorable "Casey at the Bat"; it has made more money in one form or another than *Box and Cox*, the Rus-sell Brothers, and Sidney Drew's famous skit about teeth called *Billy's Tombstones* combined; and there isn't a grown-up little boy still living who from far back doesn't delightedly remember as if it were only yesterday its pas-sage in which a pert minx seated herself at the table, im-mediately demanded the menu, and was apprised by the red-nosed comedian, upon his scrutiny of her shapely fig-ure: "You said it, baby, me 'n you!"

BROKEN JOURNEY. June 23, 1942

A play by Andrew Rosenthal, author of The Burning Deck
(*March 1, 1940*), *which holds the world's long-distance bad
epigram record and which reparteed itself off the stage in
two days. Produced by Martin Burton.*

Program

Hale Thatcher	*Tom Powers*	Dan Hardeen	*Warner Anderson*
Essie	*Helen Carew*	Christina Landers	
Belle Newell	*Phyllis Povah*		*Edith Atwater*
Rachel Thatcher Arlen		Trina	*Joan McSweeney*
	Zita Johann	Howard Newell	*Gordon Nelson*

SYNOPSIS: Act I. Scene 1. *Late afternoon.* Scene 2. *That evening,
after dinner.* Act II. *Three weeks later, Sunday afternoon.* Act III. Scene 1.
Several hours later. Scene 2. *Christmas Eve.*

The living-room of the Thatcher home, in the suburb of a city in
Ohio. Time. November 1941.

Dorothy Thompson and John Gunther while on a
joint lecture tour in the Middle West drop in on the Ohio
town where John was born. There John meets again his
childhood sweetheart, concludes that all this gallivanting
around the world is a futile business, and decides to marry
his old love and settle down. At this point the radio announces the Japanese attack on Pearl Harbor and John,
after ten minutes of agonized facial pantomime indicating
his change of heart, rushes out after Dorothy, who, having
assured him that tranquil home life is not for him, has already departed for Manila. That, although the playwright
has named Dorothy Christina Landers and John Dan
Hardeen, is the plot. It also gives you some idea.

Three scenes — one between the two women, one between Dorothy and an old fogy who proposes marriage to
her, and another between Dorothy and John — are neatly
written. But the author's juvenile hero-worship of his traveling correspondents, to say nothing of such correspondents

en masse, along with his absurd notions of the way the gentry operate, make the whole ridiculous.

The stage direction of Arthur Hopkins suggested a wrangle between George Abbott and Frank Campbell, the actors alternately comporting themselves like fire-engines and corpses. Furthermore, when will actresses realize that nothing is more disturbing to the complete acceptance of passionately emotional scenes than too immaculate dress? It is pretty hard to react properly to the emotional and mental tortures of a female character meticulously shod with the latest shining thing in fashionable footwear, clad in a series of scrupulously pressed and draped new Hattie Carnegie frocks, stockinged in the precisest of gleaming hose, and with a coiffure that indicates the three-hour assiduous pains of Charles of the Ritz.

THE CHOCOLATE SOLDIER. June 23, 1942

A revival of the Oscar Straus operetta, libretto by Rudolf Bernauer and Leopold Jacobson out of Bernard Shaw's Arms and the Man. *Produced by MM. Tushinsky and Bartsch.*

Program

Nadina Popoff	*Helen Gleason*	Captain Massakroff	
Col. Popoff's daughter			*Detmar Poppen*
Aurelia		Colonel Casimir Popoff	
her mother	*Francis Comstock*		*A. Russell Slagle*
Mascha		Major Alexius Spiridoff	
Aurelia's cousin	*Doris Patston*		*Michael Fitzmaurice*
Lieutenant Bumerli		Ballerina	*Tashamira*
	Allan Jones	Premier dancer	*Peter Birch*

Let brevity be the soul of criticism. Not content with leaving well enough alone, the producers inserted an introductory chorus of soldiers and peasant girls, a grim ballet supposedly picturing Nadina's dream, a revision of the climax to the first act, and jazzy liberties with the score. At such times as they restrained their ideology, the old warhorse delivered much of its familiar pleasure, although liberal slices of the comedy have become arteriosclerotic.

STAR AND GARTER. June 24, 1942

A glorified burlesque show produced by Michael Todd, impresario of the New York World's Fair concessions The Streets of Paris *and* Gay New Orleans. *Music and lyrics by Harold J. Rome, Will Irwin, et al.*

PRINCIPALS

Bobby Clark, Gypsy Rose Lee, Professor Lamberti, Georgia Sothern, Pat Harrington, Carrie Finnell, Marjorie Knapp, Gil Maison, the Hudson Wonders, et al.

ANY SHOW with Bobby Clark in it, whatever its faults, is bound to be amusing, and this was no exception. That select fraternity that long arched the brows of others with its rhapsodies over the comic genius of Bobby and that for its zeal was rewarded only with quizzical looks and mayhap allegations that in all probability it had had too many drinks has at length found itself esteemed as a body of veritable Aristarchi. It took one of the worst farces seen hereabout since *Call Me Ziggy* and the award of the Pulitzer prize to *The Old Maid* to do it. For it was in that sombre and depressing dose of gum-resin — the *All Men Are Alike* of the season of 1941-2 — that our hero proved himself not only all we older boys had claimed for him, but more. Single-handed and alone the great man, through sheer stunning virtuosity, turned (at least while he was on the stage) what would otherwise have been an intolerable ordeal into something funny enough to crack your buttons off. Single-handed and alone he extracted more robust, loud laughs out of material that didn't contain them than almost any other of his fellow clowns can extract from material itself already pretty tasty.

Bobby's genius, however, certainly did not on that occasion go unappreciated by my honored colleagues, the New York reviewers, albeit belatedly. No such glowing notices have been bestowed upon an artist since Salvini last acted over here or since little Butterfly McQueen showed up as the colored maid in the sporting-house scene of *Brown Sugar*. There was not a dissenting voice. As for myself, still lending my rich barroom baritone to the hallelujah chorus after all of thirty-five years, I'll give you all the profound dramas of Em Jo Basshe, along with all the profounder ones of Virgil Geddes, for even one look at Bobby in his flannel union suit making love to a six-foot blonde. I'll add to them all the acting of Walter Hampden, Stiano Braggiotti, and Ezra Stone for the histrionic technique of my man when he severely and indignantly cross-examines a friend and gradually, by virtue of his eloquent cunning, finds himself with his own shirt-tail out. And I'll supplement both with all of Michael Chekhov's Russian directorial art, Erwin Piscator's German directorial art, and the Theatre Guild's American directorial art for the privilege of beholding Bobby hopping about with a parlor rug around his middle, flirting the rear of a kilt at the customers, substituting a mouthful of gargled *g*'s and *s*'s for a naughty word, or chasing a woman upstairs to her boudoir and getting the door in his face for his chivalrous, if somewhat lascivious, pains.

If there remained any faintest doubt about Bobby's gifts, his subsequent electrification of the Theatre Guild's comatose revival of *The Rivals* set them at rest. And in this *Star and Garter* he buried them for all time. Working in the old burlesque tradition, he was a wonder. When, as the judge in the familiar *Irish Justice* courtroom scene, he blew spitballs at the prosecuting attorney; when he glaringly observed in reply to a male witness's testimony that, though there was a sofa in the fair defendant's boudoir, the witness did nothing about it: "I would have done just what you did, only I wouldn't lie about it!"; when he fell off the bench every time the fair defendant crossed her shapely legs — when he permitted himself such demonstrations of the histrionic art any man with soul so dead he didn't howl his chemise right off his back should have been either summarily put into a concentration camp (with the Huberts and their drunk act in this same show for added punishment) or deported to England and forced to look at the comedy performances of Vic Oliver.

As first assistant to Bobby the producer supplied that drollest of all xylophone clowns, Professor Lamberti, although Fred Sanborn is no mean shakes in the same classic department. And Mr. Todd's deference to License Commissioner Moss's ban on the strip-tease, which took the precautionary form of doing away with it altogether save in the single instance of the intellectual Miss Gypsy Rose Lee and instead bringing on the girls stark naked in the first place except for small rosebuds on their nipples and miniature gilt stars on their pupenda, helped materially to augment the general comedy. Thus, overlooking the inevitable equilibrists, trained monkey, team of acrobatic dancers, and concluding South America rumba number, a good, low, dirty, happy time was in the cards.

In this connection, it seems to be the firm conviction of such moralists as the above-mentioned Moss that dirt of the kind merchanted in the burlesque houses of hallowed memory is bound to inflame the libido of the customers and send them rushing out to inflict that which is worse than death upon a helpless female population, black and white. As a patron of burlesque for more than forty years and as a reporter of both myself and every other attendant I ever knew, it is difficult for me to understand how the peculiar Mosses arrive at their concupiscent philosophy. If ever there was a male over sixteen years of age who, after giving ear to two hours of uninterrupted smut, felt otherwise than going right back straight home and getting a little relief by reading *Alice in Wonderland*, I haven't heard of him. Nothing so purges the mind of indecency as too much indecency. The most moral force in this world is a really dirty burlesque show.

STARS ON ICE. July 2, 1942

A refrigerated spectacle, successor to It Happens on Ice, *with music and lyrics, to be overgenerously euphemistic, by Paul McGrane and Al Stillman. Produced by Sonja Henie and Arthur M. Wirtz.*

Principals

Carol Lynne, Skippy Baxter, the Three Rookies, Freddie Trenkler, A. Douglas Nelles, the Four Bruises, Vivienne Allen, Mary Jane Yeo, Paul Duke, Twinkle Watts, et al.

THESE ICE-SKATING SHOWS, even at their best, become monotonous before very long, since monotony is as inherent in the medium as it is in lengthy statistical tables, Powers models' faces, and holy matrimony. Nor is it prosperously to be minimized, as in the present instance, by occasionally interrupting the ice acrobatics for a few moments with mike vocalizations of such unbelievable gems as "Gin Rummy, I Love You" and with prestidigitators of lighted cigarettes.

There is no gainsaying that little is more thoroughly graceful than professional rink movement, but too insistently much of it induces the same effect as too much beauty of almost any kind, as Maugham has convincingly enough pointed out. Just as a merely pretty woman is likely to hold the interest longer than a classically beautiful one, so for a change might a little winning amateurishness amongst such uninterrupted professionalism. Two hours and a quarter of precision is more than one can comfortably endure, whether in an ice rink or Walter Pater. At least in the instance of true Corinthians, since monotony seems to be the diversion and enchantment of hoi polloi, as was amply proved by the remarkable longevity of this show's precursor and as is proved again by its own success, to say nothing of the success of the traveling Sonja Henie exhibits and others and of the ice shows in a variety of hotels like the St. Regis, New Yorker, and Biltmore. The great mass of people, in short, who year after year find refreshment and stimulation in the routine of the circus with its changeless trapeze performers, tight-rope walkers, and dancing elephants are doubtless the same who are exhilarated by the changeless rink spectacles.

Imagination might conceivably contrive to lessen the ice shows' monotony, at least in the theatre, but of such imagination there appears usually to be less than nothing. One thus gets, in a show like this *Stars on Ice,* the stereotyped skating waltz to "The Blue Danube"; the comedian who at least six times skates rapidly toward the audience and, just as he is seemingly about to be projected into its laps, brings himself up with a sudden halt, thereupon each time squealing: "I scared the hell outa you, eh?" and vouchsafing himself a broad, pleased grin; the repulsive little female blonde child who, with the self-assurance of a prima donna, grimly twirls round eight times on her skates and with a heavy humility coached into her by her mama standing beamingly in the wings coyly acknowledges the house's sympathetic applause; the male skater dressed in women's clothes who is confident that a fall on the rear that wouldn't otherwise be particularly funny becomes enormously excruciating by sole virtue of his costume; the skaters clad in red fox-hunting coats who pursue a skater dressed in a fox-skin; the woman skater in Slav costume who executes the sit-down Russian kicking dance; the obvious *Jack Frost* ballet with everyone in white costumes, the spotlight illuminating the sequins thereon; the hypothetically comical dwarf on skates; and the number in which a skater programmed as The Wind first chases one dubbed The Chrysanthemum off the stage and then busies himself chasing around the chorus representing Autumn Leaves, the accompanying lyric, surprisingly enough, being "Like a Leaf Falling in the Breeze."

THIS IS THE ARMY. July 4, 1942

A soldier show successor to the Yip, Yip, Yaphank *of World War I by the same Irving Berlin, with a cast containing three hundred men from virtually every military post in the United States, and produced to the rewarding tune of more than $3,000,000 for the benefit of the Army Emergency Relief Fund.*

Principals

Irving Berlin, Sergeants Ezra Stone and Dick Bernie, Corporals James Cross, Earl Oxford, Philip Truex, and Nelson Barclift, Privates Joe Cook, Jr., James MacColl, Fred Kelly, Anthony Ross, Alan Manson, Julie Oshins, Hayden Rorke, John Mendes, Larry Weeks, et al.

There are two points of view from which to report on the show. One is the patriotic, which would warmly assert that it was great stuff. The other is the critical, which would coolly assert that it certainly was. For in the experience of the present recorder there hasn't been a frankly designed patriotic spectacle that was in quieter and better taste, that had so much merit in it of its independent own, and that so strainlessly and modestly persuaded its audience into emotional response.

We have sampled all kinds of appeals to patriotism in both plays and musical shows, most of them of the species that have embarrassed any man still half sober into going out and making a full job of it. Ever since Mordecai M. Noah a century and a quarter ago waved the flag for the first time on our stage — in the play called *She Would Be a Soldier, or The Plains of Chippewa* — we have sniffed a long succession of melodramas like *The Ensign* and *Shenandoah,* of plays like *The American Way* and *American Landscape,* and of musicals of the George M. Cohan Yankee Doodle school that have sought to cram pride in the nation down our throats and that in the process have generally caused it to stick there like a whalebone. Nor have the exhibits of other countries been much happier. Such

French plays as *Alsace, The Unknown Warrior,* and *Lorelei* have proved to be little more than extravagantly rhetorical tricolor gargles, all calculated to induce vague traitorous impulses in any but a prime Montmartre chauvinist. And such English offerings as *Golden Wings, Heart of a City,* and, above all, *Journey's End,* with their greasepaint device of heightening bravery by an appearance of minimizing it, have in the case of intelligent Englishmen operated to much the same end. To intelligent Americans, one and all have been slightly distasteful and ridiculous.

This *Journey's End,* meant to make Englishmen proud of their unassuming fortitude, provides the nicest example of the point in question. That reticence in general is an attribute of the English character is duly appreciated. But it may be carried too far in drama and Mr. Sherriff carries it to the point where it becomes indistinguishable from nitwit lethargy. There are times in his play when, judging from the comportment of his soldiers in their dugout, one can't be sure whether what is going on outside is a war or a Pinero rehearsal. The schoolmaster lieutenant who lectures on *Alice in Wonderland* and pretty garden flowers while all hell is about to break loose above, the general nonchalant heroism painfully reminiscent of the Oh-it's-nothing-merely-a-scratch type of melodrama, and the silent-strong-man business which stubbornly suggests Edward G. Robinson having wandered out of a dead-pan American crook film and accidentally found himself in a British military uniform once owned by Haddon Chambers must cope with rebellious snickers on the part of any Briton who, for all his ferocious determination to be properly patriotic, suddenly recalls such forthright British military melodramas of the long ago as *The Cherry-Pickers,* to say nothing of such somewhat later ones as Conan Doyle's *Fires of Fate.* And the oppressive lovableness of soldiers who remain drawing-room actors to their dying moments and who wouldn't think of using even a mild cuss word if both their legs were shot off must call for copious chasers in the sentimental swallowing. I hope I may not be considered too flippant when I say that, after watching and listening for two acts to Mr. Sherriff's Lieutenant Coward, Captain Lonsdale, Sergeant-Major Van Druten, Colonel Gielgud, Second-Lieutenant Benn Levy, and Privates Ivor Novello and Terence Rattigan, I momentarily expected either Irene Vanbrugh or Vivien Leigh to show up in the dugout, dresses by Mainbocher.

The Germans have much to answer for in a direction quite apart from the consequences of their military lunacy. In the last quarter of a century they have been the worst influence on the drama since the eruption of Scribe and Sardou. Through both the first World War and the one still in operation they have inspired playwrights here and abroad to the confection of some of the damnedest rubbish known to Christendom; they have converted a recognizable portion of the stage from its quondam concern with dramatic art into a platform for the dispensation of automat propaganda, tupenny patriotic editorialization, cameraless movie junk, and boiler-factory cacophony; and they have turned the once proud theme of war — a theme that contributed to Greece's great dramatic glory — into the leit-motif of tin-pot melodrama, greasepaint gulp and tear distilleries, and portentously solemn but insubordinately uproarious dramatic belly-lettres.

The moral indignation which the Boches induced twenty-six years ago and which the Nazis have induced more recently, working its wicked will upon writers for the theatre, has exercised the evil pressure upon art that indignation of any kind usually does. During the earlier war the result was a tidal wave of foreign and domestic claptrap having chiefly to do with the shock suffered by women on discovering somewhat belatedly that the men they had been married to for all of thirty-eight years had German blood in their veins, with the possibility that even one's own beloved grandfather was a spy in the employ of the enemy, and with the penchant of the Huns for all the major crimes in the catalogue, first and foremost among them, of course, being rape. The present war has been even more productive of hot fruits, albeit of a slightly different nature. Its particular bequest has been a succession of foot-light explosions shaking the nerves out of us with fatidical implications of a Hitler-censored stage that would no longer be able to exalt us with such masterpieces as *Abie's Irish Rose,* with ominous analogies between invaded Norway and our own beloved Bronx, and with the inculcation in us of the suspicion that any man amongst us with a rigidly erect spine, a somewhat sibilant speech, and a scrupulously pressed morning coat is beyond peradventure of a doubt a scheming Nazi.

In such cases where indignation has been strainfully tempered with deliberation, what we have got from both wars has been not much better. In these instances a luxuriant rhapsodic soulfulness has taken the place of melodramatic fury and the crystallization has been a succession of exhibits, couched either in free verse or California chianti prose, which have sought simultaneously to wake us up and break our hearts with metaphorical treatises on the nobility of self-sacrifice, the ecstasy of a threatened democracy, the ignominy of defeatism, and the sacred trust of the refugee problem.

One of the leading catastrophes of the present war, moreover, has been the effect upon the drama of enemy bombing. Nor has the effect, apparently, been confined to the drama. So far as one can make out from extensive reading, this bombing business has usurped the rapt attention of nine foreign newspaper correspondents out of every ten, and of novelists, essayists, memoirists, poets, and literati generally without end. It has been difficult to pick up a Sunday newspaper or a magazine without finding in it an extended touching description of the suscitation that such bombing has had on the soul of the writer, to say nothing of on the souls of everyone else, both in and out of air-raid shelters, for a hundred miles round. While one might think that the effect might not be acutely dissimilar, so far as spiritual experience goes, to being in a Mills Hotel during an earthquake, it seems it isn't so. It seems that bombs have a peculiar and idiosyncratic way of converting everyone into sterling heroes and beatific saints, particularly if they blow one's home into smithereens and blast off one's arms,

legs, and wherever possible, head. And it has not been
much less difficult to find a novel which hasn't repeated
the psychic panegyrics of the newspaper and magazine correspondents, only more rapturously.

Frederic Hazlitt Brennan's play *The Wookey* was a forerunner of what we could expect on the subject of what may
be called the bomb in Gilead drama. Operating under the
theory of the correspondents that there is nothing like a
sufficiently puissant bomb to change the rankest poltroon
and scalawag into an immediate combination of the Duke
of Wellington, Nathan Hale, and Krishnamurti, with
slight overtones of Duff Cooper and Rabbi Wise, Mr. Brennan presented us with a lowly cockney barge captain who
stoutly opposed the British government's war policies until
one of the aforesaid eggs landed on his shack. His meta-
morphosis was thereupon instantaneous. In a jiffy he was
done with his old wisecracks, his old hesitations, his old
doubts, and off he went like another Hector to get even
with Hermann Göring. All as smoothly and automatically
as slot apple-pie, and as mechanical and doughy.

There is, of course, no reason in the world why such a
theme might not make quite as good drama as, say, the almost equally arbitrary theme of *Hamlet,* save alone the reason that the kind of playwright who is fetched by it is usually the sort that is an inferior one. And Mr. Brennan is
haplessly of that species. The measure of a good dramatist
is to be found in the manner and means by which he de-
lineates flux in character. The good dramatist maneuvers
it internally; the bad dramatist, externally. The mental
and psychical changes of the heroes of fine drama are not
wrought by bombs or collisions of papier-mâché locomo-
tives or revolvers pressed against the midriff or rescues
from the East River by moonlight. They occur in the
great inner silences, with the quiet and stealthy tread of
either tame or wild tigers. Or, in lesser men, of family cats.

Mr. Brennan is a further sample product of the fell influence in his conviction that a devil of a stage racket is
synonymous with exciting drama. What with his off-stage
Stukas, Heinkels, and Messerschmitts and his fifteen thou-

sand dollars' worth of Metro-Goldwyn sound effects, his exhibit merchanted all the noise and incidental dramatic quality, to say nothing of ear-tortured disinterest, that would be vouchsafed by a contemporary paraphrase of some such peanut-gallery melodrama of fifty years ago as *Across the Pacific,* with its gunnery din, or *The Soudan,* with its battle hullabaloo. Thinking quickly back over the war plays of all history, I cannot recall one of any authentic quality that was not practically soundless. *What Price Glory?,* with its brief uproar at the end of the second act, may be an exception of sorts, but are there any others? All the more modern ones that have gone in for gun, cannon, bomb, or dynamite have, surely, been shabby affairs from any reputable critical viewpoint.

It is commonly asserted that war is too big a subject for the drama, that the theatre and its few allotted hours are too constricted for so great a subject, and that as a consequence the stage and drama have had to fall back on its lesser aspects. This, of course, is the sheerest nonsense. The point is, rather, that war is too big a subject only for too little dramatists and that it is they who perforce have had to fall back on its minor incidentals. War was not too big a subject for the Greek dramatists, nor for Shakespeare, Schiller, or the Shaw of *Saint Joan.* It is simply too big for the Sherriffs, Howards, Storms, Brennans, and the like.

It is these small fry who think to write the modern drama of men in war either in terms of Gorki's *Night Refuge* with sound effects or Henry Arthur Jones's *The Hypocrites* with every other character in uniform. When such shenanigans do not appeal to them, there are always other equally facile paraphrases near to hand. They can always lay hold of some old melodrama, eliminate the big mechanical effect that was the show's one claim to success, rewrite the dialogue in more strictly copybook English, and incorporate into the play a few pearls cabbaged from Walter Lippmann, Dorothy Thompson, or Samuel Grafton, which is pretty sure to get them at least six or seven votes from the Pulitzer prize committee. They can, further, if their ideas are running slightly slower than usual, always resort to some such general scheme as Galsworthy's *The Mob*, set peace-lover against war-lover and in their arch-paraphrases either prove that the peace-lover is a low scoundrel who once studied German in the Milwaukee Central High School and hence is in all probability a corpsbruder of Hitler or that the war-lover has two million dollars in duPont stocks hidden away in safe-deposit boxes, is a bachelor without a son liable for army duty and cannon fodder, and is accordingly an even lower scoundrel than the other. Or they can, further still, always dig out of their trunks plays they wrote years ago and which they could not sell, make the poor old inventor a German-American with photographs of Washington, Lincoln, and Calvin Coolidge above his workbench, change the mortgage shark into a bigoted non-interventionist, cast Molly Picon as the poor old inventor's wife, put in a scene in which the phonograph ironically grinds out the Gettysburg Address the while a lot of loafers from the gashouse district beat up the old German-American, and thus prove that America is a great melting pot and the future hope of a war-plagued world.

The imagination displayed by most writers of war plays or plays touching upon war is usually not surpassed even by that displayed by writers of Cinderella and Hollywood plays, which is getting about eight thousand feet below sea-level. And the reason isn't far to seek. The war plays are generally concocted either by persons who never got nearer to the subject they are writing about than the front pages of the daily newspapers, or maybe the editorial pages, or by others who, though they have been in the thick of it, have been so overpowered by it emotionally that they remain in the position of a man composing a treatise on obstetrics while his wife is giving birth to their first baby. There is a third class of writers, too. These are they who, aloof from both battlefield and any considerable external reading, approach the subject in the mantle of philosophical dramatic poets. These, four times out of five, bring to the subject all the purple passion of teetotalers, all the wisdom of Quiz Kids, and all the lyrical grandeur of a Herbert Hoover speech.

There may be food for some meditation in the circumstance that the only two American plays of any real or relative critical quality that resulted from World War I were cast very largely in the comic mould: to wit, the before-noted exceptional *What Price Glory?* of Anderson and Stallings and the lesser *Johnny Johnson* of Paul Green. There may be even more food for meditation in the circumstance that the only Central European play of any critical quality that resulted from that same war was also cast in the comic mould: to wit, *The Good Soldier Schweik* of Carl Zuckmayer. And there may be quite as much food for meditation in the circumstance that the dismal gravity of the French contrived to produce only second- and third-rate plays at best and that, with all of England's gravity, the only reputable play to come out of that nation in turn was the witty *Heartbreak House* of Bernard Shaw. War is certainly no laughing matter, but when it comes to the theatre of today we can't be too certain. The only valid critical moments in the otherwise trashy *The Wookey,* indeed, were those ribaldly involving a watercloset and the human backside.

Thus, returning with profound relief and large pleasure to *This Is the Army,* I nominate it as one of the few exhibits produced locally during any war within memory which has achieved its proper end: to wit, the entertainment of patriotism into an audience rather than the painful injection of it with a hypodermic full of medicinal propaganda. Not once did it wave the flag; the only time the flag was allowed on the stage, indeed, was in a comedy prestidigitation act in which a rookie taken to severe task by his sergeant for his untidiness pulled out several dirty handkerchiefs and made the sergeant absurdly stand at salute by converting them into it. Not once did it proclaim the bravery and glory of our armed forces, and the one big marching song, *This Time,* was sung as quietly and as unostentatiously as if it were *Little Annie Rooney.* Beginning with a military minstrel show with a hundred men in khaki sweeping up to the flies in tiers, it went on its amiable way with song and spoof, with kitchen police juggling potatoes

instead of peeling them, with Negro soldiers hoofing hell-
bent for leather, with the Navy denouncing the Army for
trying to steal all the audience thunder, with low facetiæ
at the expense of the Stage Door Canteen, with sergeants,
corporals, and privates in beautiful girls' costumes and
dancing like the Wayburn best, and with catchy melodies
like "I'm Getting Tired So I Can Sleep," "Head in the
Clouds," and "A Soldier's Dream" (in the staging, a rare
piece of romantic raillery). And the show amounted in
sum, accordingly, to something that made any American
who hitherto had been embarrassed into a state bordering
on traitorousness by greasepaint Yankee Doodledom want
to buy a drink all around for everybody in the house.

Most of this theatrical Yankee Doodledom has, like its
English counterpart, been distasteful by virtue of the circumstance that the actors who have merchanted it have
generally seemed to be in the position of comfortable
bleachers-sitters shouting for the team to go in and knock
the other team's block off. It is pretty hard to work up any
overpowering patriotic feeling when a ham who never got
nearer to a fight than the Lambs Club bar struts down to
the footlights in khaki and, while a line of girls full of
Lindy's marinierte herring and blutwurst form a Star-
Spangled Banner in the background, sings "Let 'Em Come,
Let 'Em Come, We Are Ready!" And it is hardly less difficult (though this is somewhat irrelevant to the present
critique) to refrain from a subversive grin when, in the
drama, a man who never did anything in his life but act,
and usually badly, staggers onto the stage, his uniform
covered with sawdust, and announces that though his
horse was shot from under him he singlehanded saved the
whole damned Army of the Shenandoah. Soldiers' roles
played by soldiers are a relief — and please do not have at
me with some such infecund *mot* as Oho, so King Lear
should be played by King George! And that, as in the case
of his last war's *Yip, Yip, Yaphank,* was Berlin's recipe in
his this war's *This Is the Army.*

In conclusion, a capital show any way you looked at it,
and especially critically.

YOURS, A. LINCOLN. July 9, 1942

A play by Paul Horgan, inspired by Otto Eisenschiml's book, Why Was Lincoln Murdered?, *and produced by the Experimental Theatre, Inc.*

Program

Young Roundhill	*Del Hughes*	Herold	*Tom McDermott*
Lincoln	*Vincent Price*	Tad	*Robert Lee*
Doctor	*David Koser*	Sherman	*Bill Johnson*
First Senator	*Homer Miles*	Grant	*Harry Bellaver*
Second Senator	*Watson White*	Aide	*Harry Townes*
Third Senator	*Robert Toms*	Boarding House Keeper	
Stanton	*Sherman A. MacGregor*		*Ruth Hermanson*
Mrs. Lincoln	*Mary Michael*	Crook	*Wendell K. Phillips*
Major	*Gibbs Penrose*	Workman	*Don Valentine*
Booth	*Donald Randolph*	Roundhill	*Parker Fennelly*

Scene. *Washington, D. C.*
Time. *March 24 to April 15, 1865.*

Mr. Eisenschiml's book advanced the theory that Lincoln's assassination was prompted by Stanton for purely political reasons. Mr. Horgan's play derived from it, at least in its presentation by the Experimental Theatre group, advanced the theory that the assassination was prompted by Booth for purely histrionic reasons. For certainly a Lincoln as interpreted by Vincent Price might well be understood so to arouse the contempt of the competent actor that Booth was as to make murder in his mind thoroughly justifiable.

In the Price delineation, Abe was something. With a speech that was a cross between Hamtree Harrington's and Julian Eltinge's, with gestures which frequently suggested that the occupant of the White House was, whiskers and all, Ben Welch, and with a penchant for extended pedestrianism that threatened momentarily to land him out in Shubert Alley, the Price Lincoln, had Booth not taken the job upon himself, would have been shot on the spot by every dramatic critic present in Ford's Theatre on the fateful night, and to the accompaniment of loud cheers by the entire *Our American Cousin* company. Not since John Drinkwater's *Robert E. Lee* in its London showing suggested that the Confederate Army had been led by an uncle of Beerbohm Tree's has a notable American historical figure so made his admirers yell for Carl Sandburg and the police.

As for the play itself, it is less drama than a reading aloud of the book from which it was brewed. Mr. Horgan is apparently unaware of the difference between the two, and the result is a dead static. As placed on the stage, the so-called play resolves itself into nine scenes. The first, laid in a Washington military hospital, shows Lincoln comforting a dying Union soldier boy and, though with some historical justification, is pretty trying in its unduly protracted juke-box sentimentality. The second, laid in the office of the Secretary of War, gives us Stanton's venom for his leader and the joint political plotting of his senatorial henchmen. All it needs to make it somewhat better 10–20–30 melodrama than it is is black instead of white whiskers on Stanton. The third, placed on the stage of Ford's Theatre, shows Booth plotting against Lincoln with a young fan of his acting art and is so declamatory that it is something of a wonder Lincoln couldn't hear it in his remote White House room and take the proper precautions. The fourth, the cabin of the Presidential yacht *River Queen*, after a lengthy candy-sweet· passage between Abe and his little son Tad (in a soldier's uniform), presents us with a scene wherein Abe secretly instructs Grant and Sherman in mercy toward the South. And the sixth, which concludes the first half and which takes place on the White House porch, is chiefly notable for Lincoln's insistence that the band celebrating the cessation of hostilities play "Dixie." Whether Lincoln did actually request the number, I do not know. But whether he did or did not, it is, on the dramatic stage, altogether too obvious hokum.

The second part opens in the parlor of a boarding house and proceeds with Booth's machinations, also so proclaimed at the top of the lungs that, if Lincoln couldn't hear them before, he surely could have heard them this time, even if he happened at the moment to be as far away as Georgetown. The following scene, at the President's bedroom door in the White House, is devoted to Abe's concern over a portentous dream. The penultimate scene, set in the President's box at Ford's, shows us Booth's rehearsal of the assassination. And the last, in the White House sitting-room on the same evening — the imminent assassination itself is left to the audience's knowledge — is taken up with another stretch of sentimentality wherein Abe and the father of the dying boy he comforted at the beginning of the play go in for some moist tenderness on a heroic scale. (In the old Hal Reid melodrama it was always Abe and the boy's mother.)

What the Experimental Theatre, Inc., apparently needs as a starter is a competent reader and judge of play manuscripts.

THE MERRY WIDOW. July 15, 1942

A revival of the Viennese operetta by Franz Lehar, book by Victor Leon and Leo Stein. Produced by MM. Tushinsky and Bartsch.

PROGRAM

St. Brioche	*Michael Fitzmaurice*	Nish	*John Cherry*
Natalie	*Elizabeth Houston*	Baron Popoff	*Eddie Garr*
Camille de Jolidon	*Felix Knight*	Sonia	*Helen Gleason*
Cascada	*George Mitchell*	Prince Danilo	*Wilbur Evans*
Olga	*Elaine Ellis*	Madam Khadja	*Harriet Borger*
Novakovich	*Neil Fitzgerald*	Head Waiter	*Carl Nelson*
Khadja	*Roy M. Johnston*	Zo Zo	*Diana Corday*

It is the custom, on the occasion of most revivals, wistfully to hark back to the original productions and to recall their great superiority to the present ones. But nostalgia (that weatherbeaten noun) and the pathos of distance (that weatherbeaten phrase) often conspire against fact, as is their gentle habit. Memory is a fickle jade, particularly in the case of fat women and theatre critics, for revivals intermittently put inaugural presentations to shame.

This is true, in at least one respect, in the present instance. The original production of *The Merry Widow,* in 1907, had as its Prince Danilo Donald Brian and as its Sonia Ethel Jackson. Brian was a minor mime elevated into the role by a parsimonious management. He had a distinctly third-rate singing voice; he had all the romantic address of a Siegel-Cooper haberdashery clerk; he had little personality; and he couldn't act. Ethel Jackson's voice was second-rate; she was hardly blessed with looks or individuality; and she was quite as feeble in the matter of acting as her vis-à-vis. Both Wilbur Evans and Helen Gleason, who occupied the roles in this version, were immensely more suitable to them in every way.

Save for this improvement, however, the lang-syners had something in their favor, even though the original

Henry W. Savage production was little more pictorially impressive than this, since Savage, as has been intimated, notoriously had Scotch blood in his pocketbook. As is often the case with operetta revivals, the immediate producers were unable to resist the temptation to monkey with the book by theoretical way of modernizing it, and to this end permitted Eddie Garr, in the role of Baron Popoff, to run amuck. Popoff in the original, true enough, was scarcely a part bursting with irresistible humors; in point of fact it always drove its more sensitive auditors to the Weber and Fields Music Hall for relief. But in Garr's hands the effect it produced was akin to placing one's nose on a window ledge and then whimsically slamming down the window. That is, save the auditor was one who savored a rich humor in such remarks as "Mama done tol' me," "It's the nuts," and "That's all, brother!" in the Marsovian Embassy drawing-room, or one who considered hugely amusing interpolated allusions to priorities, Frankie and Johnnie, the conga, and — if my ears heard aright in the romantic Maxim's scene — hot dogs.

TALKING TO YOU. August 17, 1942

ACROSS THE BOARD ON TOMORROW MORNING

A forty-eight minute and a fifty-seven minute play by William Saroyan, produced and directed by the author in the Belasco Theatre, for the occasion renamed by the author in honor of himself.

PROGRAM I

THE DREAM DANCER		THE DEAF BOY	Robert Lee
	Lois Bannerman	FANCY DAN	Lewis Charles
THE CROW	Peter Beauvais	MAGGIE	Lillian McGuinness
THE TIGER	Irving Morrow	THE MIDGET	Andrew Ratousheff
BLACKSTONE BOULEVARD			
	Canada Lee		

The Place. *A basement room on O'Farrell Street in San Francisco.*
The Time. *Now.*

PROGRAM II

HARPIST	Lois Bannerman	PABLO	C. Gilbert Advincula
THOMAS PIPER	Canada Lee	PANCHO	Sam Sotelo
JIM	Bill Challee	SAMMY	Larry Bolton
JOHN CALLAGHAN		RHINELANDER 2-8182	
	Edward F. Nannary		Lillian McGuinness
HARRY MALLORY	Irving Morrow	FRITZ	Lewis Charles
HELEN	Jane Jeffreys	A POET	Maxwell Bodenheim
PEGGY	June Hayford	CALLAGHAN MALLORY	
LOIS	Carol Marcus		William Prince
R. J. PINKERTON	Arthur Griffin		

The Place. *Callaghan's, on East 52nd St., New York.*
The Time. *Continuous, for the duration.*

A<small>T ONCE</small> the easiest and most difficult dramatic form is the dream play. It is the easiest because a writer without the slightest skill in dramaturgy may, by employing it, let his deficiency run wild and periodically get away with it on the ground that a dream has no form or substance anyway. It is the most difficult because, out of countless tries, only some such master dramatist as Strindberg or Hauptmann in *The Dream Play* or *Hannele* respectively — or in the shorter length some such skillful one as Galsworthy in *The Little Dream* — has contrived to give vital form to formlessness and meaning to the essentially meaningless. In *Talking to You*, Saroyan for the major part gives us only the formlessness and the meaninglessness. Yet, as in most of his plays, good or bad, he here and there fleetingly captures and projects that peculiar cry of humanity that is his poetic gift. In the character of the Negro prize-fighter, Blackstone Boulevard, he projects it tellingly. And here once again he presents in a few strokes another of his captivating young heroines. Her name is Maggie, and this is her entire role:

> THE CROW.   Maggie's always silent.
> THE TIGER.   Not always — now and then Maggie speaks. (*Softly*) Maggie. (*Maggie looks at him but does not speak.*) What do you want — most? Most of all?
> MAGGIE (*smiling beautifully*) .   Nothing.

If that doesn't constitute one of the most desirable heroines in our modern drama, I don't know.

Nevertheless, put down the play as a whole a dud.

Patterned largely after his prize-winning *The Time of Your Life, Across the Board on Tomorrow Morning* amounts to an intermittently entertaining shorter span of typical Saroyan mad barroom fancy. While without the antic undertones and overtones of the stem-play, it contains some passages, notably a boozily fantastic end-of-the-world episode and a colloquy between two Filipino kitchenboys, that, if properly directed, would constitute tiptop humor. In general, however, it suffers badly by comparison with the play of which it is an offshoot.

Both exhibits again exhumed the old unnecessary demand on the part of various persons that they understand fully what Saroyan is driving at, which they declared they are unable to. They should recall the remark of Stokowski: "It is not necessary to understand music; it is only necessary that one enjoy it." Understanding is not always essen-

tial to enjoyment. I, like some others, sometimes do not
know exactly what Saroyan thinks he means, but that does
not interfere with my pleasure at a number of his plays.
In the same way I, like even more others, do not know exactly the meanings of such plays as Ibsen's *The Lady from
the Sea* and Hauptmann's *And Pippa Dances,* but the fact
does not materially interfere with my appreciation of them.

This passion to have every play define itself with the
prim exactitude of a schoolmarm explaining to a roomful
of children the meaning of the Fourth of July or the difference between cat and rat is the height of juvenile and un-
critical silliness. The scholars who never go to the theatre,
much more who never take a drink and never feel magnifi-
cently, beautifully, romantically, wonderfully, and intelligently cloud-woven, are still desperately arguing the precise meanings in *Hamlet.* There are, further, still prosaic
dolts who are getting bald trying to ferret out the exact
meaning of such more modern classics as *The Spook Sonata*
and who can't sleep at night for worrying what *Little Eyolf*
is about. There are yet others, Saroyan may comfort himself to recall, who wax indignant over the theoretical riddle
of some such even more modern play as O'Neill's *The
Great God Brown,* which is approximately as difficult of solution as the one demanding the name of the city whose
first syllable represents a factory that grinds wheat into
flour, whose second has to do with pedestrianism, and
whose third is what you insert into the lock of a door. And
there are a lot of others, he may beneficially reflect, who to
this day miss the warm envelopment of the beauty of the
best of Yeats because it is not as entirely clear as *Abe Lincoln in Illinois.*

It was Yeats's great countryman and fellow dramatic poet
Synge who put it all most handsomely. "The infancy and
decay of the drama tend to be didactic," he wrote. "The
drama, like the symphony, does not teach or prove anything. Analysts, with their problems, and teachers, with
their systems, are soon as old-fashioned as the pharmacopœia of Galen . . . but the best plays of Ben Jonson and
Molière can no more go out of fashion than the blackber-

ries on the hedges." Some of Synge's plays have been critically deprecated as "outlaw comedy, with gypsy laughter
coming from somewhere in the shrubbery by the roadside."
Saroyan is very far from being a Synge, but the same depre-
cation may be visited on some of his own plays, and with
the same enthusiastic hosanna.

THE NEW MOON. August 18, 1942

Joseph S. Tushinsky's revival of the 1928 beer-weeping operetta by Oscar Hammerstein II, Frank Mandel, and Laurence Schwab, with music by Sigmund Romberg, scenery apparently by the Acme Colored Postcard Company, and costumes by Joseph S. Tushinsky's Aunt Becky.

Program

Julie	*Doris Patston*	Besac	*Paul Reed*
Beaunoir	*George Leonard*	Jacques	*George Mitchell*
Captain Duval	*Gene Barry*	Marianne Beaunoir	*Ruby Mercer*
Vicomte Ribaud	*Marcel Journet*	Philippe	*Everett West*
Fouchette	*Carl Nelson*	Clotilde	*Hope Emerson*
Robert Misson	*Wilbur Evans*	Brunet	*Robert Tower*
Alexander	*Teddy Hart*	Captain de Jean	*Walter Munroe*

THE THREE ACTS and five scenes of this romantic oldster are laid, like an egg, in New Orleans, on the high seas, and on an island that looks as if it had been painted by the late Heywood Broun on one of his early off-days. The time is the year 1791. At any rate that is what the program tries to assure us. The critical mind yields reluctant to programs on such occasions, however, and the impression persists that all three acts and five scenes take place musically in a juke-box. The mind has smaller difficulty, nevertheless, in following the program as to the libretto. It is perfectly willing to agree that it is laid in 1791, if perhaps less in the localities stipulated than in a theatrical storehouse of the period.

Whenever one of these old Broadway operettas is revived, it is the habit of a number of its critics wistfully to reflect in the O tempora, O mores vein and to allow that what once was impressive is alas so no longer. The surprise is that they considered it impressive in the first place. *The New Moon,* for example, was no whit better when it was originally shown than it is today. Its book was just as dull then as it is now; its humorous passages were just as corny; and its score was every bit as saloon-piano and derivatively familiar. Yet the critics remain victims of pernicious nostalgia and the infection leads them to the museful concoction of such tender, if disillusioned, messages as the following, quoted from the full breast of *PM's* Mr. Mark Schubart: "Seeing *The New Moon* again, after a lapse of fourteen years, is like meeting an old flame, being genuinely glad to see her and at the same time noticing that she has put on weight, wears just a snip too much lipstick, and has a laugh that isn't quite as charming as you remember it. It is an interesting experience, but at the same time it makes you wonder how you ever could have been so mad about the dear old thing." It also makes some of us wonder about such critics.

Romberg's music, in this as in many of his other exhibits, is Tin Pan Alley with a high-school education. It is half-way between mediocre Victor Herbert and tiptop Rudolf Friml. Such tunes as "Softly, As in a Morning Sunrise," "Stout-hearted Men," "Wanting You," "Marianne," and above all that celebrated Broadway turtle-dove, "Lover, Come Back to Me," are undeniably successful in warming the unsqueamish musical ear and to an even greater degree the unsqueamish amorous heart, but while a Leopold Stokowski or a Cab Calloway might conceivably be influenced to hold hands and play footie when a nightclub orchestra played them, it is more than merely certain that any Toscanini, Koussevitzky or even possibly Sir Thomas Beecham, drunk or sober, would make the girl pay her own check.

I KILLED THE COUNT. SEPTEMBER 3, 1942

A mystery mummery by Alec Coppel, originally shown in London in 1937. Produced by Frank Carrington and Agnes Morgan in association with the Shuberts.

PROGRAM

COUNT VICTOR MATTONI	LOUISE ROGERS	*Doris Dalton*
Rafael Corio	RENEE LA LUNE	*Ruth Holden*
POLLY *Ethel Morrison*	SAMUEL DIAMOND	
DIVISIONAL INSPECTOR DAVIDSON		*Clarence Derwent*
Louis Hector	JOHNSON	*Edgar Kent*
DETECTIVE RAINES	MULLET	*A. J. Herbert*
Bertram Tanswell	BERNARD K. FROY	*Robert Allen*
MARTIN *Le Roi Operti*	VISCOUNT SORRINGTON	*Guy Spaull*
POLICE CONSTABLE CLIFTON		
James Ganon		

SYNOPSIS: Prologue. *10 a.m.* Act I. *11:30 a.m.* Act II. *The action is continuous.* Act III. *The action is continuous.*

Scene. *The living-room of Count Mattoni's flat, London, England, a Friday in October shortly before the present war.*

I T IS NEWS to nobody but a number of our producers that, all things considered, a mystery play is generally one of the riskiest gambles in the present theatre. The aforesaid producers, who pride themselves on their commercial cunning, continue confidently, however, to buck the machine and most often have to borrow a louis from the croupier to get home. In the last five and a half seasons, or up to the time this is written, out of a total of thirty-five plays that fell either precisely or broadly into the mystery catalogue all of twenty-nine were failures, while only four were real box-office successes and two others got by, after fair runs, mainly on the score of sales to the film companies.

True to form, the producers again this season have laid their money on these one-to-six shots and have duly hollered when they went lame at the quarter. And one to six, the statistics of the theatre indicate, are overgenerous odds.

Of all the plays in our modern theatre which have achieved Broadway runs of five hundred or more performances, only one out of the recorded fifty-three, *The Bat,* has been a mystery play.

There are, generally speaking, two kinds of these Whodunits: the Udidits and the Ididits. In the former, several persons are suspected and directly accused of the crime, with all of them denying their part in it. In the latter, several persons openly confess to the crime, with all of them regarded skeptically by the representative of the law. *I Killed the Count* is a sample of the Ididit school, and a bad one. Its badness is further heightened by the frequent employment of flashbacks, which usually help to spell a loss at the box-office; by a rubber-stamp set of characters that includes the distraught Scotland Yard inspector and his dumb assistant, the evil, brunet, titled foreigner in the inevitable fancy silk lounge-jacket, the jittery housemaid, the vulgar, wisecracking show-girl, the vengeful lover, etc.; and by the kind of playwriting that, when the situation becomes exaggeratedly complex, permits a character to exclaim: "This is getting to be ridiculous!", thus supplying its own criticism.

The mentioned producers, doubly intent upon losing their money, in connection with these mystery plays apparently never take the trouble to find out what has been going on in the theatre and accordingly often put on plays that are thematically almost exactly like plays that have been put on directly before and that have failed abruptly. If the producers of *I Killed the Count,* for example, had investigated, they would have discovered that an exhibit called *Eight O'Clock Tuesday,* presented just the season before, was much like the play they foolishly invested in and that it lasted for only sixteen performances, to a loss of many thousands of dollars.

TOBACCO ROAD. September 5, 1942

Return engagement of the record-breaker by Jack Kirkland, based on the novel of Erskine Caldwell. Produced by Mr. Kirkland.

PROGRAM

Dude Lester	*Norman Budd*	Henry Peabody	*Fred Sutton*
Ada Lester	*Sara Perry*	Sister Bessie Rice	*Vinnie Phillips*
Jeeter Lester	*John Barton*	Pearl	*Sondra Johnson*
Ellie May	*Sheila Brent*	Captain Tim	*Harry Townes*
Grandma Lester	*Lillian Ardell*	George Payne	*Edwin Walter*
Lov Bensey	*Joe Silver*		

SYNOPSIS: Act I. *Late afternoon.* Act II. *Next morning.* Act III. *Dawn, the following day.*

The entire action of the play takes place at the farm of Jeeter Lester, situated on a Tobacco Road in the back country of Georgia.

Marking on the night of its return its 3,183rd performance on Broadway, thus topping the run of *Abie's Irish Rose,* its closest statistical contender, by 856 performances, the modern American theatre's phenomenon continued to baffle the critical licentiates who still cannot bring themselves to believe that hot pornography offered in the guise of a sociological study is good, tricky box-office. That all kinds of people who squeamishly would not tolerate, for example, a scene showing a young woman horsing a man into a state of tumescence will happily accept it if it is veiled in the protective coloration of a serious folk document they seem to doubt, even while tens of thousands of such people trample over them to crowd into the theatre where it is being shown. And that, for further example, another scene presenting a woman heating up a male's libido may become equally acceptable to the bluest nose if only it be orchestrated to religious fervor, they apparently, despite the evidence, similarly doubt.

When the play opened on December 4, 1933, its prospects looked none too good, since many members of the

New York first-night audience who could not be fooled by the camouflage resented the smut and left the theatre early in the evening. But since nothing travels faster and more prosperously than indignation over something dirty, it was not long thereafter before those two boon and inseparable companions, the dirty-mind and the moralist, began packing the theatre. And when subsequently the authorities of Rhode Island, several Southern states, and the great, pure municipality of Chicago, among others, banned the play on the ground of its gaminess, its fortune was guaranteed.

It is not, however and nevertheless, that the play hasn't certain other qualities, doubtless overlooked by the majority of its customers, which merit a degree of critical favor. Along with the theatrical smell of salacity there is here and there a whiff of the authentic smell of the Georgia cracker soil, and along with the theatrical dirt a trace of the real dirt of a dirty land and its filthy, miserable, and pathetic denizens. Yet one cannot imagine that it is these attributes that over the years have attracted much the same audiences who established the unusually long runs of such other theatrical naughty postcards as *White Cargo, Personal Appearance,* and *Sailor, Beware!*

JANIE. September 10, 1942

Another session with junior misses, by Josephine Bentham and Herschel Williams, adapted from a novel by the former. Produced by Brock Pemberton.

Program

CHARLES COLBURN	DICK LAWRENCE *Herbert Evers*
Maurice Manson	TINA *Artiebell McGinty*
ELSBETH COLBURN *Clare Foley*	ANDY *Michael St. Angel*
LUCILLE COLBURN	FRANK *Franklin Kline*
Nancy Cushman	OSCAR *Paul Wilson*
RODNEY *John Marriott*	HORTENSE BENNINGTON
JOHN VAN BRUNT *Howard St. John*	*Gertrude Beach*
JANIE COLBURN *Gwen Anderson*	"DEAD-PAN" HACKETT
BERNADINE DODD	*Blaine Fillmore*
Betty Breckenridge	CARL LOOMIS *J. Franklin Jones*
PAULA RAINEY *Margaret Wallace*	JOE JEROME *Nicky Raymond*
SCOOPER NOLAN *Frank Amy*	MICKEY MALONE *Kenneth Tobey*
THELMA LAWRENCE *Linda Watkins*	UNCLE POODGIE *W. O. McWatters*

Soldiers from Camp Longstreet.

SYNOPSIS: Act I. *The Colburns' living-room, late afternoon.* Act II. *The same, the following evening.* Act III. Scene 1. *Mrs. Colburn's upstairs sitting-room, three hours later.* Scene 2. *The living-room, half an hour later.*

The action of the play takes place in Hortonville, a small city in the United States. Time. *The present.*

W HEN THE EXHIBIT was booked into the Henry Miller Theatre, the late Henry's son Gilbert, who operates it and one of whose chief attributes as man and producer is a genial candor, observed to me: "As the war goes on, only three kinds of plays will probably be feasible: those with Negro casts, those with children casts, and those with all-women casts. I'll settle, so far as my personal and private tastes go, for the women, but I've had enough of the Negroes and kids." I string along with him to a very large degree. And since this *Janie* is another of the children plays in the long line of *Junior Miss, All in Favor, The Happy*

Days, Letters to Lucerne, etc., you may have it from me, and unquestionably also from Mr. Miller, in exchange for a photograph of Henrietta Crosman.

Not that there haven't been some very good plays about children and acted by children. There have been, but they have been written by the Karl Schönherrs, Frank Wedekinds and Booth Tarkingtons, not by the Josephine Benthams and Herschel Williamses. Most of the species by the latter company are simply theatrical entertainment in its second childhood, and as such critically and artistically on a par with the Henry Aldrich radio shows and the Hollywood movies of Roddy McDowall, Shirley Temple, Mickey Rooney, Paul Muni, and other such adolescents.

In the presence of these spectacles my wandering mind for some time now has toyed with the idea of a paraphrase of Goethe's *Faust.* Contemplating these stages horribly full of theoretically lovable and charming youth, I have been bemused by the notion of a Faust who, having bargained away his soul to the devil in return for such hypothetically precious youth and having had a taste of its irritations, troubles, and general agonizing nuisances, including the blonde Marguerites, is only too glad promptly to bargain it back again for peaceful, contentful, reposeful, and happy age.

Mephistopheles, shrewd soul-broker though he was, himself quickly recognized Faust for the fool he in turn was. No sooner did Faust have at him, idiotically, with "Show me the fruits that, ere they're gathered, rot, and trees that daily with new leafage clothe them!" than Mephistopheles had back at him, sagely, with "But still the time may reach us, good my friend, when peace we crave and more luxurious diet."

Janie, which has to do with a number of young girls who, in their parents' absence, fill the house with boy soldiers from a neighboring military camp, does not, among other things, overlook the episode wherein a father seeks to instruct his young daughter in the matter of sex. Save for the scene which O'Neill wrote into *Ah, Wilderness!,* all these passages which we have encountered in the latter-day

American plays have been so much of a stereotyped piece that a little fresh imagination would be more than welcome. In this direction, why not a scene in which, when the father or mother hesitantly enters upon the old business of stern admonition and warning, the youngster will not only quietly observe that, though he or she is without experience in the matter, sex can't be the dismally dangerous thing the parent would make it out to be, but from all the child has gathered must be possessed of some beautiful thrill and pleasure and goodness, as witness not only his own dear parents but the parents of his young friends, to say nothing of the beautiful romantic stories of all the great lovers who ever lived?

These bogus stage transcriptions of youth, with youngsters conducting themselves in a manner foreign to any normal youngsters one has ever met in real life, have had no sounder critic than young Gwen Anderson, who played the leading role in the exhibit under consideration. Observed little Miss Anderson in a newspaper interview, expressing her scornful skepticism of such playwrights: "When I was sixteen years old, as I am supposed to be in the play, all my friends and myself tried to act older, not younger."

What much of our journalistic drama criticism seems sorely to need in the case of plays like *Janie* is more critics like Gwen.

THE MORNING STAR. September 14, 1942

One of England's most successful war plays, by Emlyn Williams, author of Night Must Fall, The Corn Is Green, Yesterday's Magic, *etc. Produced by Guthrie McClintic.*

PROGRAM

Mrs. Lane	*Brenda Forbes*	Brimbo Watkyn	*Rhys Williams*
Mrs. Parrilow	*Gladys Cooper*	Cliff Parrilow	*Gregory Peck*
Alison Parrilow	*Jill Esmond*	Wanda Baring	*Wendy Barrie*
Dr. Datcher (S.D.)		Sir Leo Alvers	*Nicholas Joy*
	Cecil Humphreys		

SYNOPSIS: Act I. Scene 1. *A morning in August.* Scene 2. *An evening four weeks later.* Act II. Scene 1. *A night in October some weeks later.* Scene 2. *The same, eight hours later.* Act III. Scene 1. *Eleven hours later, late afternoon.* Scene 2. *A little over 24 hours later, evening.*

The scene is the drawing-room of Mrs. Parrilow's house in Chelsea, London, S.W. 3. Time. 1940.

T̲HE Morning Star is thematically and essentially the previous season's *The Wookey* in a somewhat smarter setting. I prefer *The Wookey.* It was very bad but it wasn't nearly so bad as *The Morning Star,* which is twice as full of the greasepaint staples seemingly indigenous to most of these plays of British fortitude and soul-finding under the Luftwaffe. That Mr. Williams, who is an actor, writes like an actor (yes, I know there have been exceptions), no one familiar with much of his antecedent work need be reassured. His characters are mainly out of a theatrical warehouse; his dialogue is largely sugar-cured; and the majority of his situations have hitherto enjoyed active service in other plays. I repeat that we have now had enough of the bomb in Gilead melodrama and more than enough of English characters who need loud Hollywood sound effects to redeem their backbones. When Mr. Williams adds the old triangle of husband, wife, and miscellaneous blonde, we may be expected to call quits.

It is a paradox that it should take war to convert that

robust and hairy old institution of the popular theatre, melodrama, into something of a sissy. Yet once the cannon start to roar and the fields of the world are drenched in blood, it seems peculiarly to lose its old biff, zip, and whang and to go soft. What is more, the change does not end with war's end, but continues for several years thereafter.

The conspicuous melodramas of the last war needed little more than a butler, a sprinkling of evening clothes, and maybe three or four bad epigrams to turn them into drawing-room plays. What authentic melodrama they contained was confined largely to the wings, where a din of bass drum pounding and occasional red flares substituted for the pungent ruckus that erst was permitted the center of the stage. The climax was reached in the hereinbefore mentioned English *Journey's End*, which was demelodramatized to the extent of making its officers' battlefield dugout so closely resemble White's Club in St. James's Street with a light thunderstorm going on outside that one was disappointed when one observed that the chairs were in rather better condition.

The current unpleasantness has been even more contributive to the coating of the old gallery peanuts with sugar. Things have got to the point, indeed, where the Nazi enemy, which in the older days would have been thrown off the cliff en masse by Lieutenant Hal Desmond, U. S. A., to the cheers of the audience, is on occasion presented in so steinbeckly tender a light that the audience doesn't know which side it is expected to hiss. And when this generosity toward the enemy is more restrained, the conduct of the home team is often so pervasively debonair, even in the midst of dangers that would have scared the pants off the most fearless heroes of the old 10–20–30's, that the whole thing seems to be just a build-up for the entrance of some John Drew.

The heroes of the great melodrama of the past — the William Gillette roles alone excepted — were, frequently ridiculous as they have been, of the primitive stuff of heroes. They were men of oath and muscle, of roaring lung and derring-do, of the strength of lions and the vocabularies of barroom bouncers and Lady Astor. When they came out on the stage, the villains, however ferocious their black mustaches, knew that their goose was ultimately cooked. The heroes of today are a sadly different stripe. They speak the language of ladies' tea-parlors; they diffidently minimize their bravery; their resolution is so quiet you can hear a pin drop; they even periodically and shamefully allow that the villains may conceivably not be entirely the scoundrels they are painted. They are, in short, and many of the heroines with them, simply futile subscribers to the popular critical theory that the way to win an audience, in so far as it be compatible with official propaganda, is initially to give the villain an even break and humbly to derogate as quite ordinary, orthodox, and jogtrot their own contribution, the least part of which is death, to the dog's final undoing.

As is sometimes the way of the theatre, however, it does not always work out as it is expected to. The possibly greater critical merit of the new melodramatic dispensation doesn't entirely make up for the incidental lack of the old rousing excitement. And why should it? One goes to a war melodrama in the heat of war rooting hell-bent for one side or one either doesn't go at all or goes intelligently instead to some play of quality that doesn't depend for its life upon contemporary alarm and prejudice. (Or perhaps, by way of dutifully remembering one's responsibility in this world, to a show full of beautiful girls.) When it comes to war melodrama, if I have to take it at all, give me something straight out of the bottle in the rough, tough, bloody, battering vein of Irwin Shaw's *Sailor off the Bremen* or even something like the old Harry Clay Blaney stuff and you can have all the tame Lesley Storm *Heart of a Citys*, Steinbeck *The Moon Is Downs*, Brennan *The Wookeys,* and Emlyn Williams *The Morning Stars* from here to London and back.

The English acceptance of this Mr. Williams as a dramatist of considerable beam and heft is a source of some puzzled amusement to American critics, even at length to some of those who lost their balance completely in the in-

stance of his *The Corn Is Green*. For they have come belatedly to recognize that the theme of that play is essentially
of a piece with that of the old Stair and Havlin plays and
Essanay and Thanhouser films wherein an Eastern school-
teacher, come to the Far West, found an interest in an
uncouth cowboy and educated him into the ways of a
scholar and gentleman. They have also come to recognize
that the play's devices, ranging all the way from the initial
hostility of both the community and the pupil toward the
teacher to the eventual warm, understanding acceptance
of her, and including such jalopyan hokum as the singing
class, the blackmailing female who says the hero is the
father of her baby, and the old maid with the romantic
flutters, are hardly the mark of an imaginative craftsman.
And the writing of the play, they have come further to
recognize, is much less the authentically simple writing
they originally esteemed it to be than a kind of cagily restrained artificiality.

It isn't that there are not some fairish incidentals in the
play. One or two of its minor characters are moderately
well drawn, and one or two of the emotional passages are
deftly handled. It is rather that the writing on the whole
gives off the impression of a makeup box too near the ink-
well and that the familiar theme of the Galatea who pla-
tonically (or otherwise) carves out the future of a young
Pygmalion is consequently splotched with rouge, mascara,
and scented talcum. It may affect others differently, but
when, for instance, Mr. Williams's middle-aged school-
teacher heroine, presented as an intelligently critical
woman, reads aloud with profound awe and with intermittent rapt stares into space a composition by his young, illiterate coal-miner that would not get past the third assistant editor of *True Confessions,* I cough behind my hand.
Again, when in the brief period of two years this complete
illiterate has advanced to the point where — in addition
to having mastered many of the subjects normally mastered
by an intelligent boy only after eight years in so-called
grammar schools and four years in prep — he is fully up
on Greek, Voltaire, and the higher polysyllables, to say

nothing of being able to assimilate the entire history of Henry VIII from a moment's perusal of a sheet of paper, and where he is then successful in getting an Oxford scholarship over many long and carefully trained aristocratic rivals — when I engage all this, I cough twice behind my hand. And I make it three coughs when I am invited to regard as a remarkable and vitally fresh play one in which this genius's career is threatened because of that illegitimate bairn, in which the mama comes on at the critical moment to denounce him, in which an irascible squire is wheedled into doing her will by the *Charley's Aunt* coquetries of the school-mistress heroine, in which the hussy seduces the hero by letting him get a whiff of her perfume, in which the comical assistant school-teacher, when asked a question she can't answer, nervously and elaborately changes the subject, in which local color is achieved by periodically introducing a boy who utters a Welsh mouthful of *l*'s and *w*'s, and in which the spinster heroine, to protect the young hero, adopts as her own the latter's fortuitous child.

As for Mr. Williams's *Night Must Fall,* it was, as you who saw it will recall, just another of those London box-office mélanges of perversion, murder, and horror, rather better than a number of others of its cheap species though not nearly so expert as such as *Rope's End,* and in its entirety written with cold cream, and melodramatically ham. Two other plays, *Spring 1600* and *He Was Born Gay,* the former a feeble essay in Shakespeareana and the latter an even feebler contribution to stage literature about the overworked Dauphin, have been displayed in London, but as yet not here. As for Mr. Williams's other local revealment, *Yesterday's Magic* (known in England as *The Light of Heart*) , consider the London critical reaction: "a real play" (*Star*) , "one of the best plays of modern times" (*Sunday Dispatch*) , "a great play" (*Sunday Graphic*) , "A distinguished play welded with beautiful firmness" (*Times*) , "Williams writes like a poet" (*Sunday Express*) , "one of the best evenings in the theatre for a very long time" (*Sunday Times*) , "ladies and gentlemen, I commend to you

Emlyn Williams; cherish him!" (*News of the World*), and "magnificent stuff brilliantly mingled by this young master-playwright" (*Sunday Pictorial*).

And what is the true nature of this great treat? Its basic originality may be appreciated from its theme, which concerns a once successful actor ruined by overindulgence in the bottle, the vain efforts of his patient, self-sacrificing young daughter to reform and redeem him, and his brio end in suicide. Recovering from the initial shock of such novelty, we scrutinize the further originality of sentimental approach and treatment. I quote a sample speech, placed in the mouth of the old actor who is meditating the glory of the theatre:

"And there's that great empty place over the way, echoing with hammers and hoovers, hoovers and hammers, just a shabby factory. There's this most ordinary day; people are doing their jobs, or doing nothing, rushing about London exchanging all those worn pennies of speech we know so well. . . . And in a few hours they'll all be in that factory, waiting for the curtain to go up. And behind that curtain, in the wings, leaning on a grimy drum, a little man in dirty plimsolls will be waiting too. He hears them all, sitting out there like a lot of magpies — and then the signal. The lights fade, the voices die into sudden silence, the pulse of the world is still. . . . And like a cloud shaken from a sack, something spreads through the place from end to end. I don't know what it is, but it's magic, and there's nothing like it in the world!"

Now for a few samples of wit:

1. — "I saw in the paper about a Turk that lived to a hundred and forty."
    " 'Uman bein's is different."
    "Isn't a Turk a human being?"
    "I thought she said a turkey."

2. — "Gentleman rang up twice. A Mr. Rabbit."
    "You mean Robertson?"
    "That's right."

3. — "Laryngitis — an affectation of the throat."

We come to humorous resource in the way of character. One such is Bevan, a policeman. Here is Bevan, a paraphrase of the familiar sapient butler out of hokum plays on end:

MADDOC. But how do you account for Hazlitt's lecture on Ophelia?

BEVAN. I am not an admirer of the essayists, Mr. Thomas, and it was Coleridge.

We turn to a contemplation of fertility in the way of general dialogue. Here, some typical passages:

1. — "I feel as if I'd just gone over Niagara in a barrel."

2. — "But you know life is not as simple as that."

3. — "And please forget all this for tonight, and sit back and enjoy yourself."

4. — "It would mean you weren't happy, and you must be happy, you know, because you're doing the right thing."

5. — "It's my fault — for not realizing it was madness from the beginning — that no person has the right to make themselves indispensable to anybody else."

We sniff the device of sprinkling the text with familiar names by way of creating weight and atmosphere. A part catalogue: Covent Garden, *Daily Sketch,* the Cri, St. Margaret's, *Daily Mirror,* Selfridge's, Sarah Siddons, Ellen Terry, the B. B. C., Regent Street, Haymarket, Edward VII, *Evening Standard,* Tivoli, Charing Cross, Queen's Hall, Toscanini, Chappells', Trollope, George Moore, *The Brook Kerith, David Copperfield, Bleak House,* Henry Irving, Garrick Club, *Romeo and Juliet, King Lear, Hamlet, Peer Gynt, Vasco da Gama,* Regent's Park, Beerbohm Tree, Drury Lane, Critics' Circle, the Lyceum, the Shaftesbury, the Lyric, Mrs. Patrick Campbell, Caledonian Market, Green Room Club, Edith Evans, George Arliss, Café de Paris, Savoy Grill, Orpen, *Tristan and Isolde,* C. B.

Cochran, *Henry V,* John Gielgud, Temple Shakespeare, Dover Wilson, Kean, Kemble, British Museum, the *Times,* Goneril, Regan, Dickens, *Charley's Aunt,* Albert Hall, Chelsea, the *Star,* the *Tatler,* the Odeon, Royal Opera House, *The Merry Widow,* John McCormack, *Punch, Pagliacci,* the Embankment, Gerrard 3482. . . .

We engage virtuosity in the Tender Note:

(*Stage direction: There is sadness in the room*)

MADDOC (*drowsy*). This room's miles away from anywhere. Just you an' me, a l'il place where the rest can't get at me, back in the old days when I was a l'il chap, with the old songs.

We observe the highly original method of introducing the young male love interest:

(*A knock at the door*)

CATTRIN. Come in. (*Robert opens the door and leans round it. He is in shirtsleeves, etc.*)

ROBERT. Your father hasn't got a new Gillette blade, has he?

CATTRIN. Well, I —

ROBERT (*coming in*). Sorry, I forgot this muck on my face — I'm the nuisance who called this morning and asked for a hammer.

We savor the subsequent airy humor of the young lovers:

CATTRIN. Have you finished with the hammer?
ROBERT. I wish I'd thought of shaving with it.

We further savor the rich phraseology of the lovers' dialogue:

1. — "How do I compare with other men you know?"

2. — "I've told you enough about *me,* God knows. What is the one thing *you* want?" "As I've always known it was out of the question, it isn't really such a tragedy. It's just that by nature I'm meant to — have children."

3. — "Can't you see that I'm asking you to marry me?"

4. — "That's the thing about you, I think — you're great fun."

5. — "You might meet — somebody else."

6. — "Do you remember the things I said to you that first night, just here?" "I know them by heart."

I take it that is more than enough.

This, then, is the general complexion of a play hailed by the English critics as "magnificent stuff," "one of the best plays of modern times," "a great play," and "a distinguished play." And this the author hailed by them as a "young master-playwright."

NEW PRIORITIES OF 1943. SEPTEMBER 15, 1942

Yet another attempt to revive vaudeville. Produced by Clifford C. Fischer.

PRINCIPALS

Bert Wheeler, Harry Richman, Carol Bruce, Hank Ladd, Henny Youngman, Johnny Burke, Harrison and Fisher, The Bricklayers, The Acromaniacs, The Radio Aces, and Sally Keith.

THE TITLE of the show was obviously a typographical error. In view of the nature of its acts, songs, and jokes, they doubtless meant 1913. Save for a single bit involving Bert Wheeler and his stooge, Hank Ladd, which enjoyed some humor, and the exceptional but already all too familiar dog act, *The Bricklayers,* the bill was a compendium of vaudeville obits including everything from Harry Richman with his hat saucily over one eye vibrating his torso in stale sentimental ballads to the joke about the seasick soldier on deck who, in reply to a question as to whether the captain has come up yet, says he has if he swallowed him. If you need a further idea, there were also in evidence the travestied classical dance, the shimmy-shaker, the acrobats, the blues-singer in the split skirt, and the ditty facetiously arguing that a man's biological reaction to an agitating wench is purely a matter of mind.

If vaudeville is to be revived, its revival will hinge upon something other than the mere revival of the features that were largely instrumental in killing it. Further, what eventually drove customers away from it some years ago was the endless repetition of many of its acts. What is certain to drive them away once again, now that it is trying to stage a come-back, is a similar repetition. For however good they may be, a long succession of trapeze performers, acrobats, dog acts, equilibrists, ventriloquists, too familiar sketches, Indian-club jugglers, Volga Boatmen singers and the like is bound soon to lay audiences not in the aisles but in their seats — and flat. What vaudeville needed then and needs now is something new. And, being one angel who does not fear to tread, I address myself to some constructive bequests.

First, the matter of sketches. The one and only really acceptable one thus far shown in such vaudeville shows as *Priorities of 1942, Keep 'Em Laughing, Top Notchers,* and *Laugh, Town, Laugh* has been the Smith and Dale *Dr. Kronkheit* skit, though already familiar for almost a quarter of a century. The rest, from the old *Change Your Act* of Victor Moore's, which fell dead instanter, to the double-talk radio sketch of Willie Howard's, which was borrowed from a failure of a few seasons ago, no more belong to a vaudeville that hopes to keep on its feet for a spell than do the old trained seals or the dramatic sketches showing the man in evening dress seated before a fireplace and dreaming about his past loves.

By way of novelty — and it should be good box-office in addition to having critical merit — I suggest a half-dozen sketches such as the following:

1. A sixteen-minute sketch, one long, uninterrupted howl, consisting of that portion of the dialogue and business which Eugene O'Neill cut out (on the ground that it held up the play's movement) of the dinner-table scene in his *Ah, Wilderness!* It is as funny as all get-out and should be sure-fire.

2. The twelve-minute wordless sketch, written several years ago for the London radio by one Arbuthnot, which tells an amusing story entirely by means of sounds. It could readily be adapted to the vaudeville stage and would be a refreshing novelty.

3. The hilarious skit by Marc Connelly, originally done by the Dutch Treat Club, showing the influence of divers aquatic allusions on the physical comfort of a gentleman who has been drinking and who is unable, for reasons of punctilio, to leave the gathering.

4. Saroyan's *Once Around the Block,* a scream involving a young man who doesn't make a hit with the women because he is too persistently ebullient, who is advised that

what the girls like is a touch of languor and repose, who to achieve the desideratum runs madly around the block, jumping dozens of imaginary hurdles the better to diminish his vigor, and who then loses his girl to a cop.

5. *The Literary Approach,* a comical skit by one Moïse, in which a wily Lothario seduces a young woman of highbrow tendencies by gradually edging up to the big moment with slyly apt literary references and quotations.

6. Twelve minutes of any Frederick Lonsdale fashionable London drawing-room comedy, in blackface.

Secondly, dog acts. Just for a change, one in which an unhousebroken "sooner" convulsingly allows nature to take its course each time before going into its specialty. (Recall the mule in the musical comedy *Rainbow* who brought down the house on the opening night. No one had heard such uproarious laughter in a theatre since, years before, a horse misbehaved similarly in Beerbohm Tree's production of one of the Shakespeare chronicle plays.)

Thirdly, an abbreviated version of the previously referred to *Krausmeyer's Alley* of burlesque fame, one of the funniest acts ever heard of and not seen hereabout in its pristine form for a long time.

Fourthly, a rapid-fire act made up of the ten drollest first entrances of the comedians in such long past musical comedies as *The Isle of Champagne* (Thomas Q. Seabrooke), *Panjandrum* (De Wolf Hopper), *The Wizard of the Nile* (Frank Daniels), *The Billionaire* (Jerome Sykes), *The Rogers Brothers in Ireland* (Gus and Max Rogers), *The Press Agent* (Pete Dailey), *The Caliph* (Jeff De Angelis), *The French Maid* (Charlie Bigelow), *The Jewel of Asia* (Jimmie Powers), and *Erminie* (Francis Wilson).

And fifthly, no more trapeze acts, wire-walkers, acrobats, Indian-club jugglers, equilibrists, Volga Boatmen singers, or Keith and Proctor blackout skits.

SHOW TIME. September 16, 1942

Yet still another attempt to resuscitate vaudeville, this one produced by Fred F. Finklehoffe.

PRINCIPALS

George Jessel, Jack Haley, Ella Logan, the De Marcos, the Berry Brothers, Lucille Norman, Con Colleano, Bob Williams and dog, and Olsen and Shirley.

IN COMPARISON with the doings of the night before, these were here and there right out of the Aquavit bottle, mainly by virtue of the efforts of M. Jessel. If there is a more salubrious fellow on these two-a-day stages, I have not the signal honor of his acquaintance, though surely no reflection on the unimpeachable MM. Ed Wynn and Lou Holtz is intended. Jessel's monologue in which he figures as a Czechoslovakian refugee lecturer and the famous one in which he engages in a telephone conversation with his mama, who confuses Henry Wadsworth Longfellow with a Mr. Lowenstein who lives next door, along with his general master of ceremonies banter, are the cream of the cream. Jack Haley's amiable foolery, the De Marcos' smooth dancing (although the new Sally De Marco is not in the former Renée De Marco's class), and the dusky Berry brothers' hoofing were also assets. As for the wire-walker, the dog act, the contortionists, the joke about the mother of the female contortionist having evidently been scared in childbirth by a pretzel (Jessel, Heaven help him, was responsible), and Haley's antediluvian flute-playing business with the orchestra flutist waggishly continuing to play when Haley removes the instrument from his lips . . . !

Since dog acts seem to figure in all these tries at vaudeville rebirth, and since most of them are pretty poor, it might be a serviceable idea for the entrepreneurs to attempt to dig up another one as good as the hereinbefore mentioned *Bricklayers,* if possible. Which brings us, relevantly, to a general consideration of the important place occupied by dogs and other animals in the history of our modern stage. Without them, indeed, some of the biggest successes in our theatre could never have been produced. Think of *Ben Hur* without its chariot horses; of *Uncle Tom's Cabin* without the bloodhounds; of *Mazeppa* and *Under Two Flags* without the white horses; of *Peg o' My Heart* without Peg's dog Michael, or *The Barretts of Wimpole Street* without Elizabeth's dog Flush.

What would have become of Frederick Ballard's *Young America* if no dog had been at liberty to sign up for the role around which the whole last act revolved? The funniest skit in *Hooray for What,* Ed Wynn or no Ed Wynn, would have been impossible had no less than four dogs been available to help Ed in interpreting it. The one and only reputable comedy moment in the season-before-last's disastrous *Horse Fever* was derived entirely from the presence in the cast of a horse. Neil Burgess's greatest success, *The County Fair,* would never have been possible without its race horses. And like a silk hat without a rabbit would have been De Wolf Hopper's *Wang* without its elephant, *Siberia* without its wolves, *The Speckled Band* without its snake, and *The Prodigal Son* without its sheep. *The Wookey* called for a dachshund periodically to stimulate its faded humor and pathos. *Mr. Big* had to rely on a horse for its only real comedy moment. Sean O'Casey's *Purple Dust* needs a cow for one of its most important scenes, and if the worst comes to the worst and no cow is available properly to catch the genuine O'Casey atmosphere, the producer will sadly have to compromise to the extent of hiring a couple of mere human actors to get under a hide and try to do the damnedest they can to match the talent of a real cow. Saroyan's *Sweeney in the Trees* depends for its final curtain effect upon a dove. Without the dove the end of the play would go for naught. And at least a half-dozen other plays in the cards have been delayed because the producers have been unsuccessful in casting certain roles with the right dogs, cats, owls, horses, and — in one case — a parrot, cinnamon bear, and zebra.

If a mere black cat wandering accidentally across a stage has been known to spell the doom of a play, how many animal actors, on the more fortunate side, have been known to help spell success? The prime comedy of Noel Coward's revue *Set to Music* was negotiated by a white horse in association with Beatrice Lillie. The prime comedy of *Simple Simon*, in turn, was negotiated by a brown horse in association with Ed Wynn. And the prime comedy of *Higher and Higher*, yet again, was negotiated by a seal in association with Jack Haley.

Lionel Barrymore's career was early given a shove forward, in *The Mummy and the Humming Bird*, by a monkey. And it was a monkey, too, who helped to glorify the performance of Doris Keane in *Romance*, her biggest success. Lillian Russell achieved her comeback, in *Wildfire*, only through the aid of a horse, and Mabel Taliaferro also was lost until a horse assisted her to popular success in *Polly of the Circus*. Amelia Bingham's first New York appearance, in *The Struggle of Life*, was in conjunction with *two* horses, and Herbert Kelcey's first in London, in the Drury Lane melodrama *Youth*, was in conjunction with all of three.

Speaking of melodrama, where would it be without animal histrionic assistance to its other actors? No one would ever have seen a hundred melodramas beginning with *The Still Alarm* and *The Whip* and ending, even at the half-distance mark, with *Shenandoah* and *The Roundup*.

But of all the various animals who take up histrionism as a career, the dog, generally speaking, is the audiences' favorite. In this, of course, there is nothing surprising, since the dog, wherever you find him, is usually hokum plus. When Eugene O'Neill's play *Days Without End* failed to capture box-office trade, O'Neill remarked to me with a wry smile that it would have been the simplest thing in the world for him to have converted it into a whopping success. "All I would have had to do," he said, "is to have Blemie [his late pet Dalmatian] walk across the stage once in the first act, twice in the second, and in the third curl up at the hero's feet and gaze soulfully into his eyes. The rush at the box-office would have necessitated a couple of extra treasurers.''

It is a well-known theatrical fact that any of the old *Uncle Tom* troupes that advertised 6–Bloodhounds–6 always did twice as much business as one that offered only the usual two or three. The most sympathetic press-agency in years was that which had Katharine Cornell's dog in *The Barretts* for its subject. And for season after season two of the top drawing cards in vaudeville were Goldman's and Alf Loyal's droll canine acts.

In the many years of my incumbency as a magazine editor, it was a general, and occasionally embarrassing, fact that any even half-way good dog story usually attracted wider attention among the readers — and certainly a lot more enthusiastic letters to the editor — than almost anything else, however highly creditable to the art of belles-lettres, in the particular issue.

One of the most successful pieces of advertising copy in American advertising history has been the celebrated "His Master's Voice," with its dog listening to a phonograph. One of the most winning things in the public's mind about the current President of the United States is his fondness for Fala. And so great has been the popular interest in Fala that Howell-Soskin have published a book about the Scottie. Albert Payson Terhune was for many years one of the country's most popular magazine writers with his stories about dogs. Jack London's *The Call of the Wild,* with its dog hero, became a national best seller. Holden's dog store in East Firty-third Street, New York, with its window full of puppies, attracts almost as many people as the Stork Club situated just to the left. It was the late James Gordon Bennett's request that his *New York Herald* editors try to have a dog news story in every issue and it was his command that if the story was a better than ordinary one it must always be printed on the first page. Richard Harding Davis bought his first six top hats only after he had written a dog story.

Leaving the dog and returning to animals in the theatre

in general, it was the last Oscar Hammerstein's idea that, if everything else failed to attract New Yorkers to his Victoria roof garden, a cow grazing in an imitation pasture might turn the trick. The cow was duly installed and the mob of city folk was so enchanted by the strange spectacle that Oscar did a land-office business. When the old Christian-Pagan, Roman arena play *Quo Vadis?* in its third road season began to show signs of falling off, a senescent and mangy lion set to a ferocious growling for Christian blood by covert injections of turpentine and displayed in the lobbies as ballyhoo was sufficient to bring in the eager customers from miles around. The Middle West, when trade indicated some slackening, was galvanized into renewed action in the instance of the play *David Harum* through the mere display of a horse in front of the theatres. And the old beer-gardens from Philadelphia in the East to St. Louis in the West for a period of fifteen years got a great deal of their admission intake on the score of a performing duck named August Müller. I myself must have drunk no less than a hogshead of lager while responding, over a period of at least ten of the fifteen years, to August's drollery.

In conclusion, what screen actor, save possibly alone Charlie Chaplin, has been as universally known and attended as Micky Mouse, unless it be Donald Duck? What small illustrated book in recent years, save possibly alone *Bet It's a Boy,* has had the success of *Ferdinand the Bull?* What toy has ever achieved greater popularity than the Teddy Bear? What circus act is as necessary a part of the circus, and has been for all of fifty years, as the trick-dog act? What remains the favorite book of children if it isn't Æsop's *Fables?* And what has made the merry-go-round the one and permanent feature of all pleasure-park features if it isn't the horses, giraffes, and camels?

Mark Twain once said that the more he saw of human beings, the more he liked dogs. In and out of the theatre a whole lot of people seem to agree with Mark. And not only about dogs, but about most of the animal kingdom, excepting maybe only simon-pure skunks. Under the circumstances, therefore, it is a pity that the current vaudeville producers are spoiling the whole thing by showing us — aside only from the *Bricklayers* — dogs that for the most part could not have got a job supporting even Robert Edeson.

VICKIE. September 22, 1942

A farce by a Hollywood literatus, S. M. Herzig. Produced, in a manner of speaking, by Frank Mandel.

Program

Vickie Roberts	*Uta Hagen*	Karen	*Gerry Carr*
George Roberts	*José Ferrer*	Sandra	*Lynne Carter*
Mr. Dunne	*Taylor Holmes*	Greta *Mme. Margaret Matzenauer*	
Blanche	*Evelyn Davis*	Kay Hackett	*Wynne Boze*
Mr. Noonas	*Frank Conlan*	Mr. Corliss	*Charles Halton*
Mrs. Dunne	*Mildred Dunnock*	Mrs. Frye	*Eleanor Gifford*
Amy	*Colette Lyons*	Mrs. Arthur	*Marcella Markham*
Private Cootes	*Edmund Glover*	Mr. Hatch	*Del Hughes*
Private Carter	*Red Buttons*	Mrs. Corliss	*Sara Seegar*

SYNOPSIS: Act I. *Saturday afternoon.* Act II. *Sunday morning.* Act III. *Monday morning.*

The entire action of the play takes place in the living-room of the Roberts' apartment, in a suburb of New York City. Time. September 1942.

FARCE MAY BE DEFINED as comedy in its cups. In the case of this *Vickie,* however, it was to be defined as comedy on the water-wagon. Although hailed on its out-of-town try-out as the acme of boozy hilarity, it disclosed itself on the New York opening night to be so inordinately humorless and dull that even the close relatives of the author, actors, and management, who seemed to fill at least half the house, had a trying time making their forced laughter heard above the groans of the less descendant persons present.

The subject of women in home war service is a conceivably available springboard for some fairly good fun, but the present author took the jump in a straitjacket. Without a trace of the gaiety that Charles H. Hoyt even in the far-off days visited upon the male Home Guard in *A Milk-White Flag,* he splashed around with all the stale show-shop stuff, including the missing plans, the man hidden in the cupboard, the opera singer given at inopportune moments to bursting into arias, the frivolous woman who can't keep her mind off sex, the girl-chasing soldiers, the innocent business man mistaken for a dangerous spy, etc.

What added to the general depression was direction and acting that would not have passed muster with one of the lesser college dramatic groups. José Ferrer and Frank Mandel handled the farcical stage as if it were a combination of Sherlock Holmes radio show and meeting of the board of creditors of the old *Judge*. As for the acting, Uta Hagen, who played Vickie, was as aptly suited to farce as the late Madame Janauschek, and no less than half a dozen of the others gave the appearance of having confused farce with something written by Theodore Dreiser.

A word about farce direction in general. The idea that farce must inevitably and invariably be paced very much quicker than comedy has resulted in some of the most painful directorial antics experienced by audiences and critics. A number of the most effective and successful farces have been wisely handled not as if they were Eva Tanguay and Betty Hutton getting drunk on quicksilver cocktails but as if they were little different from straight nimble comedy. *You Can't Take It with You* is one example; *Sailor, Beware!* is another; and *A Slight Case of Murder* is, surely, another still.

You can no longer, as George Abbott once periodically and successfully did, persuade an audience to accept a veronal tablet as something exceptionally stimulating by serving it as if it were vodka. The old business of directing a play that has little more life than a Ptolemaic mummy or a novel by Mrs. Alex McVeigh Miller like the Westinghouse Electric Co. in full operation no longer fools anyone and only adds a doubled patina of boredom. If a play is in itself lively, such lively direction is appropriate, but if it isn't, all the epileptiform directorial technique from here to the Sportspalast won't do it much good. The day when Abbott and his imitators were prosperous in getting away with an impression of galvanic stage vitality by having actors read lines like "I'm so drowsy I could curl right up here by the fire and snooze for two years" as if they were written "I'msodrowsyicouldcurlrightupherebythefireand-snoozefortwoyears," the meanwhile violently rocking the rocking-chair as if it were entered in the Poughkeepsie races, is done.

WINE, WOMEN AND SONG. September 28, 1942

Not the celebrated old Mortimer M. Theise burlesque show of the same title that toured the country at the beginning of the century, but an exhibit that took its name in vain. Produced by I. H. Herk, et al.

Principals

Margie Hart, Jimmy Savo, Pinky Lee, Noel Toy, Marian Miller, Isabella Brown, Herbie Faye, Wesson Brothers, et al.

The producers' revived interest in vaudeville was accompanied by a revived interest in burlesque. But it was something of a pity that those who would restore the latter seemed to retain small consciousness of the old low art form except as regards its strip-teasers. The strip-teaser was a relatively recent development in burlesque. It was unknown in the heyday of burlesque, which flourished for all of fifty years without it, which made its reputation without it, and which was in almost every respect the better without it.

What established burlesque was not women gradually divesting themselves of their clothes, but first-rate low comedians of the stripe of Montgomery and Stone, Dave Warfield, Alexander Carr, John T. Kelly, Bert Lahr, Jim Barton, and the like, most of whom graduated in time to the Broadway stage and inspirited it with their humors. Even today such rare old acts as *On the Yukon* and *Me, Him and I* are remembered by men who forget such neoteric strippers as Margie Hart after the first drink and Ann Corio after the second, or maybe third. As a student of burlesque and its devotees since the days of the Spanish-American War, the only women I remember as having made any impression at all on either myself or the other customers were the three-hundred-pounders in Billy Watson's famous *Beef Trust,* and they were pretty sufficiently clothed in elaborately spangled, tufted fleshings and were one and all obviously as aphrodisiacal as so many tons of ice.

No, it wasn't the girls, dressed or undressed, who made burlesque the popular entertainment it was; it was the funny men. It was the floppy pants and red undershirt boys like Bozo Snyder who crowded 'em in, and the German comedians like the wonderful George Bickel, and the be-diamonded Al Reeves with his mock-serious addresses to the trade, and Sliding Billy Watson (there were three of the Watsons cavorting at one time or another on the Wheel), and all that glorious crew. Maybe a Salome dancer would show up once in a while with her seven veils, the removal of the last one of which would still disclose her with enough heavy tights on to spare the blushes of the clergy in attendance, but, aside from a few college boys in the house who had had a couple of beers, she didn't create much of a stir. Nor did most of the girls who, later on, came out on the runways and sang their flirtatious ditties. What drew the business was the comiques.

Emphasis on strip-teasers and nude women in burlesque revivals at fancy prices cannot, even if censorship refrains from interference, be conducive to prosperity in the long run. If, like Michael Todd in his show *Star and Garter,* the impresarios exercise the intelligence to safeguard the all-important low-comedy element with such old burlesque clowns as Bobby Clark and such zanies as Professor Lamberti, the money will no doubt continue to roll in as it did in the old days. But if, as in this *Wine, Women and Song,* the emphasis is on women who take their duds off, with minor regard to the comedy, burlesque, censorship or no censorship, is ultimately doomed to go the way of all flesh. Mark Twain may have been right when he remarked that he would rather look at Lillian Russell stark naked than at General Grant in his full uniform. But I doubt that even Mark would have rather looked at Lillian in that state than at, say, the before-mentioned M. Clark in his misfit suit, with his cigar butt awriggle in his mouth, and with his cane bouncing up periodically and slamming him grandly on the nose.

I don't know how you, personally, may feel about strip-teasers at this late day, but if you are anything like your commentator you don't have to tell me. When the business first began, it had a certain amount of interest, at least for men under eighteen and over eighty. But as time has gone on, what with strippers more omnipresent than bedbugs in Norfolk, Virginia, the thing has gradually taken on all the attraction, for most males even a couple of years beyond eighteen and under eighty, of Hamburger Heaven directly after breakfast.

Of all the countless females who absent themselves from clothing — there must be thousands of them in theatres, night clubs, street fairs, pleasure parks, etc., from coast to coast — there are probably not more than five or six at most who, when disrobed, do not look like the women on the German postcards that used to be sold by furtive embryo Nazis around the Monokol, El Dorado, and other such Berlin night dumps. The stimulation of the libido which they hypothetically promote is accordingly of a piece with that induced by so many chilled watermelons, at least in the instance of white Southerners and Northerners. And even in the case of the prettier hussies, repetition has exercised its familiar satiating effect. Something should be done about it.

In this great artistic crisis I offer some constructive criticism. As a novel relief from the same old revealment of the same old powdered bodies, why not a little injection of humor? When a stripper, after undulating to and fro across a platform for fifteen minutes, the while she coyly removes item after item of her wardrobe, gets to the anatomical fundamentals, why not, for example, have her show tattooed on her torso Colonel Darryl Zanuck, Dorothy Thompson, and Bennett Cerf? Or why not, on her posterior, a chromo of George Sylvester Viereck? These are only a few cursory hints. Other even more acceptably distracting ideas will occur to the surfeited spectator. It would, at the worst, be a welcome change from the current biological monotony.

If mayhap the producers look askance at such strip self-criticism and whimsy and remain intent upon the aforesaid libido stimulation, I magnanimously give them another suggestion, also gratis. When the stripper has taken

off all the layers of her outer apparel, let her reveal underneath a soft blue silk dress with a little white lace collar at
the throat. I guarantee the producers that it will, in the
case of four men out of every five, pop the libido three
times more powerfully than the dreary old expanse of cal-
cimined flesh.

The vociferous suppression by the New York city fa-
thers of the old burlesque at low prices and their delay in
doing anything about the selfsame burlesque at higher
prices, which induced widc speculation in the curious, is
readily to be accounted for in terms of Article 216 of the
American Credo. According to that article, it remains the
unsparing conviction of such parties as those in question
that a man with considerable money in his pocket is inevitably less susceptible to evil influences, including first
and foremost the wayward excitation of the Casanova
glands, than a man with little. Or, in other words, that a
man living on Park Avenue will piously run for cover at
the very sight of a beautiful blonde without any clothes on,
whereas one living on Ninth will lasciviously run for the
blonde.

The theory that a strip-teaser will arbitrarily so inflame
any gashouse district whoremonger that he will become a
menace to society but on the other hand leave absolutely
cold every member of the Racquet Club whose wife has
gone to the country is slightly difficult of assimilation. And
so, too, is the theory that a good, new, dirty joke will be
received with a frozen look by any man who went to college and will rather appeal solely to icemen, plumbers,
movie press-agents, and other such ignoramuses. It is all
pretty hard to understand. But probably no harder to understand than a censorship that prosecuted that fine play
about Lesbianism called *The Captive* and winked at the
trashy one on the same subject called *Wise Tomorrow,* that
was horror-stricken at the prostitution of the dignified *The
God of Vengeance* but acquiescent in that of the rubbishy
Behind Red Lights, that slammed the gate on Bernard
Shaw's *Mrs. Warren's Profession* but left it wide open on
Charles Robinson's junky *Mahogany Hall,* that was out-

raged by venereal disease in Gantillon's *Maya,* to say nothing of in Brieux's *Damaged Goods,* but accepted it freely in Arnold Sundgaard's amateurish *Spirochete* (and applauded the Federal Theatre Project for the performance) , and that, after clamping the lid on Margie Hart's sidestreet strip-tease at fifty cents, gave it its silent endorsement, until a few days before the show was scheduled to close, when she did it in this *Wine, Women and Song* at a dollar increase.

HELLO OUT THERE. September 29, 1942
MAGIC

A revival by Eddie Dowling of what Bernard Shaw dubbed Fatty's First Play, which Chesterton in turn dubbed Skinny's Worst Pun, preceded by a one-act tragedy by the proliferous Fresno drama rabbit, W. Saroyan.

Program I

Photo Finish	*Eddie Dowling*	Another Man	*Farrell Pelly*
Ethel	*Julie Haydon*	The Woman	*Ann Driscoll*
The Man	*John Farrell*		

Time. *Now.*
Place. *A little jailhouse in Matador, Texas.*

Program II

——	*Eddie Dowling*	Dr. Grimthorpe	*John McKee*
Patricia Carleon	*Julie Haydon*	The Duke	*Stanley Harrison*
Hastings	*Farrell Pelly*	Morris Carleon	*Jess Barker*
Rev. Cyril Smith	*Bram Nossen*		

SYNOPSIS: Prelude. *A garden in a misty twilight.* Act. I. *The duke's drawing-room, early evening.* Act II. *The same, an hour later.*

I

HELLO OUT THERE is one of the finest one-act plays in the record of the American theatre. The simple account of a man in a Texas jail cell falsely accused of rape and awaiting the approach of a lynch mob and of the little slavey around the jail who, broken and alone and defeated as he is, seeks to befriend him, it combines in its brief playing span a power and a compassion, a despair and a cry for shining hope, that have not been the portion of plays on the same general theme thrice as long. In the loneliness of its two central characters, in their ache for justice, mercy, understanding, and a touch of the outside world's beauty, there is prose poetry both vivified and infinitely moving.

II

Not the least of the consequences of war is the impreg-
nation of theatre producers and motion-picture executives
with the conviction that what their customers avidly crave
are plays and films that will reinspire them with Faith. It
appears to be the corneous belief of the theatrical impresarios that war instantaneously demolishes what divine
trust the public has hitherto unanimously enjoyed and
that the moment the guns boom a man who has never got
nearer to a church than Max Reinhardt's *The Miracle* or
closer to Christ than Walter Hampden in *The Servant in
the House,* and whose spiritual exaltation in the past has
been induced chiefly by George Gershwin's "I'll Build a
Stairway to Paradise," promptly starves for drama that will
make him see angels in every ashcan and God in every
chipmunk's eyes. And so, too, with the movie pincuses.
Once let war break and they are forthwith persuaded that
their thirty or however many million customers who have
enthusiastically been eating up Betty Grable and Bob
Hope, and whose conception of sanctity is Rita Hayworth
soulfully clasping an Easter lily, suddenly experience an
overpowering appetite for pictures which in time of peace
they would shun like poison.

That war, far from diminishing faith, increases it, these
analysts seem to overlook. War — almost all war — is the
result and consequence of faith, and faith, as should be sufficiently appreciated, battens on itself, often even more
positively in defeat than in victory. But since this is no
place for any such philosophical exercise, I proceed to the
business directly in hand and remark that, whether the
theatrical entrepreneurs be right or wrong in their deduc-
tions, the most likely, acceptable, and generally digestible
play on the subject of faith remains still this *Magic* of Chesterton's, thirty years old though it is.

The play's especial virtue is that, unlike the majority of
these hopeful faith-dispensers, it goes about its business
not, as is customary, with an air of indignant demagoguery
but with a light and easy wit and the manner of a noncha-

lant diplomat. Allowing that all divine faith is akin to the Indian rope trick, which, though no one has ever seen it done and which can't be done, is nevertheless legendarily an established fact and no more difficult of belief than the Biblical miracles or the diplomatic genius of Sir Stafford Cripps, Chesterton smiles his theme into his audience's adjudication and, for yea or nay, lets it remain there at his final curtain's fall. Those who prefer faith to be inculcated in them by solemn Charles Rann Kennedy dialectics, by William Vaughn Moody Chautauqua rhetoric and by the cow-eyed beatitudes of the *Ben Hur–Sign of the Cross* species of drama will put down a play like this as mere pleasant triviality, as in fact they have for the three decades of its life. Those who can distinguish between the triviality of resounding exhortation and the occasional greater profundity of the unspoken word will take to it, as they in turn have for those same three decades.

When the late lamented Harry Thurston Peck was editor of the old *Bookman,* he inaugurated a department devoted to words that deserved, he contended, an indefinite holiday. Among them was the overworked adjective *charming*. I agree with him, especially in the case of plays, since, if used at all, it should be associated mainly with women and snakes. Yet with hundreds of other adjectives lying around loose, I can think of no apter one to apply to this particular play, since it factually charms its theme into the consciousness instead of, as is the more usual practice, forcing it.

Plays about faith have customarily pursued routine courses. In the Wilson Barrett era of the modern stage, it was promoted into an audience's emotion in terms of Roman arena lions that viewed all Christians, whether as unappetizing as Charles Dalton or as délicieuse as Maud Jeffries, in the light of pièces de résistance especially prepared for them by Theodore of the Ritz. Barrett's side-kick in the racket was Hall Caine, who got rid of the lions, got growling actor-managers dressed up as clergymen to take their places, and had them try to convince themselves that a belief in God was a satisfactory substitute for the ravishingly beautiful heroines who would have nothing to do with them.

When the public no longer rushed to the box-office to buy such synthetic exaltations of the spirit, pitchmen like Jerome K. Jerome and the aforesaid Kennedy got out their theopathic apparatus and had at the trade with elixirs in which actors, their faces chalked into a pallor exceeding Nicky Arnstein's, were programmed as A Stranger, A Wayfarer, or Manson and, by conducting themselves for the major portion of two hours like overly verbose and objectionable pallbearers, peculiarly persuaded the come-ons that they were replicas of Christ and that the rest of the cast, a bunch of low-lifes, were converted to the faith by them.

In between and since, the theatre public has been dosed up with a wholesale pharmacopœia of anti-atheistic sulfanilamides. It has been bidden to swallow plays which have solemnly argued God in terms of everything from the defeat of the Nazis by Hershey's five-cent chocolate bars dropped in parachutes to the triumph of Christianity, peace-on-earth, and lower taxes through actors being martyred by off-stage firing squads, ecstatically wide-eyed actresses mistaking the gallery spotlight for the Star of Bethlehem, and accordions abandoned by renegade missionaries being mystically set to playing by white beams of light from the flies. But before, in between, and since, it has been privileged a minimum of plays of the species that have seen faith sharply for just what it is: a volitional remittance of cold judgment, a disbelief triumphant over itself, a puzzling, beautiful, and assuaging fairy tale told by the teller to his eager self. *Magic,* in its delicately satirical, relatively short span, is such a play. In its sheer and deliberate innocence it accomplishes what any number of pretentiously long-faced plays by such much more experienced dramatists as Henry Arthur Jones, Eugène Brieux, and their ilk have failed to.

STRIP FOR ACTION. September 30, 1942

A show by Howard Lindsay and Russel Crouse, fabricators of the successful Life with Father. *Produced by the authors in association with Oscar Serlin, who produced* Life with Father *in association with himself.*

Program

Brooklyn	*Coby Ruskin*	Jonesy	*Harold Abbey*
Jeff	*Wylie Adams*	Billy Miller	*Billy Koud*
Tony	*Richard Sanders*	Anita	*Toni Crane*
Mitch	*Owen Martin*	Wolf	*John Deshay*
Buzz	*Kenny Forbes*	Ruthie	*Eleanor Boleyn*
Dan	*Bert Freed*	Dracula	*Betty Noonan*
Eddie	*Jack Albertson*	Joey	*Joey Faye*
Hollenbeck	*Jerry Thor*	Nutsy	*Keenan Wynn*
Tex	*Don Kohler*	Harry	*Murray Leonard*
Snag	*Richard Clark*	Florida	*Jean Carter*
Gus	*James McMahon*	Traps	*Tommy Farrell*
Clint	*Charlie Kaye*	Squee	*Eleanor Lynn*
Mike	*Will J. Ward*	Capt. Adams	*Gordon Nelson*
Virginia	*Jacqueline Paige*	Major Daniels	*David Kerman*
Sally	*Olga Brace*	Lieut. Nelson	*Leonard Patrick*
Pinky	*Howard Blaine*	Commissioner Ainley	
Kitty	*Kitty Voss*		*Leslie Barrie*
Duchess	*Gary Myles*	Chief of Staff	*Harry Bannister*
Garbo	*Jeraldine Dvorak*	Gen. McPhelan	*Paul Huber*
Irene	*Evelyn Russell*		

SYNOPSIS: Act I. *Stage of the Bijou Theatre in a small town in Maryland, late afternoon.* Act II. Scene 1. *Office in the War Department, Washington, D. C., next morning.* Scene 2. *Stage of the Bijou Theatre, that afternoon.* Scene 3. *The show — Opening Number.* Scene 4. *The show — The Comics.* Scene 5. *Backstage in the wings.* Scene 6. *The show — Bedroom Scene.* Scene 7. *Backstage in the wings.* Scene 8. *The show — The Strip-Tease.* Scene 9. *Stage of the Bijou Theatre.*

THE IDEA, in brief, was to show what happens when a burlesque troupe tries to give a performance at an Army camp. The trouble with the idea is that, once you state it upon the first curtain's lift, what is subsequently going to happen is more or less obvious. One knows for a certainty that, among other things equally sure to occur, the soldiers will amorously pursue the girls all over the place, the show will encounter moral objections from the commanding officers, several of the gayer boys will get into difficulties in connection with the show, one of the soldiers will be punched in the jaw for getting naughty with the show's leading man's girl, the strip-teaser will be used heavily for comedy effect, the heroine will be made excessively pure in contrast to the show's hussies, and so on down the track. The only thing the authors can do will be a fresh handling of the details. The present authors failed to do it.

Here and there a modest laugh pried itself loose from the familiar materials, including several old Columbia Wheel acts, but in the aggregate the attempt to burlesque burlesque, a superhuman feat at best, did not come off, although the audiences, judging from their reaction, didn't seem properly to appreciate the fact. They laughed uproariously when a comedian alluded to paying for the little heroine's college intuition; when another comedian's drink of cheap whisky exploded in a cloud of smoke, as it has been doing for fifty years; when the same performer sang "Asleep in the Deep" in an exaggeratedly tragic basso profundo; when the drummer hit the drum at the wrong moments and the strip-teaser glared ferociously at him; and when the blackout skit disclosed the comedian, hidden under the woman's bed, pretending to be the voice at the other end of the telephone in the suddenly arrived husband's hand. They enjoyed no end the lecherous soldier who chased the chorus girl into her dressing-room and was peremptorily kicked out with the line: "I can't defend my country and my honor at the same time"; the dumb showgirl who persisted in turning to the left instead of the right because, she retorted to the exasperated dance director, she was left-handed; the joke about you can't come clean from Pittsburgh; and the fat soldier who returned from a walk with one of the girls with his face covered with lip-rouge. And they roared heartily at the semi-nude dancers who came on wearing the mess tins over their breasts; at the reference to the latter as goona-goonas; at another reference to the South Sea Islands as the Dorothy Lamour country; at still another to the chief stripper as the occupant of the titular role; and at the stripper herself when she observed that she didn't wear any pants and when she silently moved her lips at the drummer who banged at the wrong bump time in the pattern of the term "son-of-a-bitch."

And among those in the audience who reveled in these dramatic belles-lettres were several of the critics who the very night before allowed they were bored to death by the humanity of Saroyan and the wit of Chesterton. "I can't remember when I've had a better time in the theatre," enthusiastically wrote Louis Kronenberger in *PM*. "An excellent evening . . . countless lines and incidents are screamingly funny . . . all of these rich materials provide an exceptionally good evening," fervently wrote John Mason Brown in the *World-Telegram*. And so, also, one or two others.

It must give producers who trustingly try to do a bit better by the theatre considerable pause.

LET FREEDOM SING. OCTOBER 5, 1942

A revue by the so-called American Youth Theatre. Music and lyrics by Harold Rome, assisted by Marc Blitzstein, Earl Robinson, et al. Sketches by Sam Locke.

PRINCIPALS

Mitzi Green, Berni Gould, Lee Sullivan, Betty Garrett, Phil Leeds, Mordecai Bauman, and Buddy Yarus.

THE AMERICAN YOUTH THEATRE was launched six years ago in the mighty suburb of Brooklyn. Before invading that great cultural center it called itself the Flatbush Arts Theatre, somewhat to the puzzlement and consternation of a community that hitherto had never heard the word "arts" mentioned in connection with it and that was even a bit confused as to the meaning of the word "theatre." Its early presentations, according to a friendly salami-dealer who has served gratis as the organization's master of the records, were confined to lofts along Kings Highway for the enchantment of relatives and neighbors. With the passing of time, and after performances in several more remote lofts, the group ennobled itself with the title American Youth Theatre, although its constituent elements had by now got a bit baggy under the eyes, and descended upon the Barbizon-Plaza Hotel in Manhattan. In the small chamber that passes for a theatre in that inn it offered a collection of odds and ends under the overconfident name *You Can't Sleep Here,* chiefly over week-ends. The collection was terrible.

But youth, even youth grown a bit baggy under the eyes, is not easily disheartened and in the season of 1941–2 the little band descended again, this time in the two-by-four Malin Studio, with a revue called *Of V We Sing.* Encouraged by someone or other, this revue was subsequently brought into a long-unused theatre in the environs of Co-

lumbus Circle, where, upon professional critical investigation, it proved to be almost as terrible.

And now, in a real Broadway theatre, the intrepid amateurs had still another go at it with *Let Freedom Sing,*
which was also pretty terrible.

I give you a rough idea of the exhibit, enthusiastically
fashioned out of the revolutionary philosophy that freedom is a desirable condition.

After the amateur orchestra, resplendent in Tuxedos and
yellow shoes, had negotiated the overture, which consisted
of Harold Rome's rewriting of his own stale tunes, came
the staple opening number, "Ring Up the Curtain," in
which six faded youths, male and female, dispensed the
usual facetious lyric involving references to the Shuberts
and their own fortitude in entering upon the evening to
come. Followed a number, "It's Fun to Be Free," during
the rendition of which the ensemble threw balls at chromos
of Hitler, Mussolini, and Hirohito. The frantic applause
of the relatives and neighbors subsiding, out then came two
young men who, evidently under the impression that they
were comedians, purveyed a skit called *Tactics,* wherein
each offered his idea of the proper military strategy to win
the war. Miss Mitzi Green, billed as the star of the proceedings and clad in a blue-gray uniform, next obliged
with a ditty entitled "The Lady Is a WAAC," a patriotic
paraphrase of "The Lady Is a Tramp," which she sang
in a show some years ago. Following that came a sketch,
A Night in Washington, a steal from the long familiar *The
Rest Cure,* which had to do with the difficulty in finding
a peaceful place to sleep in the overcrowded capital. The
comedian in the sketch took off his clothes preparatory to
retiring and disclosed himself in a red flannel union suit.
Someone also put a cake of ice on his lap.

Now again Mitzi with a song called "I Did It for Defense," frequently embellished with the phrase "I dood it"
in place of "I did it" and relating how she surrendered her
most priceless possession to a young soldier in the cause of
her country, the most priceless possession in the last line of
the lyric turning out to be not her virtue but her collection

of tin foil. Then — "We Have a Date," a sentimental duet relating what happiness would be the loving couple's when the war was over. During the duet the lights were lowered and through a scrim one beheld half a dozen other loving couples lovingly dancing a waltz. (All the songs were be-volumed by loud speakers.)

One of the aforesaid males who was under the impression that he was a comedian was next with a number in which he impersonated a senator urging everyone to be calm and in which he so worked himself up that two attendants finally removed him in a straitjacket. He sprayed his throat waggishly during the act and now and then even more waggishly gulped at a whisky bottle. Two funny boys followed him, also pretending to be senators, who, after a friendly colloquy, turned around and revealed knives stuck in their backs. A teacher-and-pupils number — the background was a little red schoolhouse — now vouchsafed a ditty called "History Eight to the Bar," in which the teacher cracked whimsicalities about George Washington, Abe Lincoln, et al., and in which the pupils tossed their heads up and down in a lyric accompaniment. Again then Mitzi in dialect imitations of soldiers at the Stage Door Canteen, orchestrated to a sentimental ditty concerning her heartbreak over missing Private Jones before he left for his overseas destination. And finally, before the first intermission, a paraphrase of Rome's old "Franklin D. Roosevelt Jones" number called "Little Miss Victory Jones," in which the father of triplets decided to name them Franklin D. Jones, Winston C. Jones, and Joseph V. Jones.

The second half of the bill, to shorten the story, was made up of pseudo-satirical allusions to blackouts, rich European refugees, Noel Coward, women in uniform, and hoarders.

A bove majori discit arare minor.

THE EVE OF ST. MARK. OCTOBER 7, 1942

A play by Maxwell Anderson, originally written for the amateur stages of the National Theatre Conference and presented by seventy-nine of them. Produced in the professional theatre by the Playwrights' Company.

PROGRAM

DECKMAN WEST	*Matt Crowley*	CORPORAL TATE	*Charles Mendick*
CY	*Grover Burgess*	PRIVATE FRANCIS MARION	
NELL WEST	*Aline MacMahon*		*James Monks*
NEIL WEST	*Carl Gose*	PRIVATE GLINKA	*Martin Ritt*
ZIP WEST	*Clifford Carpenter*	SERGEANT RUBY	*George Mathews*
RALPH WEST	*Edwin Cooper*	SERGEANT KRIVEN	*Robert Williams*
PETE FELLER	*Stanley G. Wood*	LILL BIRD	*Joann Dolan*
JANET FELLER	*Mary Rolfe*	SAL BIRD	*Toni Favor*
PRIVATE QUIZZ WEST		WAITER	*Charles Ellis*
	William Prince	FLASH	*Dorothea Freed*
PRIVATE THOMAS MULVEROY		DIMPLES	*Beatrice Manley*
	Eddie O'Shea	PEPITA	*Joven E. Rola*
PRIVATE SHEVLIN	*David Pressman*		

SYNOPSIS: Act I. 1. *Nell West's kitchen, April 1942.* 2. *The barracks at Fort Grace.* 3. *Janet's room.* 4. *The Moonbow Restaurant.* 5. *Nell's kitchen, September.* Act II. 1. *A gangplank, October 1941.* 2. *A field.* 3. *The cave on the island, April 1942.* 4. *A corner of the cave.* 5. *The same.* 6. *The cave on the island.* 7. *Nell's kitchen, June 1942.*

THE DIFFICULTY with war plays written and produced in time of war lies in the arbitrary censorship which playwrights must inevitably impose upon themselves. If they do not impose it, the public will do the job for them. They have no way out. They must accept the public's attitude toward the war; they must hew to the line of popular thought and prejudice; they must, whether they will it or not, for the most part resign themselves to being mere cheer-leaders, or perish. John Steinbeck, for example, found that out all too soon. His *The Moon Is Down*, which pictured the Nazis in a fairly human light, was spurned by the public until, for its road engagement following the New

York débâcle, the enemy was presented in a more villainous manner and hence was more publicly acceptable.

It is only in the way of minor and thematically unimportant detail that a dramatist in war time may let himself go. If O'Neill, say, were to write the finest play in all American dramatic history with a pro-Nazi or pro-Japanese theme, not only could it not presently be produced but, were it produced, it would be hooted off the stage by its first audience, including — as was proved by the Steinbeck play — most of those theoretically unwarped connoisseurs, the critics. At this moment Steinbeck, I hear, has a new play that he refrains from offering for production simply because its theme and treatment differ from the necessarily conventional dramatic war philosophy. And at this moment, too, Sean O'Casey's eminently worthy *Purple Dust* and less worthy but greatly superior-to-the-general-run *The Star Turns Red* cannot be shown because the former presents Englishmen in a ridiculous light and because the latter hits at the democratic theory.

The war play in war time can at best only reflect the common denominator of public prejudice in a relatively novel manner. Originality, free thought, unorthodoxy are taboo. Patriotism, admiration of one's allies, contempt and hatred of one's foe must ride high in the saddle. That all this is admirable from a national point of view, even from an individual point of view, there is no gainsaying. That it is equally admirable from an artistic and strictly critical point of view — from the point of view of sound and independent classicism — is, to put it mildly, more than doubtful. And it is for this reason that the great majority not only of this war's plays but of the previous war's are and have been, for all their occasional popularity, such critically mediocre affairs.

It amounts to no answer to reply that the plurality of playwrights write only what they honestly and truly feel. Of course they do, and due praise be theirs. But honesty of feeling alone does not, alas, automatically result in fine drama. If it did, *The Morning Star*, to name but one example out of scores, would be a stunning masterpiece, su-

perior even — if we appreciate the inner history of the
play — to *King Lear*. The answer, again, is rather that
the playwrights would not be permitted to think and feel
otherwise even if they would. The general situation is akin
to that which in times of peace would prevent a playwright
from showing a mother-in-law as anything other than a
venomous witch, an errant woman as anything other than
a foul prostitute, and Fritz Kuhn as other than a combination of Little Eyolf, Rudolf Rassendyll, Sir Miles Hendon,
and Hänsel und Gretel.

The direct consequence is that our stages are unremit-
tingly and surfeitingly devoted to telling us, in one way or
another, what we already sufficiently know and sufficiently
feel. To wit, that the Nazis are odious, that the Japs are
odious no less, that the Jews are persecuted, that the English can bear up under bomb attacks, that we Americans
are, for all our appearance of being somewhat too lacka-
daisical, right in there pitching, both physically and spir-
itually, in times of crisis, and that freedom is a rare and
wonderful thing to have lying around the house. Since the
changes to be rung may only, as has been noted, be in the
direction of superficial detail, it is natural that a long succession of the plays should become tedious, as, with small
exception, they do. The reaction is much as, under other
circumstances, would be that to an equally long and arbitrary series of exhibits which constantly and unvaryingly
apprised us that true love triumphs over all obstacles, that
marriage for money is a grievous mistake, and that George
Washington slept there, and always alone.

Which brings us to this particular war play. Forgoing
for the most part his Maxwell Bodenheim Anderson vel-
veteen verse, which has often in the past been so trying, and
writing with an unaccustomed simplicity, the author has
contrived out of the routine chronicle of an American farm
boy's pilgrimage from home, family, and sweetheart to military training camp and eventual death in the Philippines
a satisfactory popular if not always satisfactory critical play,
yet withal the best of the indifferent lot he has negotiated
in some years. Embroidering his rooting theme with hu-

morous and occasionally touching threads, he manages to
make much of the standard stuff effective audience-bait.
But here again we take little more out of the theatre than
we have brought in, and only the details linger, which is
ever the way of all that is fundamentally hokum. For hokum periodically deodorized with a humorous and feeling spray is what the play is: the boy torn from his sweetheart, his temptation by the juke-joint tart, his agonies in
the malarial Philippine swamps, his visualized dream of
home and beloved, his fortitude under fire, his ultimate
sacrifice, his family's heroic dispatch of his younger brothers to follow him in battle, the final curtain speech about
fighting to make the world a decent place to live in. Nevertheless, to repeat, a more plausible play than several of the
author's previous Sardoodledandys.

That the majority of our critics become patriotic sheep
in the sensitized contemplation of such drama in war time,
I have already suggested. Consider just one example in
illustration of the pretty general reviewing picture, the
John Mason Brown hereinbefore mentioned. Thus, in his
critique of the Anderson play, Mr. Brown: "Whether *The
Eve of St. Mark* is a good play or not almost seems beside
the point [*sic*]. It is deeply affecting. It speaks to the heart
irresistibly even when the head says No [*sic, sic*]."

The closing months of the previous theatrical season
were devoted by the critics to acrimonious denunciations
of Steinbeck's *The Moon Is Down* on the ground of its
sentimentalization of the German soldiery. The closing
months of the season before that were devoted by the same
critics to fulsome commendations of Lillian Hellman's
Watch on the Rhine, which was just as sentimental in its approach to the German underground movement. The closing months of the season still before were devoted by the
same critics to almost equally warm endorsements of Robert Sherwood's *There Shall Be No Night,* which was even
more sentimental in its treatment of the Finns, whose land
had been invaded by the Russians, then anathema. What
you got, in other words, was not dramatic criticism, which
you paid your money for, but — as you often do in such

cases — mere emotional prejudice. And that, if I may be allowed to say so, is a juvenile trick to play on any dramatist, whether good or bad.

Steinbeck's play was a poor one, but certainly not because he exercised his artist's privilege to view the Nazis as here and there possibly gifted with a few of the qualities of human beings and not necessarily and inevitably all Frankenstein monsters liberally crossed with the attributes of Robert G. Ingersoll, Boss Tweed, Al Capone, and divers other such memorable Americans. In the same way Miss Hellman's and Sherwood's plays were somewhat better ones, but equally and certainly not because they were similarly generous in their views of pre-Nazi Germans and the Finns, the latter subsequently, like the Russians at the time, in locally bad odor.

This present criticism of drama in ratio to the acceptability of its themes is just a small step removed from the older criticism of drama in proportion to its morality, chiefly sexual, and must lead to the same artistically dubious end. If carried to its natural conclusion in relation to drama dealing with the Germans, it would quite logically denounce as worthless such famous plays as Lessing's *Minna von Barnhelm,* Goethe's *Götz von Berlichingen,* and Schiller's *Cabale und Liebe.*

Let us be patriots all, surely, but let those of us whose job is dramatic criticism not confuse it with the job of flying a bomber over Berlin.

COUNT ME IN. October 8, 1942

A musical tort by Walter Kerr and Leo Brady, with tunes and lyrics by Ann Ronell. Produced by the Shuberts in association with Olsen and Johnson, et al., misguided souls.

PRINCIPALS

Charles Butterworth, Luella Gear, Hal Le Roy, June Preisser, Mary Healy, Gower and Jeanne, Melissa Mason, et al., misguided souls.

WAR IS SURELY no funny matter, but neither is it the dull one that many of our playwrights make it out to be. And among those playwrights include especially and particularly the soi-disant humorists, *vide* the authors of *Vickie* and, above all, those of this *Count Me In*. If war is to be used in certain of its aspects for comic effect, as Aristophanes proved possible, what we need, if impossibly not Aristophaneses, is at least playmakers and showmakers with a considerably more piquant wit than those who have been freezing us stiff with their feeble satirical whimsies about women in war service and the droll like.

Count Me In, originally produced by the amateurs of the drama department at the Catholic University in Washington, D. C., and since revised by a pair of Broadway hands, the Messrs. Lester Lee and Jerry Seelan, has to do with a married man who fought in the first World War, whose family, composed chiefly of strident females, are engaged in all kinds of activities in connection with the second and current, who is brushed aside as too old when he aspires to do his share toward subduing the Axis, and who by hook and crook finally manages to horn in. That Aristophanes or even the Carl Zuckmayer of *The Good Soldier Schweik* might have made something amusing out of the not too sauceful idea is possible. What the present authors made out of it constituted one of the most stupefyingly somniferous shows seen in the local theatre in years. Among other things, when they did not know what else to do, which was often, they could think of nothing better than collaborating with their producers in the introduction of a trio of female acrobats, and if anything is more terrifying or nauseating than female acrobats, who invariably suggest the spectacle of large hunks of raw, muscled meat in a butchershop window, I, among ten thousand others, have not experienced the agony of encountering it.

A general picture of the catastrophe:

Sample character names: Sherry Brandywine, Teddy Roosevelt Brandywine, Alvin York Brandywine.

Sample humor: Sergeant Brandywine (female), surveying a line of female recruits, observes to one with a large posterior: "Your food must go to the rear," whereat another recruit: "It had better go to the front." Again, when Papa Brandywine suddenly appears after having effected his escape from a concentration camp in a laundry hamper and is asked how he managed it, the reply is: "I came out in the wash." Still again, when he comes on in a white smock embellished with a map and, turning around, discloses Germany on his behind, he observes to a character who inquires whether that is the real location of Germany that if it isn't it should be.

Sample stage business: The female sergeant orders brave volunteers to step forth from the line of women, whereupon the line steps backwards and leaves forward a distraught and trembling member.

Sample lyrics: One in which the singers allow they know who the various other generals are but can't make out who General Staff may be. Another, called "The Women of the Year," in which a ballet dancer in white poses as Columbia. Still another entitled "Why Do They Say They're the Fair Sex?"

Sample of unanimous critical report: Phew!

THREE MEN ON A HORSE. OCTOBER 9, 1942

A revival of the successful 1935 farce by John Cecil Holm and George Abbott. Produced by Alex Yokel.

PROGRAM

AUDREY TROWBRIDGE	*Kay Loring*	PATSY	*Sid Stone*
THE TAILOR	*J. Ascher Smith*	MABEL	*Jean Casto*
ERWIN TROWBRIDGE	*William Lynn*	MOSES	*Richard Huey*
CLARENCE DOBBINS	*Fleming Ward*	GLORIA	*Iris Hall*
HARRY	*William Foran*	AL	*James Truex*
CHARLIE	*Horace MacMahon*	MR. CARVER	*William Balfour*
FRANKIE	*Teddy Hart*		

SYNOPSIS: Act I. Scene 1. *The living-room of the Trowbridge House, Ozone Heights, New Jersey.* Scene 2. *A barroom in the basement of the Lavillere Hotel, New York.* Act II. Scene 1. *Ozone Heights.* Scene 2. *A room in the Lavillere Hotel.* Act III. Scene 1. *Ozone Heights.* Scene 2. *The hotel room.*

THE SEASON at this point promised to take on the aspect of a séance, with producers in the roles of so many Madame Celestes applying themselves to the hopeful business of raising ghosts of the dead. These ghosts, or revivals, are seldom happy in persuading the more tasty customers that they are other than three-sheets on wire frames, and as lifeless as ghosts commonly are. Here and there the revival of some little-known play like Chesterton's *Magic* piques the more cultivated interest, attention, and curiosity, but for the most part familiarity with the plays exacts its penalty. For, the ageless classics aside, little is more disquieting than an invitation to engage again — and sometimes for the third and fourth time — some modern play or show that even on its initial revealment failed overpoweringly to agitate us.

With the advent of *Three Men on a Horse,* we already so early in the season had been requested to heat ourselves up over no less than six such revivals, not including the *Magic* aforesaid. And announced for the early future were numerous others. The situation began to acquire an alarming look. I, for one, am perfectly willing to see something like this *Three Men on a Horse* once, which was and is more than enough, but when I am asked to sit through it a second time and not only sit through it but quietly grin and bear it, I am ready to yell. In the case of some good musical like *The Merry Widow,* things aren't so bad, although I have had my fill of even *The Merry Widow* by now and would much prefer to stay at home and snooze privately and unobserved by the fireside or mayhap go around for a second helping of Bobby Clark or George Jessel, which, damn you, is infinitely less lowbrow of me than your going around to look at such inferior *Merry Widow* revival comics as Eddie Garr and John Cherry.

I duly appreciate that there has been a serious shortage of worthy new scripts and I also appreciate that there is something to be said for the interest evoked in contemplating new actors in the old roles. Nevertheless and notwithstanding, if we must have revivals why not plays less well known to us and surely, here and there, possessed of more quality?

Three Men on a Horse, you will recall, adheres to George Abbott's old pet farce formula of putting three men in a room and worrying them to death in their search for a solution of their difficulties. The first acts are devoted to a succession of wisecracks accompanied by fairly normal physical movement. The second acts bring about a prodigious brow-wrinkling on the part of the beset trio, the brow-wrinkling accompanied by excessively abnormal physical movement. The third acts, as the screwballs' problems incline toward liquidation, return momentarily to the fairly normal movement, proceed then lustily again to the abnormal, drop back to the fairly normal, and end on a wisecrack which it probably took half a dozen men besides Mr. Abbott at least three months to sweat out and which is hopefully designed to send the audience into the night laughing its hat off.

The formula has become tiresome from too much repetition. And so, also, has the species of stage direction spon-

sored by Abbott and presently duplicated by his imitators.
You can't hope to make the unfunny excruciatingly funny
simply by pacing it so rapidly that the audience won't have
time to realize it isn't funny.

Having seen *Three Men on a Horse* once as a farce, once
as a movie, and once as a musical show *(Banjo Eyes)*, the
average customer may be forgiven for crying quits.

OY, IS DUS A LEBEN. October 12, 1942

A biographical play in Yiddish (with songs) about the Yiddish actress Molly Picon, by the Yiddish Jacob Kalich, her husband. Produced by Edwin A. Relkin.

Program

PROLOGUE		IN THE PLAY	
Theatre	*Leon Gold*	Molly	*Molly Picon*
Achashverosh	*David Lubritzky*	Mr. Kay	*Jacob Kalich*
Vaschti	*Jennie Casher*	Mrs. Picon	*Dora Weissman*
Vaizuso	*Esta Saltzman*	Ziggie	*Izidor Casher*
Jacob P. Adler	*Boris Auerbach*	Rosalia	*Anna Appel*
David Kessler	*Izidor Casher*	Misha	*Leon Gold*
Sigmund Mogilesco	*Sam Kasten*	A Comedian	*Sam Kasten*
Boris Tomashefsky		Sylvia	*Esta Saltzman*
	Michael Wilenski	Nadya	*Jennie Casher*
Bessie Thomashefsky		Zelda	*Tillie Rabinowitz*
	Tillie Rabinowitz	Rebbitzen	*Rosa Greenfield*
Keni Lipzin	*Celia Pearson*	Schlome	*Charles Cohen*
		Zalmyn	*David Lubritzky*
		Getzel	*Boris Auerbach*
		Chayeh-Sura	*Rebecca Weintraub*

SINCE YIDDISH is a tongue unfortunately not embraced by my worldly education, since the only term in it I can recognize is the *Ish kabibble* borrowed by American slang, and since, further, I don't even know what that means, I fear I cannot properly enlighten you as to this exhibit. True enough, the playbill contained a brief synopsis in English but, though I understand English, I have seldom been able to achieve any real idea of what a play in a strange language is about merely from reading some such scant digest of it. On such occasions I usually speculate how a Hindu audience, say, that had never heard of *Hamlet* could appreciate all that was going on on the stage from a brief synopsis in Hindu something as follows: "A young man's mother marries her brother-in-law, who has slain her hus-

band. The young man plans revenge, traps his new step-
father, and, after various adventures, slays him in turn. His
mother also dies from accidentally drinking poison, he in
the meantime having lost his intended in death (she
went crazy over unrequited love). He is finally killed by
her brother. During all this time he is given to profound
philosophical meditations, which are full of wisdom."

There is, accordingly, nothing left for me but to report
on Miss Picon's art and Miss Picon's husband's story of her
life through the reviewers of the New York newspapers,
apparently all intimately familiar with Yiddish since early
childhood.

Therefore:

Yiddish scholar Richard Lockridge, of the *Sun:* "Molly
Picon proving all over again why her fame has spread so
very far from Second Avenue. Without, apparently, being
at all literal, it [the play] recapitulates things that have happened to her, or might have happened to her, from the time
she was a small girl beginning in the theatre until just now.
Miss Picon is grand."

Yiddish authority Wilella Waldorf, of the *Post:* "Miss
Picon touches the high spots of her early career with carefree insouciance. The first half seemed only intermittently
interesting to this reviewer . . . but the second half of the
evening devoted to some of Molly's experiences in Europe
. . . offered some fantastic clowning . . . that turned out
to be the hit of the show. Its [the play's] better parts are
strangely arresting."

Yiddish expert John Mason Brown, of the *World-Telegram:* "When she [Miss Picon] looks back on the days leading to her stardom she has much to recall that is colorful,
amusing, even exciting. After a prologue has sung the
glories of the Yiddish theatre and reminded us of such of
Miss Picon's distinguished predecessors as Jacob P. Adler,
David Kessler and Boris Thomashefsky, Molly bounds onto
the stage. Thereafter her life story begins. Miss Picon first
appears as the impish little girl who in 1910 in Philadelphia's Arch Street Theatre was working for fifty cents a
performance. Then it was that, after an audition, a Yid-

dish stage manager urged her to forget acting and turn to some useful profession. In Philadelphia Molly first met Mr. Kalich, who was then a member of the troupe. Some years later in Boston, when he was managing another successful Yiddish theatre, Mr. Kalich persuaded Molly to join his company and marry him. After she had scored a hit in a quaint musical comedy Mr. Kalich had written for her, the both of them set out for Europe." (And so on, at confiding length, about the heroine's trouble with anti-Semitic students in Bucharest, her visit to her husband's mother in Poland, her New York triumphs, etc.) "It is an unpretentious biography, if ever there was one. Its comedy is broad; its sentimentalities are unblushing. Some of the character acting is reliable if unsubtle."

Yiddish honor scholar Burns Mantle, of the *Daily News:* "Her [Miss Picon's] sense of comedy is sure and her feeling for character, both in comedy and drama, wins a response that is definite."

Yiddish solon Joseph Pihodna, of the *Herald Tribune:* "Miss Picon is justly honored by an entertainment that takes in the high lights of her career."

Yiddish luminary Robert Coleman, of the *Mirror:* "It delighted the first-nighters. [Follows a revealing description of the plot and its details.] The new vehicle permits Miss Picon full scope for her remarkable talents. She holds the stage most of the evening, giving an amazing demonstration of versatility. Even without a synopsis the story is not hard to follow. *Oy, Is Dus a Leben* is the best of the many Picon vehicles we've seen. It sets a new high for the Yiddish stage. Miss Picon and the Molly Picon Theatre, in sum, have a big hit."

Yiddish medallist Brooks Atkinson, of the *Times:* "Although Broadway is not Second Avenue, Yiddish can be understood uptown too. . . . Miss Picon runs the whole gamut in her autobiography. By underplaying she can oftentimes make Broadway performers sound loud and look coarse and she can put their manners to shame. If you do not take a firm grip on yourself she can also break your heart with a simple song about the course of true love."

BEAT THE BAND. OCTOBER 14, 1942

A musical comedy by George Marion, Jr., and George Abbott, with music by Johnny Green and lyrics by the Marion aforesaid. Produced by Mr. Abbott.

PROGRAM

BUSTER DA COSTA	*Romo Vincent*	TRUMPET PLAYER	*Johnny Mack*
VERONICA	*Joan Caulfield*	BAND GIRL	*Evelyn Brooks*
HUGO DILLINGHAM	*Jerry Lester*	MAMITA	*Juanita Juarez*
WILLOW WILLOUGHBY		QUERIDA	*Susan Miller*
	Toni Gilman	DON DOMINGO	*Averell Harris*
MR. PIROSH	*Ralph Bunker*	HOTEL MANAGER	*Cliff Dunstan*
PRINCESS	*Eunice Healey*	BELL GIRL	*Doris Dowling*
DAMON DILLINGHAM	*Alfred Drake*	HOTEL OWNER	*John Clarke*
DRUMMER	*Leonard Sues*		

SYNOPSIS: Act I. Scene 1. *A theatrical agent's office.* Scene 2. *The terrace. One week later.* Scene 3. *The apartment.* Scene 4. *Theatrical agent's office.* Scene 5. *The terrace.* Scene 6. *The apartment, one week later.* Act II. Scene 1. *A corridor.* Scene 2. *The apartment.* Scene 3. *The lobby of the Savoy-Perkins Hotel, Washington, D. C.* Scene 4. *The boiler-room of the Savoy-Perkins Hotel.* Scene 5. *The lobby.* Scene 6. *A peach orchard outside of Washington, D. C.* Scene 7. *The lobby.* Scene 8. *Opening night of The Boiler-Room Café.*

THE ATTITUDE of a portion of our theatrical producers seems to be that what people want in war time is not serious drama but entertainment, and then providing them with none of it. At least in the opinion of this particular recorder. Far from being the don I am sometimes accused of being, no one relishes such entertainment more than I do. My demand of it, however, is that it entertain, for if it doesn't it cheats its label and I'd rather go around and have the time of my life laughing at some solemn dramaturgy like *The Morning Star.*

I don't say that some people aren't different. They must be, judging from their pleasure in a number of these entertainment filibusters. But when, whether as professional reviewer or private sitter, I am invited to feel wildly carefree and inordinately gay when in *Strip for Action* a comedian paraphrases that facetia about the impossibility of coming clean from Pittsburgh, when in *Wine, Women and Song* a semi-nude contortionist shows a pair of phosphorescent hands painted on her behind, and when in *Let Freedom Sing* a funny man delicately dabs at his armpits with a handkerchief after a bit of acrobatics, I fear I am left pretty chilly. Nor do I find myself exploding with mirth when, still further, a female in *Vickie* pretending to be an igneous Mata Hari squirms temptingly around a small, bald, timid man, when in *Janie* a little brat stands on her head and discloses an expanse of diaper, or when in one or another vaudeville revival a comedian says he told his sergeant that it was too cold for him and the sergeant told him where he could go to be comfortable.

Maybe I am difficult to please. It isn't that I am such a fogy that I think the strip-tease should be spelled socrates or that there hasn't been any genuine entertainment since comedians last came on in suits six sizes too big for them with red electric bulbs on their noses, with carrots and turnips as boutonnières and with hatchets in their rear pants pockets or since Lionel Barrymore acted Macbeth, but when I am bidden to a show to be amused I am strangely ill at ease when no amusement is vouchsafed me with which to be amused. I faithfully go to that something called *Count Me In* and politely hark to such hereinbefore alluded to jocosities as involve a comedian's body covered with a map and, upon his turning around, revealing Germany on his rump, yet my features remain peculiarly immobile. I hopefully repair to something like that *Priorities of 1943* and my midriff remains disturbingly calm and unbusted when one of the zanies speaks his lines with his mouth full of sandwich. And I optimistically hie me to a musical show like this *Beat the Band* and find that the entertainment it seeks to gladden me with consists for the major part in a lyric-writer who apparently believes that *Who's Who* is a source of great wit and who in rattling off familiar names achieves the high in something or other by rhyming "get the morons" with "Gertrude Lawrence"; in a 240-

pound comedian who bumps an intruder out with his ample belly and thereupon excruciatingly exclaims: "Now I know what it's good for!", in a hip-rolling señorita who says she hails from Mexico and is sexico; and in a plot which has to do with a man who discovers, as men have been discovering in musical comedies, etc., for the last forty years, that his little god-daughter whom he has never seen is a beautiful grown-up girl and who falls in love with her.

The truth seems to be that what the producers have sanguinely been dishing out as entertainment isn't actually one-hundredth so entertaining as what is commonly regarded as somewhat heavier theatrical fare. There is, for example, more genuine entertainment in three single little scenes of Maxwell Anderson's war play, *The Eve of St. Mark,* albeit the play as a whole has been ridiculously overestimated by the reviewers, than there is in three entire musical comedies like *The Time, the Place and the Girl* (*q.v.*) . There is more forthright fun to be extracted from the performances of the Lunts, whether their vehicle be Shakespeare or the Behrman of even *The Pirate* (*q.v.*), than there is from those of a dozen such vaudeville and revue clowns as Henny Youngman, Jimmy Savo, Romo Vincent, Berni Gould, Phil Leeds, Zero Mostel, Johnny Burke, and the like. And there is at least two or three hundred times the lift of the spirit, whichever way you choose to look at it, in a Saroyan's short *Hello Out There* that you will experience from all these recent musical comedies representing aggregate investments running into many hundreds of thousands of dollars and, as in *Beat the Band,* giving you for your own $4.40 stages full of hoptoad jam sessions that blast your eardrums, songs called "Let's Comb Beaches" with the lights going down and showing through a scrim a man in BVD's chasing a hula dancer, and comedians whose idea of rib-cracking humor is getting tangled up in the telephone cord.

BIRD IN HAND. OCTOBER 19, 1942

A revival of the John Drinkwater comedy after a period of thirteen years. Produced by Ronald T. Hammond.

PROGRAM

JOAN GREENLEAF	*Frances Reid*	CYRIL BEVERLY	*Romney Brent*
ALICE GREENLEAF	*Viola Roache*	AMBROSE GODOLPHIN, K.C.	
THOMAS GREENLEAF	*Harry Irvine*		*Nicholas Joy*
GERALD ARNWOOD	*Henry Barnard*	SIR ROBERT ARNWOOD	*J. W. Austin*
MR. BLANQUET	*Harry Sothern*	BARMAID	*Elizabeth Sutton*

SYNOPSIS: Act I. *The bar parlour (evening)*. Act II. *Beverly's bedroom (the same night)*. Act III. *The bar parlour (the next morning)*. The *"Bird in Hand"* Inn, Gloucestershire, England.

Oₙₑ OF THE CHARMS of the theatre is its playwrights' intermittent delightful habit of making monkeys of its critics. Often no sooner do the latter stoutly assert that this or that dramatist not only follows a set and invariable pattern but apparently couldn't do anything different if he tried than the defendant ups and not merely does something completely different but does it confoundingly well. Thus the critics were positive that Brieux was a single-track sociological dramatist when he suddenly abashed their sapience by writing in *Les Hannetons* one of the drollest comedies of the modern French theatre. Shaw, they deposed, was incapable of sentiment and he proved them foolish with *Candida,* one of the finest sentimental plays in the modern English theatre. O'Neill, they insisted, was all metaphysical gloom and he embarrassed them sorely by confecting in *Ah, Wilderness!* one of the most thoroughly enjoyable comedies in the modern American drama. And so on to and including, at least to a degree, John Drinkwater.

This Drinkwater, they were convinced, if he had any talent at all was gifted solely in the way of historical biographical drama. He was, they were sure, a solemn fellow, even something of a stuffed shirt, and humor as foreign to him as to Cal Coolidge or, to be more extreme, Sir Arthur Quiller-Couch. So Drinkwater, grossly inconsiderate of their critical omnipotence, tossed off *Bird in Hand,* which not only made them merry with chuckles but on its original presentation ran for a solid 500 performances in New York to happy audiences.

Dealing with an innkeeper who snobbishly objects to his daughter marrying above her station, and utilizing the simple theme for satirical thrusts at English class distinctions, the comedy, while certainly no great shakes, combines some good, if now rather dated, talk with some lively tomfoolery and amounts in the aggregate to an amiably diverting evening. But you would never have suspected it from this shabby revival presentation, which was so wretched in every respect that the newer generation of reviewers were to be forgiven for not being able to see the pleasant quality of the little play through it. It was a tough job even for us ancients.

THE TIME, THE PLACE AND THE GIRL
OCTOBER 21, 1942

A revised version of the musical comedy of the same name by Will M. Hough and Frank R. Adams, originally presented A.D. 1906. Revisers: Will Morrissey and John Neff. Tunes by Joe Howard, lyrics by William B. Friedlander. Produced by Georges D. Gersene.

PROGRAM

MRS. TALCOTT	*Evelyn Case*	MR. SPREE	*Rolfe Sedan*
MOLLY KELLY	*Vickie Cummings*	LAWRENCE FARNHAM	
HJALMAR SWENSON			*Richard Worth*
	Clarence Nordstrom	MARGARET SWENSON	*Irene Hilda*
BUD SWENSON	*Bert Lawrence*	WILLIE TALCOTT	*Duke Norman*
TOM CUNNINGHAM	*Paul L. Wendel*	JOE HOWARD	*Joe Howard*
JOHNNY HICKS	*"Red" Marshall*		

SYNOPSIS: Act I. *Grounds of the sanitarium, afternoon.* Act II. Scene 1. *Grounds of the sanitarium, evening of the same day.* Scene 2. *Main gate of the sanitarium, an evening two weeks later.* Scene 3. *Grounds of the sanitarium. A few minutes later.*

Scene. *Sanitarium and hotel of the famous Keely Cure in the mountains of Virginia.*

HOUGH AND ADAMS in their day wrote a number of the musical shows for the old La Salle Theatre in Chicago, several of them having germinated while they were still students at the University of Chicago. It was their custom, so the story goes, to clip out of such college humor magazines as the Princeton *Tiger,* Cornell *Widow,* Columbia *Jester,* etc., any appealing jokes they discovered therein and to drop them into a box in the dormitory room which they shared. When they were ready to write another show, they simply opened the box and got going. The revisers of their exhibit seem to have retained most of the antediluvian wheezes. The least they might have done, one would think, would have been to subscribe for some rather later issues of the undergraduate periodicals. But one way or another, the affair remains just what it originally was: a college show without an education.

As samples of the jocosities offered to the 1942 trade I submit the following:

1. — "Did you graduate from college?"
   "No, I quit after seven years."

2. — "He thinks he's a dirty shirt."
   "Why?"
   "We took the starch out of him."

3. — "I've got a mind as sharp as a whip."
   "That's funny; I always connected a whip with the hind end of a horse!"

4. — "Why are they carrying him off backwards?"
   "Oh, he doesn't care where he's going; he only wants to see where he's been."

The plot is even more hilarious. It is laid in the Keely Cure, which is naturally invaded by a bevy of schoolgirls. A case of measles breaks out and everybody is quarantined. With nothing else to do, the inmates and the girls, including some performers cleverly billed as The Sophisti-kids, gather round and pass the time singing songs named "I Can't Get Along without You," "The Custom of Dressing for Dinner," and "A Penny for Your Thoughts, Junior Miss," crack the jokes noted above, and fall miscellaneously in love.

The younger reviewers, apparently under the impression that the show was representative of the musical comedy theatre of thirty-six years ago, expressed their gratitude that what they ironically alluded to as "the good old days" were no more and that the contemporary theatre, for all its weaknesses, boasts musical shows so immensely superior. They should be interested to know that *The Time, the Place and the Girl* no more represented the musical comedy of its distant period than *Count Me In*, for example, represents the musical comedy of the present. In the general period when *The Time, the Place and the Girl* was produced, musical comedy was represented on our stage by such eminently creditable entertainments as, among others, Oscar Straus's *The Waltz Dream,* Lehar's *The Merry Widow,* George Ade's *The Sho-Gun,* John Philip Sousa's *The Free Lance,* Pixley's and Luder's *Woodland,* and Reginald de Koven's *Happyland.* Not to mention George M. Cohan's *Forty-five Minutes from Broadway,* Richard Harding Davis's *The Yankee Tourist,* and some of Victor Herbert's very best.

THE DAMASK CHEEK. October 22, 1942

A comedy by John Van Druten and Lloyd Morris. Produced by Dwight Deere Wiman.

Program

Rhoda Meldrum	*Flora Robson*	Daphne Randall	*Joan Tetzel*
Miss Pinner	*Ruth Vivian*	Calla Longstreth	*Celeste Holm*
Mrs. Randall	*Margaret Douglass*	Michael Randall	
Nora	*Mary Michael*		*Peter Fernandez*
Jimmy Randall		Neil Harding	*Zachary Scott*
	Myron McCormick		

SYNOPSIS: Act I. *Afternoon.* Act II. Scene 1. *Early that evening.* Scene 2. *Later that evening.* Act III. Scene 1. *The next morning.* Scene 2. *The same afternoon.*

The action takes place in the upstairs living-room of Mrs. Randall's house in the east sixties, New York City; mid-December 1909.

Among three or four other discomposing things in this otherwise literate and amiable, if overly leisurely, comedy is its authors' conviction that actresses in the Year of Our Lord 1909 were generally regarded as outcast fish hardly acceptable to anything bordering on polite society. Upon that point a share of their plot hinges. They might have profited from some of the research which they suggest in certain other directions. In the period in question, they would have discovered, the facts ridiculed their thesis. The wives or wives-soon-to-be of such social figures as August Belmont, William Astor Chanler, Jimmy Elverson, Thomas B. Clarke, Jr., Peter Duryea, Antonio F. de Navarro, Benjamin P. Cheney, Jr., Russell Griswold Colt, James Brown Potter, Oscar Lewisohn, Bradlee Putnam Strong, et al., were all actresses. So, also, were the wives of such well-known scholars as Brander Matthews, such leading dramatists as Augustus Thomas, such literary lights as Justin Huntly McCarthy, John Fox, Jr., and Richard Harding Davis, such titans of the steel industry as William E. Corey, such critics as Max Beerbohm and James Metcalfe, such diplomats as George H. Butler, such naval men as Admiral Marix, such men of big business as G. W. Bird and William Patterson, such nobles as the Marquis de Otero and Count de Guerbal, such London clubmen as Rene Webb and Percival Mitchell, such Southern aristocrats as Rezin Davis Shepherd of Shepherdsville, such conspicuous descendants as Stephen A. Douglas, such military figures as Captain Charles Nesbit Frederick Armstrong, such high-born journalists as Almyr Wilder Cooper, and so on. It was an actress of the period who rejected the marriage proposal of the richest and most socially eminent man in New York; it was an actress who was presently to lead the international society set on the Riviera; it was an actress who married an illustrious Senator and who was soon to exercise a tonic influence on a President of the United States.

A second discomposing item is the authors' belief that in 1909 an Englishwoman of mature years who demonstratedly knew her Shakespeare by heart might have been deeply offended if her male cousin humorously started to enunciate the word "bastard."

A third and even more discomposing item is the authors' seeming conviction, placed sympathetically in the mouth of one of their leading characters, that the music of Victor Herbert's *The Red Mill,* Emmerich Kalman's *Sari,* and Leo Fall's *The Dollar Princess* is so extremely bad it is a pain to have to listen to it.

A fourth discomposing item is the authors' attempt to induce nostalgia in their audiences through the familiar mention of the names of bygone theatres, plays, actresses, restaurants, and the like. It does not work, and for a simple reason. At least half their audiences probably never heard of most of the names and would not know what exactly they stood for even if they had — and would sentimentally care still less. But the authors introduce one such device that does work, and for an equally simple reason: the allusion to a drive in a hansom cab through Central Park in the snow. It works because that beautiful drive is of the present no less than the past and because audiences can thus recall a sentimental past they may never have experienced through a sentimental present which they have.

The title of the play derives from Viola in *Twelfth Night* who "never told her love, but let concealment, like a worm i' the bud, feed on her damask cheek." As the ugly duckling who in the end wins her love from the tempting actress, Flora Robson, while expert in a light comedy medium hitherto strange to her, regrettably followed most of the company in maintaining throughout the evening that set stage smile deemed by the acting profession to be an integral factor in the projection of great charm. What, after a steady hour or two, it usually projects is rather a deep-dyed suggestion of great imbecility.

NATIVE SON. OCTOBER 23, 1942

A revival of the dramatization of the Richard Wright novel by the author and Paul Green. Produced by Louis and George W. Brandt.

PROGRAM

BUCKLEY, D.A.	*Alexander Clark*	ERNIE JONES	*C. M. Bootsie Davis*
BIGGER THOMAS	*Canada Lee*	MR. DALTON	*Graham Velsey*
HANNAH THOMAS	*Evelyn Ellis*	MRS. DALTON	*Nell Harrison*
VERA THOMAS	*Helen Martin*	BRITTEN	*Ralph Bell*
BUDDY THOMAS	*Rudolph Whitaker*	PEGGY	*Frances Bavier*
MISS EMMETT	*Eileen Burns*	MARY DALTON	*Anne Burr*
JACK	*Thomas Anderson*	JAN ERLONE	*Herbert Ratner*
CLARA	*Rena Mitchell*	JUDGE	*William Malone*
G. H. RANKIN	*Rodester Timmons*	PAUL MAX	*John Berry*
GUS MITCHELL	*Wardell Saunders*		

SYNOPSIS: Prologue. *Courtroom.* Scene 1. *The Thomas room, early on a midwinter morning.* Scene 2. *A street, the same morning.* Scene 3. *The Dalton study, the next morning.* Scene 4. *Mary Dalton's bedroom, before dawn, a day later.* Scene 5. *The Dalton study, that afternoon.* Scene 6. *Clara's room, night of the same day.* Scene 7. *The basement of the Dalton house, afternoon of the same day.* Scene 8. *A room in a deserted house, the next night.* Scene 9. *A courtroom.* Scene 10. *A prison cell, some weeks later.*

The action takes place in present-day Chicago.

IN HIS REVIEW of the play upon its original production, Richard Watts, Jr., of the *Herald Tribune,* observed: "It all goes to indicate that, when a story was intended for one medium of expression and was entirely successful in employing that medium, it is dangerous to use some other narrative form for which it was not essentially planned." Although the reflection on the dramatization of this particular novel is well taken, the argument in support of it is hardly so. Surely there are countless instances that confound the contention, and they range all the way from satisfactory plays made from the old *Pride and Prejudice* and the later *Dodsworth* to equally satisfactory ones fash-

ioned from the old *Uncle Tom's Cabin* and the later *Rain*.
(In the latter case, Maugham had been steadfast in his conviction that it would be impossible for anyone to make a
play out of the tale, originally called *Miss Thompson*.)

The fact about this individual play is simply that it is
the dramatization which is at fault. But there is no sound
critical reason why more expert hands might not have
evolved one that would have captured and projected the
spirit and essence of the novel with complete effect. All this
talk about the limitations of the stage is too frequently
arbitrary. The stage, to be sure, has certain obvious limitations, but a first-rate dramatist finds a way to triumph over
most of the theoretical others. The history of the progress
of dramaturgy is a long record of such triumphs. Imagination, daring fancy, and poetic inventiveness have successively lessened the limitations, until today the only ones
still left are for the most part those which have been will-
ingly and even happily given over to the cinema for the
cinema's childishly proud exploitation.

Even so, the play made from the Wright novel is here
and there not without some superficial dramatic power.
This is due partly to the ready-made melodramatic kick in
certain of the materials, partly to the vigorous quality of
the direction, and partly to the merit of Canada Lee's performance of the role of Bigger Thomas. The debility of the
whole lies, first, in the surrender of the subjective elements
of the novel to purely objective action; secondly, in the
gradual diminuendo of the dramaturgy; and, thirdly, in the
final impression that out of the whole little more emerges
than a blackface version of Patrick Kearney's dramatization of Dreiser's *An American Tragedy* — the theatrical
image being heightened by certain similarities in the staging of the two exhibits, as, for example, the pleader sta-
tioned in the orchestra pit, etc.

But the play's greatest weakness rests in its attempt to
evoke compassion and sympathy for the Negro simply on
the score that he is a Negro. With the novel's penetration
into the depths of Bigger's mind, character, environment,
and the like scarcely flicked, what we get is not much more

than a straight-out melodrama about a white law-breaker made black to purely sentimental ends. The environment that wraps its rebellion around Bigger becomes on the stage merely the stereotyped overcrowded and sordid tenement room. We have had that rather regularly in the case of dramatic white Biggers. The hostility aroused in Bigger by superiority and condescension has been often similarly aroused in dramatic white Biggers. And so throughout most of the play. Yet where in the case of a white character guilty of various crimes from blackmail and theft to murder we would rationally be willing to let the law take its course, we are here invited to break our hearts simply because the character is black. That is not the novel, to be sure, but it *is* the play.

LITTLE DARLING. October 27, 1942

A comedy by Eric Hatch, currently resident in Hollywood, financed, appropriately enough, by Hollywood money. Produced by Tom Weatherly.

Program

Katherine Wilson	*Karen Morley*	Doctor Jarvis	*Gerald Cornell*
Wong	*Peter Goo Chong*	Miss Fairchild	*Betty Kelley*
Kenneth Brown	*Leon Ames*	Alice Bushfelter	*Phyllis Avery*
Cynthia Brown		Sully Peters	*James J. Coyle*
	Barbara Bel Geddes	Ralph Pabst	*Erik Martin*
Teddy Graves	*Arthur Franz*	Danny	*Dick Landsman*

SYNOPSIS: Act I. *Late on a Saturday afternoon in November 1941. (During the act the curtain will be lowered to denote the passage of several hours.)* Act II. *Another Saturday afternoon, two months later.* Act III. *Twenty minutes later.*

The entire action of the play takes place in the living-room of Kenneth Brown's house in Connecticut, about forty miles from New York.

IT IS A RARE SEASON that does not bring with it the comedy about the middle-aged man and the young female. Most often the ancient (in the eyes of all but one of the fledglings in the cast) finds that his attempt to renew his youth is a bore and is only too happy to return to his former comfortable existence, represented either by an already acquired spouse or a presently to be wedded adult, understanding, and long worshipping secretary. On a few occasions the protagonist alters the scheme and marries the young girl, also generally his secretary (since he is usually a literary fellow), who, to the secret delight of the octogenarian members of the audience, philosophizes that any male under forty-five is just an intolerable college boy, going to bed with whom would be like sleeping with a copy of *Physical Culture* magazine. When the play happens to be written by a Hubert Henry Davies, as in *A Single Man,* a witty comedy is the result. When it is written by a Samson Raphaelson, as in *Accent on Youth,* a considerably less witty but diverting comedy is the result. When it is written by an Eric Hatch, as in the exhibit here reported on, the result is largely what one might expect from a cinema belletrist.

It isn't that Mr. Hatch has not provided several amusing moments and at least one good scene (that wherein the middle-aged man gently explains to his skeptical and disgusted young daughter that a little romance is welcome in his long-humdrum life) ; it is rather that his collective treatment of the familiar theme is for the most part commonplace, obvious, and cheap. Consider, for example, the prevailing quality of the humor. His literary hero remarks that he is working on a story in which a brother unknowingly marries his own sister. "I have a good title for it, too," he says. *"Keep It in the Family."* His Chinese houseboy intermittently ejaculates "O Lell!" and shakes with mirth every time the name of Miss Bushfelter is pronounced. The city of Milwaukee takes the place of Yonkers, Flatbush, and Oshkosh as laugh-bait. When the hero, upon bringing the young blonde into the house, observes to the servant: "My bag's in the car," the juvenile retorts: "The hell she is!" Merriment is beseeched in the reiteration of the term cutie-pants. The daughter operates for hilarity with an allusion to her father as a concubine. The Chinese servant looks for laughter in pronouncing the word "bury" as "belly." A grandfather's clock periodically strikes the normal tones followed by a cacophonous bang. . . .

As for the general complexion of the chestnut, the tweedy writer hero is almost constantly pulling at a pipe; the young blonde who represents his platonic romance shocks the rest of the cast by coming downstairs in a saucy négligé; the hero's suddenly acquired youthfulness is indicated in terms of an unaccustomed lapel flower; the Yale undergraduate is presented as a complete moron given apropos of nothing to college cheers for Old Eli; when the hero first lays eyes on the young blonde he waggishly begins fortifying himself with a whisky and soda; the young daughter enters unexpectedly and believes the worst when she beholds the blonde asleep on the sofa and her father seated close by; the secretary slaps the daughter's face when the latter implies that there is something between her and her writer-father; the fiancé of the blonde indignantly rushes in and threatens to beat up the hero, who, he believes, has compromised his girl; and so on.

The drama, it would seem, still strangely calls for a somewhat higher skill than the movie scenario.

ROSALINDA. October 28, 1942

Johann Strauss's operetta Die Fledermaus *under still another title. Adapted from the Max Reinhardt version by John Meehan, Jr., and Gottfried Reinhardt, with lyrics by Paul Kerby. Produced by Lodewick Vroom for the New Opera Company.*

Program

Alfredo Allevanto	*Everett West*	Falke	*Gene Barry*
Gabriel von Eisenstein		Dr. Frank	*Paul West*
	Ralph Herbert	Fifi	*Shelly Winter*
Adele	*Virginia MacWatters*	Prince Orlofsky	*Oscar Karlweis*
Rosalinda von Eisenstein		Aide de Camp	*Edwin Fowler*
	Dorothy Sarnoff	Frosch	*Louis Sorin*
Blint	*Leonard Stocker*		

SYNOPSIS: *The action takes place in a summer resort, near Vienna, in the year 1890. Prologue. Outside Von Eisenstein's house at sunset. Act I. Living-room of Von Eisenstein's house, a few hours later. Act II. Ballroom of Prince Orlofsky's palace, a few hours later. Act III. The warden's office at the local jail, 6 a.m. the following morning.*

I T IS HARDLY NEWS in this day that whether it be called *Die Fledermaus, The Bat, One Wonderful Night, The Merry Countess, Night Birds, Champagne Sec, Rosalinda,* or whatever else, the libretto of the operetta afflicts Strauss's grand score with the pox. It was, in point of fact, hardly news when it was first uttered and duly groaned at in 1874. If the tale of the philandering husband who goes to a ball and there encounters his wife in a two-inch mask and, not recognizing her, makes loving overtures to her, to say nothing of embarrassed obbligatos to her maid, who is present under false colors — if the tale was stuporous almost seventy years ago, its deficiency in enormous dynamic power may be understood in the present era. Worse, when the libretto, as in the production under consideration, is treated to acting that seems persistently to be beset by the conviction that high Alt Wien spirits are best to be interpreted by comportment indistinguishable from a number of chamois frisking with an equal number of kangaroos, that deficiency becomes doubly apparent. There were times during the evening, indeed, when one couldn't be sure that what one was watching was not a mixed troupe of high divers and flying trapeze artists.

The stage was unfortunately also graveled in other directions and was only in the Strauss spirit when director Felix Brentano stepped aside and allowed George Balanchine to take over with the ballet that brilliantly concluded the second act. This Mr. Brentano appears to be infected with some peculiar ideas, one of which he shares with most directors of the musical stage. I allude to drunks. Whereas on the dramatic stage a gentleman in his cups is generally presented as bearing some slight resemblance to a gentleman in his cups, on the musical he is invariably pictured as an unrecognizable cross between an adagio dancer and a case of Parkinson's disease, with overtones of the late Antonio Scotti on one of his off days. A portion of the second act, laid in Prince Orlofsky's ballroom, and a larger portion of the third, laid in the warden's office at the jail on the following morning, consequently offered the appearance less of ladies and gentlemen of old Vienna who had looked upon the champagne when it was amber than of a crowd of current Bowery boulevardiers full of wood alcohol.

There was also the matter of legs. Whoever selected many of the ladies, the dancers foremost among them, must have a mother who in childbirth was not scared by a grand piano.

But if the physical stage on the whole suggested considerably less the romantic Vienna of yesterday than a Broadway night club of today, the Strauss score, led by Erich Korngold and amplified by the interpolation from other Strauss sources of "Wiener Wald," "Wein, Weib und Gesang," etc., — and in the main ably sung — made more than sufficient amends. But I can only pray that the next time *Rosalinda* is produced they will have the orchestra play it and the singers sing it with the curtain down. Or at least not raise it until the second-act waltz ballet and then again promptly drop it.

WITHOUT LOVE. November 10, 1942

A comedy by Philip Barry fabricated for the purposes of Katharine Hepburn. Produced by the Theatre Guild.

Program

Patrick Jamieson	*Elliott Nugent*	Peter Baillie	*Robert Shayne*
Quentin Ladd	*Tony Bickley*	Paul Carrel	*Sherling Oliver*
Anna	*Emily Massey*	Richard Hood	*Robert Chisholm*
Martha Ladd	*Ellen Morgan*	Robert Emmet Riordan	
Jamie Coe Rowan			*Neil Fitzgerald*
	Katharine Hepburn	Grant Vincent	*Royal Beal*
Kitty Trimble	*Audrey Christie*		

SYNOPSIS: Act I. Scene 1. *Late afternoon, May 9, 1940. Scene 2. Early the following morning. Scene 3. Afternoon, ten days later. Act II. Scene 1. Late afternoon, April 1941. Scene 2. Night, the following June. Act III. Scene 1. Evening, early October 1941. Scene 2. Night, the first of last December.*

The action of the play takes place in the course of two years in the living-room of the late Senator James Owen Coe's house in Washington.

Such recent productions as the Van Druten-Morris *The Damask Cheek* and, to an infinitely greater degree, this *Without Love* again bring home the fact that in late years American light comedy has declined from its high even more than B. & O. common, H. G. Wells, and the Bluepoint oyster. Van Druten (he has lived over here for years, has taken out citizenship papers, and so may be regarded as an American), while still indicating skill, has not negotiated anything in seasons to equal his early *Young Woodley* and *There's Always Juliet*. Barry has gone off precipitantly since the days of his *Paris Bound, Holiday,* and somewhat later *The Animal Kingdom*. And Behrman, the most adroit of the lot, has not done anything that has come anywhere near his *Rain from Heaven*, produced in 1934.

As for the others, Rachel Crothers, never of much consequence, has since not touched even her *Let Us Be Gay*

and *As Husbands Go,* done in 1929 and 1931 respectively.
A. E. Thomas, after *No More Ladies* in 1934, has critically disappeared. Paul Osborn did a nice job in *The Vine-
gar Tree* and a fairish one in *Oliver, Oliver* a decade or so
ago and has latterly gone off in other dramatic directions
with minor accomplishment. Arthur Richman, who began
promisingly, has done little worthy of record since *The
Awful Truth* in 1922. Vincent Lawrence, with all indica-
tions of a fine talent, wrote two or three intelligently amusing comedies, went to Hollywood, and, like so many others,
died there. After her *The Marriage Game,* produced many
years ago, Anne Crawford Flexner faded into nothingness.
Lynn Starling, who began with *Meet the Wife,* subsequently confected several lesser comedies and then went
down the Hollywood chute. Donald Ogden Stewart, author of the entertaining *Rebound* in 1929, ditto.

Aside from some of these obvious cases and regarding
only the better writers who have persisted in the light comedy field, what may be the reasons for the collapse, either
complete or comparative? The first that comes to mind is
the war and the upset state of the world, allegedly hardly
conducive to the writing of such comedy. But recollection
proves the reason hollow. During the last World War there
came from both America and England a plenitude of variously deft light comedies, including among others Alfred
Sutro's *The Clever Ones* and *The Two Virtues,* Monckton
Hoffe's *Things We'd Like to Know,* the Smith-Mapes *The
Boomerang,* the Ditrichstein-Hatton *The Great Lover,*
W. S. Maugham's *Caroline* and *Our Betters,* Clare Kummer's *Good Gracious, Annabelle* and *A Successful Calam-
ity,* and the Harwood-Jesse *Billeted.* Also Haddon Chambers's *The Saving Grace,* Jesse Lynch Williams's *Why
Marry?,* Milne's *Belinda,* Maugham's *Too Many Husbands, Love in a Cottage,* and *Cæsar's Wife,* Arnold Bennett's *The Title,* Kummer's *Be Calm, Camilla,* Cyril Har-
court's *A Pair of Petticoats,* and Gladys Unger's *Our Mr.
Hepplewhite.* So war and the upset state of a world do not
seem to be exactly the answer.

A second commonly heard argument is that our America

is not, and never was, possessed of the right social background and tone for the comedy of manners. That it may not have been in the past is more than possible, although out of it even then emerged such commendable exhibits as Langdon Mitchell's *The New York Idea,* Clyde Fitch's *The Truth,* and divers others. But that it has in later years been at least the equal of England in that respect should be more or less evident. This largely and paradoxically has been brought about by the English themselves, who for the past twenty years have flooded the American metropolitan social scene and become, to a considerable extent, part and parcel of it. Thus, more and more, what with economic conditions in England what they have been, with manifold British-American intermarriages, and with similar phenomena of time, New York gradually grew to be the capital of fashionable society, where things came to such a pass that one could no longer familiarly throw a champagne bottle across the room without hitting at least a couple of lords, three dukes, and several ladies, not to mention various French and Italian counts, Rumanian princesses, Russian grand-dukes, and maybe a Greek or Spanish royalty or two. And the scene, accordingly, became so much meat for comedy of the Maugham *Our Betters,* Lonsdale *The Last of Mrs. Cheyney,* and even general Haddon Chambers-Hubert Henry Davies sort. So that doesn't seem to be exactly the answer either.

Then what is the answer? I answer the question simply and confidently. I don't know.

The specific and personal case of Philip Barry, however, is an exception to the otherwise baffling problem. Once content to write at least an approximation to pure and unadulterated light comedy, he some years ago became obsessed by the notion that, in addition to his talent in that direction, he was a creature of puissant brain and that it was his duty, along with his pleasure, to share its pearls with the public. From this hallucination there presently issued not only a quota of pseudo-philosophical opera that sorely grieved that portion of the public whose mental capacities were slightly in excess of those of the average ballet critic but, further, a proportion of comedies which were not satisfied to be merely comedies but which deemed it incumbent upon them to include a variety of solemn passages confiding their author's profundities on divers cosmic enigmas. The result was and is a species of entertainment that sacrifices light comedy to heavy platitudinizing and that in sum suggests an undergraduate at a small Methodist college wildly celebrating the completion of a cribbed thesis with a couple of beers.

This *Without Love* provides a sterling example. Borrowing the time-honored theatrical plot of a hundred or more marriage-of-convenience and marriage-in-name-only plays, Barry has overlaid it with political symbolism analogically having to do with English-Irish national relations. Therefrom it is his apparent idea to prove that a little hot love would not be and is not a bad idea in either case and, in the English-Irish case in particular, that it might lead to mutually profitably co-operation, especially in war time. (He elects to overlook that the platonic relationship between the two nations in point has been somewhat one-sided and that Ireland's frigidity has not restrained England in the past from seducing her good and plenty.) His stated argumentation in proof of his point is additionally so juvenile that even the most bellicose Anglophile would have some trouble in rationalizing it, taking as it does the vaudeville viewpoint that whereas everybody objects to Ireland's neutrality in the present war, nobody objects to Switzerland's and contending further that it is Ireland's duty to have consideration in a dire hour for a country which never showed it consideration in an almost equally dire hour.

Not only has such political brain exercise invalidated much of Barry's comedy but his comedy writing itself shows an increasing inner debility. Once not without some wit, it has now descended to such Balaban and Katz humors as alluding to an inebriated character as "my little tipsy sweetheart" and patriotically observing of a highball layout that "it has everything but Vichy." Once given to some originality, it now presents itself as little more than a pastiche of materials from its author's antecedent plays, as well as

from the plays of others on end. Thus, in *Without Love,*
we get again Barry's sentimental "shining face" love dialogue from his *Bright Star* of some years back, his final curtain out-of-step, in-step business from the final curtain of
his *The Philadelphia Story,* and his piano-playing business
accompanying a love passage from his *Paris Bound,* along
with such character stencils as the unhappily married man
seeking refuge in drink, the hard, sophisticated female with
the heart of gold, and the amorous Frenchman to whom
an attractive and possibly available woman is, in Barry's
phraseology, worth all the delicate preparation of an appetizing dish — and further not forgetting such dazzling
sexual philosophies as "Men seem to understand their own
love lives well enough, but they don't seem to know anything of women's needs."

If Mr. Barry regards what I write of his mental gifts as
unkind, let me give him some comfort. Let him reflect that
some of the best comedies the modern theatre has disclosed
have been written by men of no especial cerebral voltage.
Unlike him, however, they have duly appreciated the fact
and have contented themselves with the achievement of
merely very brilliant light entertainment.

A word on Miss Hepburn, for whom Barry has tailored
his last two boons. An actress of such strikingly limited
ability that, in professional company, she seems almost
amateurish, she is nevertheless paradoxically a constantly
prehensile and inveigling stage figure. You know she can't
act, yet you do not particularly mind. In this respect she
resembles a child's toy choo-choo. You know that it is only
a poor imitation of the big, real article but it none the less
exercises a fascination even for a paternal locomotive en-
gineer.

Of the most charming young actress in our theatre, Richard Bennett several years ago remarked: "I wouldn't give
five cents for her acting, but I'd rather have her on a stage
than any other young actress in the American playhouse."
Although it was not Miss Hepburn to whom he referred
— the young actress in question, despite Bennett, has a
very considerable ability — his observation rather fits her

also, though with certain heavy reservations. That Miss Hepburn's acting would have brought from Bennett a slightly less handsome pecuniary offer is more or less obvious, since, as noted, when it comes to the business of histrionism she is little more than an accomplished tyro. But that she is oddly, as also noted, a creature who nevertheless holds the attention while she is on the stage is equally obvious. What it is that brings this about may be variously guessed at. Although she is not beautiful, she has an admirably slim figure and striking features, so maybe that is part of the story. Although her speaking voice is not particularly engaging, it none the less has in it a peculiar quality that, while occasionally monotonous, refractorily fetches the ear, so that may also be part of the story. Although her physical movements are often without grace, there is something about them that is awkwardly attractive, so maybe that is still another part of the story. And although she is hardly the possessor of any overpowering sex attraction, she is appetizing in the same chill way that a whisky sour is, so maybe that is yet still another part of the story. But whatever it is, she seems to have a substantial following, and that substantial following seems in turn to be perfectly willing to remit its judgment (if it has any) so far as her acting performances go and to accept in its stead the spectacle of its pet in mere propria persona.

MR. SYCAMORE. NOVEMBER 13, 1942

A fantasy by the Hollywood literata, Ketti Frings, derived from a short story by Robert Ayre. Produced by the Theatre Guild as its gesture toward dramatic art.

PROGRAM

TOM BURTON	*Harry Townes*	REVEREND DOCTOR DOODY	
NED FISH	*Harry Sheppard*		*Russell Collins*
JOHN GWILT	*Stuart Erwin*	JANE GWILT	*Lillian Gish*
MYRTLE STAINES	*Leona Powers*	FRED STAINES	*Otto Hulett*
ABNER COOTE	*John Philliber*	MR. OIKLE	*Albert Bergh*
ESTELLE BENLOW	*Enid Markey*	EMILY	*Mary Heckart*
JULIE FISH	*Louise McBride*	MR. HAMMOND	*Jed Dooley*
ALBERT FERNFIELD	*Buddy Swan*	DAISY STAINES	*Pearl Herzog*
MR. FERNFIELD	*Walter Appler*	MR. HOOP	*Ray J. Largay*
FLETCHER PINGPANK	*Franklyn Fox*	MR. FINK	*Harry Bellaver*

SYNOPSIS: 1. *A street.* 2. *Reverend Dr. Doody's study.* 3. *John's back yard.* 4. *The same.* (*Intermission.*) 5. *John's back yard.* 6. *Outside the church.* 7. *John's back yard.* 8. *The same.*
The Place. *Smeed, a small town.*

THE DEMAND of fantasy is that it shall possess either charm, poetic wisdom, or humor, or at its best all three in combination. If it fails in the charm of, say, Max Beerbohm's *The Happy Hypocrite,* the poetic wisdom of the short plays of Dunsany, or the humor of even Pedro Alarcón it is lost. Lacking all three elements, *Mr. Sycamore* is accordingly not only lost but completely sunk.

Little is sadder than amateur fantasy, and this treatment of the fable of a postman who, recalling the old Greek legend of Philemon and Baucis, decides to convert himself into a tree to get away from the bickerings of the human race and do some thinking is amateur with a vengeance. Real dramatic fantasy, after all, rests in something more than giving characters such names as Gwilt, Fish, Pingpank, Doody, Coote, Oikle, Hoop, and Fink, in causing the central figure to stand unhumorously motionless in the center of the stage for most of two acts, and in providing a number of the characters with dialogue that stems from Lottie Blair Parker.

The basic scheme of the play has possibilities for fantasy, but all that has been realized is much the kind of entertainment variously recommended to amateurs in the Samuel T. French catalogue under the headings: "parlor comedies," "charade plays," and "plays for school, college and camp." Viewing the exhibit and hungry for just a little humor, I couldn't help thinking, with a deplorable facetiousness it may be, that Miss Frings's postman might better have taken a hint from Ilka Chase's *Past Imperfect* and, longing to get away from a postman's dull and puritanical existence, have converted himself not into a tree in the small community of Smeed but into a bush in Hollywood. But since a tree in Smeed it is, I also couldn't help thinking, with considerably less facetiousness, that another idea was overlooked. A small dog figures in the play, at the final curtain of which the postman-tree waves its leaves in a signal of satisfied peace to the postman's wife seated in its shade. After the signal, I meditated, the dog should be brought on just as the curtain is falling and be caused to lift its leg moistly against the tree. Not only would the business provide a welcome laugh against the antecedent dullness but it would also provide a valid criticism of both the play and the sappy philosophy inherent in its arboreal theme.

Fantasy may be superficially described as being weak serious drama filtered through a poetic imagination into beauty. In the case of the exhibit under consideration, however, all we get is a fantastic idea filtered through a prosy imagination into dismally weak comedy. Fantasy consists in something more than a mere extravagant conceit. It is the quasi-realistic conversion of such a conceit into wonder and charm and loveliness and ache and laughter and commiseration through the wonder and charm and loveliness and ache and laughter and commiseration of a literate and whimsical mind.

In the production of *Mr. Sycamore* the Theatre Guild experienced the shortest-run failure in its history, even many of its paid-in-advance subscribers withholding their attendance.

HOMECOMING. November 16, 1942

A comedy by Edward Peyton Harris. Produced by New Plays, Inc.

Program

Lot Eborn	*Georgia Simmons*	Sam	*Thurman Jackson*
Nate Eborn	*Augustin Duncan*	Liz	*Andrea Duncan*
Ruth	*Elena Karam*	Jace	*Scott Cooley*
Hen	*Robert Berger*	Guilf	*Immanuel Duval*
Alice	*Margherita Sargent*		

SYNOPSIS: Act I. *The kitchen of the Eborn home, on the outskirts of Greenville, N. C., a Friday night early in June, some years from now.* Act II. Scene 1. *The cabin of a boat, mid-afternoon, the first of July.* Scene 2. *The same, before dusk, toward the middle of August.* Act III. *A hilltop, one instant later.*

After more than twenty years' disappointing experience, there are still some persons, a number of the critics amongst them, who apparently believe that in some mysterious way the hope of the American drama lies up a sidestreet. For twenty years or more, ever indeed since the Provincetown Theatre down in dingy MacDougal Street gave birth to Eugene O'Neill and the Washington Square Players hidden away in beery Yorkville uncovered a promising talent or two, these ardent souls have been taxicabbing and sledding up remote alleys and distant bypaths pursuing possible new glorious epiphanies and, as regularly as winter colds, have found nothing. Yet undismayed their conviction persists that sooner or later something pretty tasty will surely turn up.

In this regard the sanguine voyagers resemble the suckers who trust the people who are always discovering wonderful new little restaurants down near the Brooklyn Bridge or in some other such inaccessible locality where you can get a remarkably fine dinner (with wine) for eighty-five cents, the aforesaid restaurants upon due investigation and trial turning out to be fit only for the less connoisseur dogs and vaudeville acrobats. Although countless eager amateurs and semi-amateurs have been in operation now for two full decades in sidestreets near and far, little or nothing they have disclosed has been the equal, and certainly not the superior, of even the lower run of Broadway drama, and the lower run of Broadway drama, you need no stage whisper to apprise you, is low-double-low. I myself, being at times just as gullible as my critical brethren, have followed their hope and trust into the dark recesses of the metropolis and, like them, have returned to civilization, such as it is, with nothing for my pains. Whether dramatic or musical, what I have seen has for the overwhelming part been zero. Once, maybe, in forty or fifty tries something may provide something to write about, but even on such rare occasions the productions and the acting are so atrociously bad that only a long-practiced professional eye can see through them to the script. The Broadway theatre these days is certainly nothing to brag about, but in comparison with the sidestreet theatre it is the cream right off the top of the bottle.

Homecoming, produced down in the Provincetown Theatre of hallowed memory, is a fair sample of what you get when you foolishly wander afield. A parable brewed from the Biblical tale of Noah's ark and told in terms of poor white trash on the outskirts of Greenville, North Carolina, at the end of the current war, it amounts to the kind of exhibit in which an old cracker Noah sits placidly to one side solemnly spouting Biblical quotations the while the younger generation's speech leans toward the Cocacola, in which the food on the Ark, as the reviewer for the *Times* pointed out, is kept in a small box and somehow lasts eight persons for all of the flood's forty days, and in which the author, having seen the old play called *The Deluge,* causes his repentant characters, once the flood has receded, to return promptly to their former sinful ways, chief among which is shamelessly amateur acting.

Moral: Never spend more than sixty cents' taxi fare to get to a theatre.

THE SKIN OF OUR TEETH. November 18, 1942

A fantastic comedy by Thornton Wilder. Produced by Michael Myerberg. Awarded the Pulitzer Prize.

Program

ANNOUNCER	*Morton DaCosta*	USHER	*Harry Clark*
SABINA	*Tallulah Bankhead*	GIRL, DRUM MAJORETTE	
MR. FITZPATRICK	*E. G. Marshall*		*Elizabeth Scott*
MRS. ANTROBUS	*Florence Eldridge*	GIRL, DRUM MAJORETTE	
DINOSAUR	*Remo Buffano*		*Patricia Riordan*
MAMMOTH	*Andrew Ratousheff*	FORTUNE TELLER	*Florence Reed*
TELEGRAPH BOY	*Dickie Van Patten*	CONVEENER	*Stanley Weede*
GLADYS	*Frances Heflin*	CONVEENER	*Seumas Flynn*
HENRY	*Montgomery Clift*	BROADCAST OFFICIAL	
MR. ANTROBUS	*Fredric March*		*Morton DaCosta*
DOCTOR	*Arthur Griffin*	DEFEATED CANDIDATE	
PROFESSOR	*Ralph Kellard*		*Joseph Smiley*
JUDGE	*Joseph Smiley*	MR. TREMAYNE	*Ralph Kellard*
HOMER	*Ralph Cullinan*	HESTER	*Eulabelle Moore*
MISS E. MUSE	*Edith Faversham*	IVY	*Viola Dean*
MISS T. MUSE	*Emily Lorraine*	FRED BAILEY	*Stanley Prager*
MISS M. MUSE	*Eva Mudge Nelson*		

SYNOPSIS: Act I. *Home, Excelsior, N. J.* Act II. *Atlantic City boardwalk.* Act III. *Home, Excelsior, N. J.*

THIS PLAY once again reinforces the conviction that Thornton Wilder remains merely a talented dilettante. Apparently determined at all costs to be different, his stage writing, while it accomplishes that end, does not succeed in investing the difference with enough weight to give it an even relative importance. He is at times agreeably humorous; he is at moments remotely inventive; he is at times even moderately moving. But it is all on the surface; there is little or no plumbing of the depths; and the final impression, after the pleasant little moments have been forgotten, is of one of those imitation gold bracelets hung with newfangled charms that one sees in the so-called novelty shops.

It is pretty and it is cute, but it isn't the real article, and its novelty very quickly wears off.

The Skin of Our Teeth, announces a program note, "is a comedy about George Antrobus, his wife and two children, and their general utility maid, Lily Sabina, all of Excelsior, New Jersey. George Antrobus is John Doe or George Spelvin or you — the average American at grips with a destiny sometimes sour, sometimes sweet. The Antrobuses have survived fire, flood, pestilence, the seven-year locusts, the ice age, the black pox and the double feature, a dozen wars and as many depressions. They have run many a gamut, are as durable as radiators, and look upon the future with a disarming optimism. Ultimately bewitched, befuddled and becalmed, they are the stuff of which heroes are made — heroes and buffoons. They are true offspring of Adam and Eve, victims of all the ills that flesh is heir to. They have survived a thousand calamities by the skin of their teeth, and Mr. Wilder's play is a tribute to their indestructibility."

What Mr. Wilder's play, aside from that, essentially is is an old-time morality play of the *Everyman* species related in terms frequently identical with the celebrated pre-war Berlin-Piscator production of *Hooray, We're Alive!* Adam, Eve, Lilith, Cain, Moses, etc., are here presented as people of today, and through fantastic anachronisms and analogies and equally fantastic stage tricks, involving loud speakers, lantern slides, flying scenery, and actors in the auditorium the playwright seeks to depict the struggle of humanity down the ages. Some of the result is mildly amusing and some of the devices are fairly diverting, but a strain for originality and an often embarrassing archness make the whole considerably less effective than the author hoped. Tallulah Bankhead, as a combination eternal temptress and critical commère of the play, accomplished wonders in infusing the exhibit with a vitality that it hardly on its own possesses. In short, while respect is due Mr. Wilder for his eagerness to bring fresh life into the theatre, his manner and means for the doing are still sadly wanting.

In this general connection, two terms commonly employed by journalistic drama criticism call for clarification: to wit, *imagination* and *originality*. Both are indiscriminately held to be synonymous with virtue, yet close scrutiny proves that often they are not. Some of the best plays are lacking in such "imagination," as some of the worst are full of it. And so, too, in the case of such "originality." There is no more imagination, in the above accepted critical use of the word, in some such relatively worthy play as, say, Brieux's *The Red Robe* than in some such unworthy one as, for example, Brieux's *Woman on Her Own*. There is, in all truth, more of this so-called imagination in a rubbishy play like Davis's reincarnation nonesuch, *The Ladder*, than in an upright play like Ibsen's *A Doll's House*. As for originality, there is surely far more in a mystery and detective play like *The Bat* than in a rather greater contribution to dramatic art like Sudermann's thematically and basically stale *Honor*.

Imagination, it seems, is too often critically identified with a fancy flight into space, however meaningless, whereas the greater imagination frequently exercises itself with its feet firmly planted on the ground, as witness, in the first instance, Albert Bein's mediocre *Heavenly Express* and, in the second, Hauptmann's *The Weavers*. Originality, it also seems, is too often identified less with treatment than with first theatrical use of theme, and a second-rate play like Yeats's *Deirdre* consequently is accorded the compliment and a first-rate subsequent one like Synge's *Deirdre of the Sorrows* arbitrarily deprived of it.

That Mr. Wilder's *The Skin of Our Teeth* has both relative imagination and originality in the above dubious Broadway sense is to be granted. Its scheme of showing mankind's fight for certainty and security down the centuries through anachronisms visited upon the present is both theatrically novel and fanciful. But it is emphatically not the kind of play that results from imagination and originality in the higher, finer, and purer Joycean sense. (The play unacknowledgedly paraphrases much that is in Joyce's novel *Finnegans Wake*.)

On the old-time vaudeville bills one used from time to time to encounter pairs of performers who proudly billed themselves as "Those Somewhat Different Comedians." The chief difference between them and the comedians who were content to appear simply under their own names and without any further parsley was that the latter were really funny and that, unlike the former, their vests didn't have three-inch pearl buttons on them. Although thus far Mr. Wilder has not billed himself as "That Somewhat Different Playwright" (over Saroyan's dead body), there is small doubt that the billing nevertheless remains in his secret mind.

Mr. Wilder's desperate effort to be different not only takes the form of the three-inch pearl buttons but raises them to six inches, and for added measure embroiders the vest with gilt pretzels. In *Our Town* he laid hold of an essentially standard small-town play and successfully put it over on the Keith-Albee intellectuals by ridding it of scenery, cagily employing a narrator to substitute for the more difficult job of playwriting which suggests all the thematic color of past and present within itself, purveying charadish pantomime for a humor that neither his action nor dialogue contained, and giving pseudo-size to the whole with a last-moment discourse on life after death, of the metaphysical calibre of a tank-town Baptist church pulpit. In *The Skin of Our Teeth* he presents evidence that he considers his antecedent *Our Town* just another pea in a pod, throws off his coat and trousers — though leaving the Pantages vest in its place — and goes in for difference with an assiduity that has not been matched since Glenn Warner tucked a football up the back of a Cornell player's jersey and scored a touchdown while the bewildered Penn State team was searching for the ball in Renwick Park half a mile away.

Wilder does everything with his stage but bring on Billy Rose in a swimming tank. He peoples it with a maid out of Jerome K. Jerome who spoofs the stage doings, a prehistoric mammoth the size of a Schnauzer, a dinosaur whose wide-open mouth leads one to anticipate that it believes itself to be a Dinahshore, a house whose walls tumble in when they are dusted, a blaring Salvation Army band, a glowing fireless fireplace, and just about everything else that the Messrs. Olsen and Johnson haven't yet got around to thinking about. And at the end, as in the instance of *Our Town,* he makes himself up as a philosopher by way of letting his audience know that Philip Barry and all the rest of those boys have nothing on him, falling back for his eloquent proof on this occasion upon quotations from Plato, Aristotle, and Spinoza.

In short, when it comes to being a Joyce, Mr. Wilder remains nine parts Peggy to one part James.

ONCE OVER LIGHTLY. November 19, 1942

An "Americanization" of Beaumarchais's The Barber of Seville, *with the music of Gioachino Rossini, the whole edited and conducted by Laszlo Halasz. Dialogue by Louis Garden. Produced and quickly withdrawn by Saul Colin.*

Program

Figaro	*Igor Gorin*	Dr. Bartolo	*Richard Wentworth*
Rosina	*Grace Panvini*	Bertha	*Ardelle Warner*
Almaviva	*Felix Knight*	Fiorella	*Myron Szandrowsky*
Don Basilio	*Carlos Alexander*		

SYNOPSIS: Prologue. *A street in Seville, dawn.* Act I. *A room in Dr. Bartolo's home, later that day.* Act II. *The same, several hours later.*

T HE ATTEMPT to make a Broadway show out of this Metropolitan Opera House old reliable was akin to an attempt to make a Metropolitan Opera House exhibit out of *Beat the Band,* and as gratuitous. The gesture in question rested largely in a reduction of the libretto to what the producer and his aides evidently considered pretty saucy George Abbott. We were thus regaled with such old Spanish locutions as "what's cookin'?" "I'll say it's a racket," "you'll get your dough," "it is my motto, never be blotto," "tell the world," "phony," "who in hell are you?" "just a local yokel who made good in a big way running a clip joint," "for the love of bacteria!" and "I'm the well-known barber of Seville who gets in everybody's hair," along with stage deportment that the singing histrios apparently deemed suitable to the articulation of the academic pearls of speech.

There can be no sound critical objection to Americanizing any such libretto. The trouble, when the job is undertaken, is that the jobbers appear usually to believe that America is bounded on the north by the Bowery, on the south by Billy Bryant's river showboat, on the east by an Asbury Park billiard parlor, and on the west by a Hollywood gag factory, and that it is inhabited entirely by descendants of George Primrose and Junie McCree.

For the occasion, the Sterbini libretto was abandoned in favor of the Beaumarchais original, the noted wrench-throwing being visited upon the latter. Add to this voices that intermittently indicated their projectors' seeming belief that Rossini composed exclusively for trumpets, and stage direction that periodically suggested Seville was the birthplace of Milton Aborn, and the picture becomes sufficiently clear.

YANKEE POINT. November 23, 1942

A war play by Gladys Hurlbut. Produced by Edward Choate and Marie Louise Elkins.

Program

Miz Bekins	Elizabeth Patterson	Captain Trueman	
Jeremy Adams	Dorothy Gilchrist		Donald McClelland
Bob Adams	John Cromwell	Coast Guard	John Forsythe
Mary Adams	Edna Best	Sandy Martin	K. T. Stevens
Doctor Nickerson	James Todd	Uncle Pete	Arthur Aylsworth
Miss Higgins	Ann Dere	George Fitch	Richard Rudi
Ruth Lapo	Dora Sayers		

SYNOPSIS: Act I. *The living-room, morning.* Act II. *The observation post, afternoon.* Act III. *The living-room, evening.*

Scene. *The Adams home at "Yankee Point" on the eastern sea coast.*
Time. *The present.*

THIS IS ESSENTIALLY an American paraphrase of the English *Mrs. Miniver* plus the English *The Morning Star,* treating of the effect of war on a family living on Long Island in the neighborhood of the Nazi saboteur landing of newspaper headline memory. All the expected ingredients are present, from the comedy-relief servant to the veteran of the last war who longs to do his duty again in this one, from the fortitude of little people under a bomb raid to the brave, patient ministrations of the mother of the family, and from the German spy to the daughter with pacifist leanings who turns patriot on all cylinders and espouses the dramatic stencil that "we must fight to make a better world for the childen that are to come into it."

The general devices duly follow the cliché pattern: the wife who sends her husband to war with a gallant, heartbroken smile; the feeble but brave old retainer who refuses to seek shelter (like a damn fool) when danger threatens; the widow of a war hero who throws aside her grief to sell war bonds and beseech men to enlist; the unsung pluck of men and women in civilian defense; the old man who

goes out hunting for the enemy with an ancient blunder-
buss; etc. And the general writing is of a piece.

These many duplications of war plays, most of them,
like this one, doomed to early failure, only further em-
phasize the stupidity of what flatteringly knows itself as
show business. Consider, in immediate relevance to the exhibit under discussion, the story, for example, of five New
York theatrical producers of thirty or so years ago who became wildly excited over the critical and commercial possibilities of a certain play. The producers were Sam S.
Shubert, Lee Shubert, J. J. Shubert, John C. Fisher, and
Frank Perley. The play was *The Nazarene*, by Hal Reid. In
association, the five enthusiastic gentlemen put on their
great treasure in Newark, New Jersey, sat back, and prepared themselves for the flood of gold that was to come.
Then something happened. Just before the curtain was due
to go up on the opening night — in fact, just ten minutes
before it was due to go up — they got word from a rather
inconsiderate friend that their potential gold-mine had
been presented exactly two years before at the Murray Hill
Theatre in New York under the title *The Light of the
World*, that the audience had gone sound asleep at it on
the first night, that the critics the next morning had roasted
the life out of it, and that it was one of the most awful
duds of its season. The rest may be imagined, including the
consternation of the five producers and, obviously, the immediate failure of their hypothetical mint.

But let it not be imagined that this is an exceptional
tale about the craziest of all trades. Furthermore, if anyone
believes that things have changed materially since those
days, he is corybantic. It is true that in that era there were
many incidents that would take a lot to beat them, but
when it comes to the show business you can usually trust
it to be sufficiently vertiginous at any and all times.

It would seem, for example, pretty hard to outdo the
old witticism of the eight Hurtig brothers who got their
start as theatre managers and producers by dividing themselves into two groups of four each, sending one group on
the road ahead of Sarah Bernhardt quietly to buy up all

the tickets in advance and then following it around the country with the second group to sell the tickets, before the Divine One opened, at a stiff premium. Or to surpass the intellectual effort of J. Austin Fynes, the first dramatic critic of the New York *Evening Sun* and thereafter manager of the Union Square Theatre, to inaugurate three-a-day opera at his theatre with a lone piano-player in the orchestra pit and with a variety show added as a bargain. Or to excel the producer who, upon being offered Remenyi, the famous Hungarian violinist, as an attraction, demanded to know "what the sketch is about, how many actors it calls for, and how much scenery it uses." Or, surely, to top the story of the Gilbert and Sullivan troupe that was pursued to New Haven, Connecticut, by half a dozen indignant hotel managers who had been beaten out of their bills in near-by towns and who, when the show was threatened by the sheriff with immediate closing in New Haven and when the male chorus struck, allowed themselves to be persuaded that for financial self-protection they should substitute as the peers of high and lofty station in *Iolanthe*. Or, again surely, to beat the record of George Jones, known as Count Joannes, who made a fortune playing Romeo and Hamlet behind a net and whose large audiences came nightly solely to razzle-dazzle the tights off him. Or, finally, the whimsy of Joseph Tooker, manager for Jarrett and Palmer, who introduced seven different Juliets, among them Marie Wainwright, in as many scenes in the Shakespearean tragedy wherein George Rignold, the English actor, played Romeo.

However, coming to present times.

When the Theatre Guild in the season before this announced as the first of its revivals Eugene O'Neill's *Ah, Wilderness!* and issued a call for actors, one of those who went around to see Theresa Helburn, in charge of the casting, was a little actress named Ruth Gilbert. "But what role did you have in mind?" asked Miss Helburn, not without some impatience. "The role of Muriel," replied Miss Gilbert. "Muriel!" exclaimed Miss H. "Nonsense! You are altogether too young for the part!" Miss Gilbert took her departure, with no small humorous difficulty restraining herself from informing Miss Helburn that it was she herself, now apparently much too young for the role, who had played it all of eight years before when Miss Helburn and the Guild had originally produced the play.

Incidentally, when Philip Moeller was directing the original production he stopped suddenly short at one point and said to O'Neill, who was in rehearsal attendance, that he believed it would be a fine idea to put in a comical line — he gave a sample — at that particular juncture. O'Neill, who never accepts outside suggestions for his plays from anyone, gazed at Moeller long and hard. "Your line is funny, all right," he observed sarcastically, "but, if you insist on a laugh in that spot, it would be a much finer idea and a lot funnier if you yourself came on during the scene, very slowly turned around, the meanwhile dropping your trousers, and disclosed to the audience your arse painted a brilliant Alice blue."

The week after *Shadow and Substance* had scored a big success in New York, the Shuberts, who shared financially in the production, sought to economize on the overhead and so guarantee larger profits. It was thus that, when on the second Monday night Sir Cedric Hardwicke in the role of the aristocratic Canon came on stage and delivered his famous testimonial to his friend Don Miguel Barzan y Perdito and the taste in personal surroundings which he had acquired from him, his eyes suddenly rested not on the rare antique furniture that had been in the parochial house before but horrifiedly on some of the doggonedest stuff ever seen outside a kitchen in a Mississippi hotel.

The following year, when Sinclair Lewis played the Canon in summer stock, he found that the necessarily fine reproductions of Velasquez's *Philip IV Entering Lerida*, Murillo's *Immaculate Conception*, and Raphael's *Dispute of the Sacrament*, to which the Canon addresses one of his most telling speeches, were beyond the financial resources of the theatres. His loud protestations to the several managements being of no avail, he was driven to substitute for the Canon's grand speech the following paraphrase: "I have no pictures on that wall, and why? Because if there can hang no beautiful reproduction of Velasquez's *Philip IV Entering Lerida,* and there another of Murillo's *Immaculate Conception,* and there another of Raphael's bitter *Dispute of the Sacrament,* I want no compromise with beauty and prefer no pictures at all. But were they to hang there, could they be called secular if we know anything of the might of the thing that has given us birth?" The audiences esteemed the speech as one of author Paul Vincent Carroll's very best.

Throughout its prosperous run in New York and other cities, critics and audiences at *The Time of Your Life* deplored the momentary shifting of the scene from the waterfront saloon to a hotel bedroom, arguing that the shift slowed the action and that the bedroom scene could just as well — in point of fact, much better — be played in the saloon and be made sufficiently convincing in a pictorial direction simply and merely by the use of lights. Lawrence Langner of the Theatre Guild, which had a financial interest in the production, stubbornly refused to consider any such change. "We spent a hundred dollars on that bedroom set and we aren't going to throw it away for anyone!" he insisted.

When the young actress named Julie Stevens read for a part in *Brooklyn, U. S. A.,* the producers told her that she was satisfactory except for one thing. "Your hair is much too dark," they said to her. "You'll have to dye it. You play a Polish girl and, naturally, all Polish girls are blonde." So, despite the fact that every authentic Polish woman who has ever appeared on the American dramatic stage — from Janauschek to Josephine Victor — has had dark hair, Miss Stevens became a blonde. The producers evidently got their idea of Polish girls from Lyda Roberti, of musical comedy fame, who was as blonde as Hollywood makes them. If ever they put on another play with a Polish woman in it and hire the dark Polish Pola Negri for the role, watch for a taffy-topped Pola.

When William Saroyan put on his *The Beautiful People,* he told the agents to send around for his inspection actors for the role of Jonah Webster, described in the text as a carelessly dressed, poetic, impoverished, boozy old bird. Of those who showed up, one, Cooksey by name, what with his indifferent clothes and genial slouch, struck Saroyan as just right, and he engaged him on the spot. During the weeks of rehearsal Saroyan further warmly congratulated himself on his sagacity in having picked exactly the man for the part. Then came the opening night — and Saroyan fainted. Proud of himself for sharing in the great occasion and determined to make the most of it in every direction, Cooksey had gone out and bought himself an elegant new wardrobe and, when he appeared on the stage, it was nigh impossible to distinguish between the bum that Saroyan had written and John Drew, or even William Faversham, in his fashionable prime.

COUNSELLOR–AT–LAW. November 24, 1942

A revival of the eleven-year-old play by Elmer Rice. Produced by John Golden.

Program

Bessie Green	Ann Thomas	George Simon	Paul Muni
Henry Susskind	Leslie Barrett	Cora Simon	Joan Wetmore
Sarah Becker	Clara Langsner	Lena Simon	Jennie Moscowitz
Zedorah Chapman	Betty Kelley	Peter J. Malone	John L. Kearney
Goldie Rindskoff	Frieda Altman	Johann Breitstein	Barrie Wanless
Charles McFadden	Jack Sheehan	David Simon	Philip Gordon
John P. Tedesco	Sam Bonnell	Harry Becker	Joseph Pevney
Regina Gordon	Olive Deering	Richard Dwight, Jr.	
Herbert Howard Weinberg			Buddy Buehler
	Kurt Richards	Dorothy Dwight	Norma Clerc
Arthur Sandler	John McQuade	Francis Clark Baird	
Lillian Larue	Frances Tannehill		Elmer Brown
Roy Darwin	Alexander Clark		

SYNOPSIS: Act I. *A morning in the spring of 1939.* Scene 1. *Reception room.* Scene 2. *George Simon's private office.* Scene 3. *The reception room.* Scene 4. *Simon's office.* Act II. *The next morning.* Scene 1. *Simon's office.* Scene 2. *The reception room.* Scene 3. *Simon's office.* Act III. *A week later.* Scene 1. *Simon's office.* Scene 2. *The reception room.*

For some reason that often has no basis in sound critical ground, an actor's performance on second view frequently seems much better than it did on first, even when it is not and when the first performance was itself plenty good. Why this is, I do not know, but any reviewer who tells the truth will admit that it is so. Perhaps it is the reviewer's increased acquaintance with the role that obliquely leads him to believe it is the actor's increased acquaintance that leads the latter, in turn, to give a better account of himself in it. Or perhaps a second view allows the reviewer, already familiar with the aspect of the exhibit in its entirety, more greatly to concentrate on the actor and hence to see things in his performance that, while originally there, he had on the first visit overlooked. Or perhaps again, and most likely, the whole business is nonsense and the reviewer simply mistakes such obvious histrionic tricks as slightly longer pauses, intermittently slower readings, and the like for an increased mentality and perception on the part of the actor.

Whatever it is, it frequently gives issue to critical writing that augments actors' popular conviction that critics know very little about acting. This conviction was not long ago again brought to light by a survey conducted by the trade periodical, *The Billboard.* Polling the actors playing at the moment on the New York stage, the survey indicated that there was close to a unanimous agreement among them that, when it came to writing about acting, the reviewers were a lot of fish. At this point it will naturally be expected of me, as one such reviewer, that I will in turn denounce the actors as a lot of idiots and observe with a stale facetiousness that they often seem to know even less about acting than the critics. But I fear that I shall disappoint you. I shall do no such thing. What I shall do is rather simply to allow that both of them often play a scoreless tie.

That critics betray their defective knowledge of the acting craft in these instances of second-view appraisal is readily to be admitted. That they also betray it in their periodic confusion of the player with the role, whether in the way of favorable or unfavorable opinion, in their visiting upon the actor praise or blame that properly belongs to the director, and in other such aberrations is similarly to be acknowledged. But that actors themselves frequently usurp to themselves credit that properly belongs to directors alone and to roles to a considerable degree should not be forgotten. The bulk of the acting business is fraud plus, a fortuitous incidence of extrinsic good or bad dramatic and theatrical luck, and it no more approaches sheer individual governorship, which is the mark of the true artist, than do the constituent elements of a swing band. There are, of course, actors apart from the general who do not come under the animadversion, but they are few and far between. There are also, it may be allowed, critics apart from the general who exercise a sharp eye upon the acting business. But by and large it is on both sides often a case of cheating cheaters. So let both take it as they find it — and genially chuckle to themselves.

In the original presentation of *Counsellor-at-Law,* Paul Muni, generally an actor who in almost any theatre but the American would be assigned to minor character roles, offered a performance that, though richly filigreed with ham, was for the purposes of the play nearly all that might be demanded. In this revival he duplicated that performance, nothing more, nothing less. Yet there were the notices attesting to the "increased stature," the "greater understanding," and the "larger surety" of it. The critical answer is: fiddlesticks.

As to Rice's play, which treats of a poor East Side Jewish boy who rises to eminence in the legal profession only to be threatened with disbarment for an early lapse and who turns the tables on the snobbish lawyer who is out to get him, it remains, despite minor changes, just what it was in the first place: a skillful and successful exercise in Broadway commercial theatrical art.

THE PIRATE. November 25, 1942

A romantic comedy by S. N. Behrman, derived from a thirty-year-old German play by Ludwig Fulda. Produced by the Playwrights' Company in association with the Theatre Guild.

Program

PEDRO VARGAS	*Alan Reed*	TRILLO	*Maurice Ellis*
MANUELA	*Lynn Fontanne*	DON BOLO	*Walter Mosby*
ISABELLA	*Lea Penman*	ESTABAN	*Robert Emhardt*
MANGO SELLER	*Juanita Hall*	SERAFIN	*Alfred Lunt*
INES	*Estelle Winwood*	THE HERMIT	*William Le Massena*
CAPUCHO	*James O'Neill*	LIZARDA	*Muriel Rahn*
FISHERBOY	*Albert Popwell*	VICEROY	*Clarence Derwent*

SYNOPSIS: Act I. Scene 1. *The patio of Pedro Vargas' house, a hot midsummer day.* Scene 2. *A mountain road.* Scene 3. *The public square.* Act II. *Manuela's bedroom, same day.* Act III. *The public square, that evening.*

The action takes place in a small village in the West Indies early in the nineteenth century.

M R. BEHRMAN magnanimously allows in a program note that his play was "suggested by an idea in a play by Ludwig Fulda." In view of the fact that he has taken over most of Fulda's play, including the title, main plot scheme, characters, and even characters' names, this is much like allowing that *Rosalinda* was suggested by an idea in *Die Fledermaus* or that an English translation of *Rosmersholm* was suggested by an idea in a play by Ibsen.

Fulda, who was the German Maxwell Anderson of his day, was frequently given to a form of spurious romantic versification that was more suited to the operetta than to the dramatic stage. Both in the case of this *Der Seeräuber*, which was a failure when originally shown in the Vienna Burgtheater, and in such of his other plays as *Master and Servant* and *Talisman,* one felt oneself in the presence of potential librettos rather than drama, and feeble librettos at that. This libretto feeling rebelliously persists in Behrman's version of *Der Seeräuber,* so much so that the *World-Telegram's* Burton Rascoe was to be complimented on reacting to the impression forthwith if hardly on believing that Fulda, because his play was laid in Andalusia and Behrman's adaptation of it in the Spanish West Indies, was a Spaniard [1] and the play "an opera bouffe faithfully adhering to the Spanish style of comic opera, even to the Spanish type of humor, which is that of sententious exaggeration." (Which the Spanish type of humor, incidentally, is not: *vide* the Quintero brothers, Benavente, Alarcón, et al.)

As to the local production. Whatever else may be said against the Lunts — and as for me I can't think of anything — they surely constitute one of the genuine acting pleasures of the American theatre. That there may be more talented actors, it is true; but when it comes to squirting bright color into a stage they have few peers. It is the heirloom argument of some of their devotees that the reason lies in the circumstance that "they always seem to be enjoying themselves." Whether they are always enjoying themselves, I of course have no means of knowing. But, even if they are, that is a pretty silly reason to assign for their salubrious effect upon their audiences. The best comedy actor and actress of our generation, the late Charles Hawtrey and Marie Tempest, seldom gave the impression that they were having any particular whale of a time. In point of fact there were many occasions when, even at their best, a certain grimness about their immediate jobs betrayed itself. The reason for the Lunts' success is probably that they know their business just a little better than most of the other players of light comedy hereabout and that as a team they work together more proficiently than just about anything since Notre Dame under Rockne, or even Williams and Walker.

A favorite vehicle of the duo is the slightly risqué comedy, something in the vein of *The Guardsman, Reunion*

---

[1] Fulda thus also became a Spaniard in the appraisals of the critics for the *Post* and *The New Yorker.*

in Vienna, Caprice, Design for Living, Amphitryon 38, or
this *The Pirate.* Their present conveyance is a flimsy bit
of foolery about a minstrel Beau Caccio who sets his cap
for the fair wife of a respectably retired buccaneer and who,
to gain his end, indulges in a little shrewd blackmail on
the side. As a contribution to the art of the drama it ranks
considerably less than a buck private, but though here and
there haplessly halting it contrives to serve its purpose as
a Luntish lark, which is something. It would be easy to
urge the Lunts to give us a play of more substantiality and
merit — and I hereby do it. But even mild fun is not to
be sniffed at and I am not going to press the point any more
than I am going to sit down and write a piece urging Bobby
Clark immediately to get into touch with the agent for
Björnstjerne Björnson.

THE GREAT BIG DOORSTEP
NOVEMBER 26, 1942

A folk comedy by Frances Goodrich and Albert Hackett, from the novel of the same name by E. P. O'Donnell. Produced by Herman Shumlin.

PROGRAM

EVVIE CROCHET	*Joy Geffen*	COMMODORE	*Louis Calhern*
TOPAL CROCHET		MR. DUPRE	*Nat Burns*
	Jeanne Perkins Smith	TAYO DELACROIX	*Ralph Bell*
MRS. CROCHET	*Dorothy Gish*	DEWEY CROCHET	*Clay Clement*
GUSSIE CROCHET	*Dickie Monahan*	BEAUMONT CROCHET	
PAUL CROCHET	*Gerald Matthews*		*Morton Stevens*
ARTHUR CROCHET	*Jack Manning*	ED	*Robert Crawley*
MR. TOBIN	*John Morny*		

SYNOPSIS: Act I. *A morning in early April.* Act II. Scene 1. *Late afternoon, Wednesday of the next week.* Scene 2. *Early evening, ten days later.* Act III. Scene 1. *Three days later.* Scene 2. *The next day.*

The entire action of the play takes place at the Crochet home in Grass Margin, Louisiana.

T HE COMEDY DEALS with Cajuns of the Mississippi delta. Living in quarters so squalid and crowded that a problem presents itself when their numerous offspring approach maturity, the family one day comes upon a fancy doorstep that has been washed up by the river and the play proceeds to show its efforts to finance an appropriate new house around it. Considering the slenderness of the basic idea, one is reminded of the comedian in the old Victor Herbert operetta *The Fortune Teller* who spent the whole evening searching desperately for a good joke around which to build a musical comedy.

What the authors have managed to build on the idea is an only moderately recreative comedy that in some of its aspects suggests a parlor *Tobacco Road*. A certain monotony and a deficiency in quick humor make some of the going rather rocky. Contributing further to the weakness of the evening was the customarily skillful Herman Shumlin's surprisingly inept casting, staging, and direction. If in place of Dorothy Gish and Louis Calhern, obviously the wrong actors for the leading roles, he had cast, say, Arthur Hunnicutt and Doro Merande, who proved their mettle for such roles in *Love's Old Sweet Song*, if he had presented the scrubby Cajun womenfolk as looking somewhat less like actresses pleasantly determined to preserve at least a semblance of their natural physical and sartorial attractiveness, and if he had done several other such things, the play might have made a fair impression and not, as in its immediate manifestation, a mere dent.

Even a good folk play loses much of its reality because of the all too painfully obvious rouge and greasepaint makeup on the actors, and when you are asked to accept as authentic Cajuns actors who, for all their abject surroundings, are as neatly and prettily pinked of face as the characters in *The School for Scandal* or a Noel Coward comedy and who, in the instance of the women, are as smoothly powdered of bare legs and backs as the dancers in a Felicia Sorel ballet — when you are asked to do this you are asked just a little too much. Add in the present exhibit shoes evidently from Abercrombie and Fitch's Madison Avenue shop, costumes supervised, according to the program, by Peggy Clark, and hair-do's carefully maneuvered by some Fifth Avenue coiffeur, and you are asked even more than that little too much. And add still further a group of supposedly low-down, impoverished Cajuns with such symmetrical, white, and fictionally beautiful teeth as one seldom sees this side of a Hollywood movie lot, to say nothing of illiterate Cajuns who indulge in such terms as "coronary thrombosis," of a stage as spick and span as a Versailles garden, and of lighting pretty enough to suit a Ziegfeld stage, and you may be forgiven for wondering if it is a group of beggarly Cajuns in beggarly surroundings you have been invited to look at or a revival of *Lord and Lady Algy*.

WINTER SOLDIERS. November 28, 1942

A war play by Daniel Lewis James, accorded the Sidney Howard Memorial Award by the Playwrights' Company. Presented by Erwin Piscator on behalf of Shepard Traube.

Program

General Kessel	Ross Matthew	Antomin	Daniel Schatt
Marshal von Seldte		Jan	Geza Korvin
	Lothar Rewalt	Karel	Boris Tumarin
Tieck	Herbert Berghof	Stefan	Guy Sorel
Marshal von Falken		Nikolai	Boris Marshalov
	Ronald Alexander	Masha	Sara Strengell
Colonel Gerhardt	John Altman	Katya	Paula Bauersmith
Colonel Kranz	Hanns Kolmar	Grigori	R. Ben Ari
General Holz	Theo Goez	Red Army Lieutenant	
Colonel Schreiber			George Andre
	Alfred L. Linder	Hauser	Gilbert Leigh
Janez	Vaughn George	Weiskopf	Mason Adams
Major Bauer	Paul Jones	German Lieutenant	
Lieutenant Tilsen	Sterling Mace		John Stephens
Professor Hoffman	Paul Marx	Russian Commissar	
Maxo	Max Leavitt		David Alexander
Franke	Rolf Bayer	Sergei	Nick Perry
Girl	Dolly Haas	Marshal Lechner	
Gestapo Officer	Alexander Day		Robert G. Lance
Marya	Miriam Goldina		

SYNOPSIS: Act I. Scene 1. *German staff headquarters, somewhere in Russia.* Scene 2. *A Yugoslav peasant hut, three hours later.* Scene 3. *A mountain cave near by, at the end of the same day.* Scene 4. *Vienna, a day later.* Scene 5. *Prerau, Czechoslovakia, the following night.* Scene 6. *A Polish railroad station, a day later.* Act II. Scene 1. *German staff headquarters, three days later.* Scene 2. *A Russian collective farm, the same day.* Scene 3. *German front lines before Moscow, that day, just before dawn.* Scene 4. *Russian front lines, immediately following.* Scene 5. *German staff headquarters, that afternoon.*

The time of the play is the end of November 1941, during the main German advance against Moscow.

Here, for a welcome change, is a good, honest, full-fisted, intelligent war melodrama. By way of testing it at small expense, Mr. Traube, who so ably produced that psychological thriller of the season before, *Angel Street,* had recourse to the little Studio Theatre operated by Piscator, but it remained no sidestreet dispensation, as might have been inferred from its habitat, but simply Birnam Wood come downtown to West Twelfth Street for economy's sake. Put on with an often sure professional touch, its rightful residence was considerably farther uptown.

The play is none of your usual mincing, parlor war stuff. Dealing with saboteurs in countries occupied by the Nazis, it shows how the best calculations of military masterminds, failing to reckon with the unmathematical emotions and acts of human beings, may be upset and put to naught. It shows, in short, and with a pointed vigor that failed Steinbeck in *The Moon Is Down,* how the conquered may conceivably prevail over their conquerors with little more at their disposal than small railway switches, morale-breaking radios, labor strikes, ounces of dynamite, earth-scorching brands, guerrilla sniping, and other such humble means left to them. And it shows it, through Yugoslav peasant huts to mountain caves and through Polish railroad yards to Russian collective farms, with all such exciting adjuncts of roaring, bloody, old-fashioned, elemental melodrama as sounds of rushing trains, nervously clicking telegraph instruments, rifle fire, breathless telephone messages, intercepted plans, murderous chokings, and the like — and, gratefully, with a minimum of rhetorical philosophizing. Save in two or three regrettable particulars as, for example, a rather trying parallel between the defenders of Thermopylæ and the little people of the vanquished countries and some such hokum special as the German general's final speech to the effect that, in the face of the little people's determined heroism, his side cannot hope to win — save in such lapses the play, which doesn't abandon all humor, has a crude drive and power that have been the portion of scarcely any of its tonier rivals. Its frank and unaffected blood and thunder is tenfold more persuading than pale literary ink and $15,000 Sam Goldwyn Jovian tin-sheets.

Here for a change, to repeat, are no bogus intellectual didoes corrupting straight-out, hard-hitting, purely emotional melodrama but straight-out, hard-hitting, purely emotional melodrama naked and unashamed. In other words, the essential, primitive stuff of the theatre of the people.

In the headlong rush of the play, faulty production and other details were overlooked and quickly forgotten. Nazi generals who pronounced it "the Foohrer," Gestapo agents who advised the marshals as to the conduct of their military campaigns, Nazi soldiers going about bareheaded on the freezing Russian steppes, a German general staff that seemed resolutely to abstain from even the suspicion of schnapps — such things that might have induced a critical snigger under other dramatic circumstances were lost sight of in the melodrama's swirling flight. The dear old peanut-gallery was back again, with improvements.

LIFELINE. November 30, 1942

*Another English war play, this one by Norman Armstrong,
nom de drame of Norman Lee and Barbara Toy. Produced
by Gilbert Miller.*

Program

Casey, Steward *Dudley Digges*	Captain J. McGrath, Master
Ronnie, Apprentice *Bob White*	*Rhys Williams*
Larry Oulton, 2nd Mate	Jim Lloyd, 1st Engineer
Stanley Phillips	*Whitford Kane*
Peter Launder, 1st Officer	Ed Murgess, Bosun *Edward Hunt*
Colin Keith-Johnston	'Oppy Parker, Able Seaman
Dennis Comber, 3rd Mate	*Victor Beecroft*
George Keane	
Fred Judd, Wireless Operator	
Everett Ripley	

SYNOPSIS: Act I. Scene 1. *In port, Canada.* (*Morning.*) Scene 2.
At sea, Atlantic. (*Three days later.*) Scene 3. *Atlantic.* (*The following
day.*) Act II. Scene 1. *In convoy.* (*Later the same day.*) Scene 2. *Out of
convoy.* (*The following day.*) Act III. Scene 1. *Out of convoy.* (*Three
days later.*) Scene 2. *Approaching the British Isles.* (*Ten days later.*)
Scene 3. *In port.* (*Seven days later.*)

The action of the play takes place in the saloon of a 5,000-ton
tramp ship, Clydesdale.

Gilbert Miller has by now produced more English
plays attesting, in time of peace, to the irresistible charm
of English persons of title and, in time of war, to the silent
fortitude and insouciant heroism of the English than Al
Woods in his long heyday ever produced American plays
uniformly denying, in Walter Prichard Eaton's old phrase,
that beds are sometimes also used for sleeping purposes. It
seemingly has come to the pass where Mr. Miller finds it
impossible to resist any script sent to him with a stamp
bearing the likeness of King George. Let even something
like *Popsy,* that local finnan haddie, come along with the
scene laid in England, with Popsy named Basil Mountjoy
and with an allusion in it to the way Popsy, alias Basil, bore

up under the Nazi air blitz or the way in which he quietly is doing his bit to help win the war by joining the Royal Navy in the capacity of Admiral Sir Esme Ivor Devonshire's valet and, provided it contains a tribute to the R. A. F. for good measure, Gilbert is right in there pitching to Sullivan, with the band playing *Onward, Christian Soldiers* on all twenty bass drums. That he missed producing *The Wookey* can be accounted for only by the circumstance that the stamps on the script bafflingly bore the features of Abe Lincoln. That he missed producing the English *The Morning Star* simply can't be accounted for at all.

Mr. Miller doubtless likes to believe that his productions of these British testimonials are in the cause of desirable propaganda, though how a succession of very bad and very dull plays can be expected to foster a deep respect for our English allies I, for one, cannot make out. Aside from the obvious fact that any British propaganda, even if tiptop, was at this stage of the game (1942) as wholly unnecessary and quite as redundant as propaganda designed to persuade us that the Nazis were lowdown, nogood sons-of-boches, it seems to me that Mr. Miller does the England he cherishes a considerable disservice in putting on these many exhibits that, by virtue of their total lack of merit, reflect disastrously on her playwrights, make unintentional mock of her men at arms and civilians by presenting them as greasepaint hams, and in the aggregate bore the ears off even the most sympathetic American theatregoer.

This *Lifeline*, which opened and closed in the same week, amounted to just another waste of Mr. Miller's fond faith, time, and effort. The tale of the brave boys of the British Merchant Marine and of how through thick and thin they take their ships through submarine-infested waters and bring their much needed cargoes from Nova Scotia to British ports, it was so sketchily amateurish that the essentially heroic theme was reduced to the proportions of some such melodramatic comic strip as *Vic Jordan*. If its fabricators overlooked any old sea-play stencil, one didn't know what it was. The gruff, surly, bewhiskered old seadog of a captain, the serio-comic steward, the awkward young apprentice who trips over himself every time he carries a tray in or out of the galley, the sailor who worships his wife as an angel of purity and the revelation that, unknown to him, she is a loose fish, the wistful playing of sentimental phonograph records, the mouth-watering description of the delicious meals to be had on land, the ailing master who gags when they give him water in place of rum, the first officer who placidly takes over when the captain is killed — all were present, and many more with them. And, incidentally, it was not overly easy, for all of patriotism, to accept as admirably heroic a crew which took pride in reporting that, coming upon four German castoff sailors drifting about in a small boat, it promptly let go with its ship's gun and slaughtered them.

Which again brings us to the fact that, tottering and bleeding, drama criticism emerges as yet another victim of the war. While it can still get on its legs in the presence of a farce, a vaudeville show, a musical comedy, or even, in certain instances, some play that has no concern with immediate events, it falls flat on its face when asked to contemplate any play that deals with the current world struggle. The veteran of a thousand peaces has cracked with the boom of the first gun.

The noble old fellow's wounds were first observable some three years ago and now cover his entire body. And they drip anew and mortally on the occasion of almost any drama that has to do with us or our allies in arms. Patriotism then triumphs over the once analytical old fox and, try as he will, he can come out only a bad second. For one critic who can't see just how a mediocre play is arbitrarily converted into a good one simply because its theme is soothing to the national or allied sensibilities there are half a dozen who seem to be able to see it with their eyes closed.

It isn't, true enough, that all these plays of war are invariably praised as masterpieces. A number very surely are not. But even where criticism manages heroically to retain a little of its old poise, its grievous injuries are still discernible. In evidence whereof I set down literally six sample comments on the plays in point culled from the present New York practitioners of the craft of Aristotle:

1. — "No one whose heart is burdened by the human misery of a cruel war can face Mr. Anderson's play with equanimity. After the war it may be possible to have a detached point of view about *The Eve of St. Mark*. There is, in short, some ham in it. But as things stand in the world today no one is prepared to cavil at [such] minor details."

2. — "It is easy to forgive the grave faults of Mr. Williams' *The Morning Star* in view of the bravery of our English brothers which it so sympathetically pictures. The mind may say no, but the heart proclaims a loud yes."

3. — "The matchless heroism of our British allies makes Lesley Storm's *Heart of a City* what it is: a play deserving of the plaudits of criticism. Who would dwell on dramatic defects when moved by such a theme?"

4. — "The nobility of Mr. Steinbeck's drama, *The Moon Is Down*, comes from the fact that he demonstrates, however now and again faultily in a dramaturgical sense, that the Nazis are in the end doomed."

5. — "In *Watch On the Rhine*, Miss Hellman evokes the high admiration of criticism with her sympathetic delineation of the anti-Nazi underground movement in Germany. Her theme is hard to resist."

6. — "Mr. Sherwood's *There Shall Be No Night* preaches the folly of unpreparedness. What more, in these days, can one demand of a play?"

And, with immediate relevance to this *Lifeline*, stuff like this:

"The heroism of such men is too often taken for granted. Few are the medals that come their way. But they don't squawk. They have pride in the merchant navy and love of country. They can take it and dish it out. A moving tribute to the men of England's navy, those heroes who

fight subs, bombers, ice, storms and fire to get the vital sup-
plies across the Atlantic that keep their country in the war
and insure its eventual victory . . . the play somehow does
not tug at your heart and emotions as it should. *Rather is
it content to command your admiration.*"

There are many other such examples of what once was
dramatic criticism. The craft would seem to be in increasing need of the ministrations of the Red Cross.

R. U. R. December 3, 1942

A revival of the fantastic melodrama by Karel Čapek, originally shown in 1922. Produced by David Silberman and Daniel Blank, it lasted for four performances.

PROGRAM

HARRY DOMIN	*Gordon Oliver*	MR. ALQUIST	*Hugo Haas*
SULLA	*Gudrun Hansen*	CONSUL BUSMAN	*Reginald Mason*
MARIUS	*Lewis Wilson*	NANA	*Marie Louise Dana*
HELENA GLORY	*Edith Atwater*	RADIUS	*Sydney Smith*
DR. GALL	*Horace Braham*	HELENA	*Katharine Balfour*
MR. FABRY	*Hunter Gardner*	PRIMUS	*Wendell K. Phillips*
DR. HALLEMEIER	*Louis Hector*	ROBOT	*Loy Nelson*

SYNOPSIS: Act I. *Central office of the factory of Rossum's Universal Robots.* Act II. *Helena's drawing-room, five years later, morning.* Act III. *The same afternoon.* Epilogue. *A laboratory, one year later.* Place. *An island.* Time. *The future.*

THE PROGRAM, with a great show of relevance to the play, quoted President Franklin D. Roosevelt: "It is the young, free men and women of the United Nations and not the wound-up robots of the slave States who will mold the shape of the new world." Since Čapek obviously had not the slightest notion, when he wrote his robot play, that any other interpretation could ever be placed upon it than that, very simply, automata bred of an economic, machine age must be lacking in soul, the use of the quotation only goes to show once again the lengths to which the later theatrical passion for parallels and analogies to current events sometimes carries itself. Things have come to the point where one would not be overly surprised to encounter in the program of a revival of, say, *A Doll's House,* a quota-tion from Winston Churchill arguing that Nora's final slamming of the door is symbolic of the occupied little na-tions' determination to be free of the yoke of the fascist Helmers. Or in the program of a revival of *Three Men on a Horse* a message from Raymond Gram Swing stating that the three men are to a degree counterparts of Hitler, Mussolini, and Hirohito and that the play metaphorically proves that, for all the hypothetical sagacity of their private counsellors and tipsters and for all the fact that they have been lucky for quite a spell, they must one day find that they have been betting on the wrong nag.

It is, of course, possible with considerable stretching to identify the manufactured robots of Čapek's play with the slave soldiers of the Nazi state, but to do so remains nevertheless as far-fetched, considering Čapek's original intention, as it would be, with seemingly equal justice, to identify them with the husbands of rich society women or Congressmen created by powerful business for its own ends. I am only surprised that the producers didn't insert another note in the program suggesting that Čapek clairvoyantly named his play *R. U. R.* (the title is derived from Rossum's Universal Robots) in anticipation of the bombing of the Ruhr, particularly since the final revolt of the robots might also be regarded as a parallel to the revolt of the long acquiescent British diplomats and statesmen against the Nazis who had taken advantage of them.

Several minor changes in the play's script only made matters worse for the analogy maniacs, since those responsible for the alterations, who hoped to give the theme immediate implications, went but part of the distance and apparently overlooked the fact that the play was still laid in the far future. Absurdity was thus laid upon absurdity and was further nourished by failure to eliminate such lines as those of a man of the future who viewed with sober moral alarm the circumstance that a young woman was traveling alone and unchaperoned. The producers should have gone the whole hog or left the play as it originally was, with no seeking for contemporary militaristic significations. All things considered, they might have been more freely forgiven if they had frankly designated Domin, manager of the robot factory, Hitler, made up the board of directors to resemble Göring, Goebbels, Ribbentrop and Co., dressed the robots like Storm Troopers, and changed the name of the protesting heroine from Helena Glory to Clare Luce.

THE SUN FIELD. December 9, 1942

A bill of sale by Milton Lazarus, from the novel by the late Heywood Broun. Produced by Howard Lang.

PROGRAM

Lefty Hendricks	*Jay Brassfield*	Warren Yost	*Tom Tully*
Bill Doyle	*Robert Lynn*	"Tiny" Tyler	*Joel Ashley*
Carl Randolph	*Karl Malden*	Karyl Dumont	
Jack Kennelly	*Frank Otto*		*Florence Sundstrom*
Whacky Cassatt	*Fred Sherman*	Judith Winthrop	*Claudia Morgan*
Mrs. Doyle	*Betty Kean*	Hugh Coler	*Richard Gordon*
Jim Rocco	*Lewis Charles*	Mildred Deagon	*Fay Baker*
Mrs. Rocco	*Katherine Meskill*	Bessie	*Georgia Burke*
George Wallace		Samuel Dickerman	*Herbert Duffy*
	Donald Randolph		

SYNOPSIS: Act I. Scene 1. *Tiny Tyler's suite in the Pilgrim Hotel, July.* Scene 2. *Judith's apartment, three weeks later.* Act II. Scene 1. *A restaurant table on the "road," a week later.* Scene 2. *A section of hotel lobby, two weeks later.* Scene 3. *The Tylers' hotel room, an hour later.* Scene 4. *Tiny Tyler's suite in the Pilgrim Hotel, a week later.* Scene 5. *Judith's apartment, four hours later.* Scene 6. *Same as Scene 1, an hour later.* Act III. Scene 1. *The back porch of the Hotel Lee, Coldhaven, Florida, the following March.* Scene 2. *Tyler's room, immediately following.*

It is still another idiosyncrasy of the American theatre that the national sport apparently becomes the national bore immediately it is moved indoors. While all kinds of plays dealing with relatively less popular sports have succeeded, there is no record of a play dealing directly with baseball that has. From the now remote day of Rida Johnson Young's and Christy Mathewson's *The Girl and the Pennant* to Ring Lardner's *Elmer the Great* and from last season's *The Life of Reilly* to this *The Sun Field,* all such exhibits have either closed within a few days or at best have achieved only minor runs. Football plays like *The College Widow, Strongheart,* and such have made all kinds of money. Prize-fight plays like *Is Zat So?, Golden Boy,* and such have also prospered. And so have horseracing plays all

the way from *In Old Kentucky* and *The Whip* of the long
ago to the more recent *Three Men on a Horse*. But aside
from *Brother Rat,* which, while it touched to a degree on
baseball, cannot be considered strictly a baseball play, there
has been no bat and ball parcel that has interested theatre
audiences sufficiently to turn its producer a profit. Why this
should be so is rather puzzling, since some of the plays have
not been any worse than some of the plays about football,
prize-fighting, and racing that have succeeded.

The Sun Field, however, could hardly hope to succeed
even if it dealt with one of these other sports, since its plot
scheme would discourage even the most rabid fan in any
direction, having to do once again after all these decades
with the high-born, educated young woman who succumbs
to the physical attraction of a dumb man of muscle and
who subsequently finds as much difficulty in adjusting herself to the situation as the meatball himself. Make the
baseball aphrodisiac in this case a young husky with Com-
munist sympathies as in John Howard Lawson's *Gentle-
woman,* or a brawny lackey as in Strindberg's *Countess
Julie,* or a bruiser as in Shaw's *Cashel Byron's Profession*
and, if you can write only one-fifth so well as Lawson and
not one ten-thousandth so well as Strindberg or Shaw, you
get the inevitable Lazarus result. And add further the kind
of obsolete humor which consists in a woman encountering
a man clad only in shorts and exclaiming: "Now I know
everything!" along with the kind that brings down a curtain on the whimsy about marriage being like buying a
cow when you already have all the milk you want, and you
may as well call up the storehouse service instanter.

The business of losing money in the theatre, once something of a problem, has in recent years become so simpli-
fied, however, that even some of the less canny producers
like this Mr. Lang with his *The Sun Field* are apparently
gradually catching on to the trick. And in many instances
they do not need even baseball plays to complete their education.

There was a time, and not so very many years ago, when
the theatre usually guaranteed a pretty certain profit on

investment, whatever its nature, and when more men got rich out of it than you could shake a cocktail at. That was the time before the films drained out of audiences their less intelligent component parts. And that was the time, ac- cordingly, when plays which today would go to the store- house by the next Saturday night, or before, still drew cus- tomers in sufficient numbers to fatten the box-office.

It was in that era that Al Woods made so much money out of pork melodrama that at one period in his producing career he actually kept half a million dollars in surplus cash in safe-deposit boxes. It was then that the Stair and Havlin circuit made a fortune by booking plays that now- adays could not run half a week in even a summer barn theatre; that the road — then in its heyday — permitted producers to wear thirty-two-carat diamonds achieved from such claptrap as *A Trip to Chinatown, Under Southern Skies,* and *In the Palace of the King;* and that stock com- panies spread throughout the country reaped a harvest from such dramatic chow as *Sweet Lavender, The Chris- tian, Hearts of Oak,* and *The Silver King.*

You simply couldn't kill the stock companies, however bad the plays they offered, in those benighted days. There was one in Baltimore, for example, whose manager once approached H. L. Mencken, then serving briefly as a dra- matic critic on a local gazette, for advice on what play to produce in a following week. Mencken, who had no stom- ach for the theatre and wanted to rid himself of his job and drink his beer in peace, thought he saw a way to ruin the stock company. "Put on *East Lynne,*" he gravely ad- vised the counsel-seeker. The latter swallowed the sugges- tion, put on the rubbish, and the house played to the big- gest business it had ever played to.

Overjoyed, and now completely sold on what he believed to be Mencken's extraordinary acumen, the manager again sought him out and beseeched of him advice on what play to follow the big success. Mencken was sure that this time he knew the way to knock out the stock company for good and all. "There are two versions of *East Lynne,*" he sol- emnly apprised the manager. "Since the first one seems to have gone well, why not follow it up with the second version?'' The manager thought it was a great idea, fell for it hook, line, and sinker, and — to Mencken's loud anticipatory glee — put on the other version. It was an even bigger success than the first.

It was in those facile money-making years that the theatrical syndicate headed by Klaw and Erlanger became inordinately wealthy not merely through theatre ownership and control of bookings, as is most commonly believed, but also through the production of plays most of which had a minimum of critical quality. *Ben Hur,* that Saturnian chattel, is just one example. The three Shubert brothers, coming down from Syracuse and also sniffing the rhino, inaugurated their celebrated successful fight against the syndicate and soon not only began to make large money by running theatres in opposition to it but by producing plays that weren't an iota better. And things continued so that such an actor as the late William Hodge could make a personal fortune through appearing in shameless hokum like *The Man from Home,* that such a producer as Belasco could coin money out of juvenile realism involving steaming coffeepots and authentic flapjacks, and that such playwrights as Charles Klein could achieve hefty bank accounts with pap like *The Lion and the Mouse.*

You couldn't dish it out sour enough for them in that palate-paralyzed era. Compared with some of even the grade-A plays then, the present grade-B movies are authentically colossal. I have mentioned stock companies. There was one in Cleveland, Ohio, that will serve as another illuminating example. On one occasion, just before a matinée presentation of the balderdash called *The Charity Ball,* one of the lesser actors in the troupe who nevertheless had a pretty important role in the second act appeared at the theatre under the influence of the alcoholic cup. Believing that they could get him back into shape before his entrance in the play, they rang up the curtain. But when the first act was over, they found that the job was hopeless — at least for the immediate moment — and that something had to be done, and done quickly.

A hurried consultation and it was decided to play the third act in place of the second act and then, certain that the actor could be iced and massaged into normality in time, to play the second where the third should have been. The stratagem was duly put into operation; the audience didn't know the difference; and the play went bigger at that particular matinée than it had gone at any other performance during the week.

One of the road box-office magnets in those days was a consignment of old hoke dubbed *Zeb*, the brain child of one Samuel Young. In the last act of the play there was introduced the character of a country gawk named Sis Hopkins. Played by Rose Melville, it was a sensation. Associated with the company was Rose's sister Ida, who was the wife of the play's author. One day when the run of the play indicated signs of fading, Sister Ida was seized with an idea. "If," she said to her husband and Sister Rose, "two Topsys have proved such a hit in some *Uncle Tom's Cabin* companies, why not two Sis Hopkinses?" Ida's idea was instantaneously accepted as something rather wonderful and, with Ida in the duplicate Sis Hopkins role, the show went on to even greater acclaim that it had in the first place.

When *Zeb* eventually closed on the road, the two sisters went to New York and it wasn't long afterward that they were a dual Sis Hopkins sensation in still another show, *Little Christopher*. Upon the withdrawal of Sister Ida later on, Sister Rose was able successfully to incorporate the same character into both *The Prodigal Father* and *By the Sad Sea Waves*. And then, as a climax, she appeared in a play called *Sis Hopkins* that ran steadily for more than nine years and made a mint. Imagine in these present days of the theatre some such character as one of the Day brats in *Life with Father* being prosperously reincorporated into a lot of other plays and shows for all of a dozen years!

It is true that a downright bad play may still occasionally make money for its producer, but it is a rare exception to the current rule. The plays that make real dollars in the American theatre today are for the larger part plays of at least some relative merit. And the plays that lose their producers' shirts are generally the kind that in another period might have made the gentlemen enough to lay in several trucks of silk chemises. This is the lesson the producers are slowly learning: to wit, that the way to drop money in the present theatre, and to drop a pile of it, is sedulously to avoid quality.

The hereinbefore alluded to Al Woods, who made a fortune in the old theatre, lost it in the improved modern one. "I can't understand," he once said to his fellow producer Sam Harris, "why exactly the same kind of melodramas that used to bring in the heavy dough now only get the razzoo." "Al," replied Sam, "Jess Willard was once also a big winner and you're still trying to cash in with a bunch of Jess Willards."

Another thing. It is generally accepted nowadays that the critics know pretty well what they are talking about when they turn thumbs down on a bad play and that there isn't much use in fighting back at them and trying to force a run in the face of their adverse opinion. Once in a great while it can be done, but even then, as in the freak case of *Separate Rooms* — which, at that, was reviewed by the second-string newspaper critics — what results is largely and merely a cut-rate or two-tickets-for-one attraction.

Edgar Selwyn was one of the first producers to recognize and magnanimously admit the change. Some seasons ago he put on a play of his own authorship called *Anything Might Happen*. Observing the reviewers during the course of its first and second acts and gifted with a touch of clairvoyance, he knew that they were certain to roast the play to a turn. What was more, seeing his play in production before an audience, he appreciated that it was hardly what he thought it would be. So he hurried out into the rear of the box-office, seized a sheet of paper, wrote something on it, and ordered his press-agent to hustle forth, dig up some all-night printer, and have a dozen copies of what he had written struck off instanter. Barely had the reviewers returned to their offices to write their scathing reports on the play — Selwyn shrewdly saw to it that the third-act curtain was sufficiently delayed — than they received this card:

"Mr. Edgar Selwyn humbly apologizes to the critics for his play, *Anything Might Happen,* and asks their forgiveness for having inflicted it on them."

The apology, of course, couldn't kill the critics' first-night notices, but it took all the wind out of any subsequent Sunday blasts they may have had in mind.

As for actors, the first to follow Mr. Selwyn's principle was, several years ago, Fredric March, who had come on from Hollywood to appear in a production of his own backing called *Yr. Obedient Husband.* Lambasted by the critics and taken off after a run of only eight performances, it resulted in March's insertion of an advertisement in the newspapers containing a cut of himself falling off a trapeze and underneath it the line: "Oops, sorry!"

In the now far past, things were considerably otherwise. Not only did the producers and actors fight the critics but the critics themselves often found themselves at severe variance with the public's taste. Play after play that they denounced prospered nevertheless. Dozens upon dozens, literally, made all kinds of money. And for many years their influence on dramatic art was even less than the average vain idiot's influence on his wife, intelligent woman. From the day they unanimously knocked the tar out of Mark Twain's collaborative effort, *The Gilded Age,* which thumbed its nose at them and ran for an entire season, and Benjamin Wolf's *The Mighty Dollar,* which also ran for a whole season and in which Mr. and Mrs. W. J. Florence had the biggest success of their careers, on and up to the considerably more recent time of *Abie's Irish Rose,* which most of them pooh-poohed as ignominious hooey but which none the less ran for years, the public often told them to go chase themselves. But very, very seldom so nowadays.

You can't trick the public any longer in any amusement direction and expect it to lay out its good money. The day when you could humorously bill the Cherry Sisters as the world's worst act and get a crowd to the box-office is gone. Even the movie exhibitors discovered that not so long ago when they humorously billed the Jimmy Savo picture, *Once in a Blue Moon,* as the world's worst. And the theatrical producers and the actors are discovering it month by month when they should in all truth and in all seriousness make similar announcements in the case of some of the plays they produce and act in — and don't.

THE WILLOW AND I. December 10, 1942

A psychological drama by John Patrick. Produced by Donald Blackwell and Raymond Curtis in association with David Merrick.

Program

Bessie Sutro	*Barbara O'Neil*	Dr. Oliver	*Robert Harrison*
Tinny	*Amanda Randolph*	Robin Todd	*Gregory Peck*
Mara Sutro	*Martha Scott*	Duke Todd	*Alec Englander*
Bailey	*Edwin Lewis*	Mabel	*Pauline Myers*
Theodore Sutro	*Edward Pawley*	Kirkland Todd	*Gregory Peck*
Millie Sutro	*Cora Witherspoon*	Dr. Trubee	*Francis Compton*

SYNOPSIS: Act I. Scene 1. *Spring, 1900.* Scene 2. *A year later.* Act II. Scene 1. *Autumn, many years later.* Scene 2. *The following week.* Act III. A few weeks later.

The action takes place in the Sutro living-room.

Mr. Patrick is an elementary playwright in more senses than one: not only does he write in school copybook terms, but he relies upon climate to further his dramaturgy. The elements seem to be as necessary to the pursuit of his art as beds to an erst Palais Royal playwright or, forsooth, to an ambitious Palais Royal actress. In the two meteorographs he has thus far vouchsafed us, there are enough climatic phenomena to satisfy even the most particular customers of the old pleasure-park rides known variously as *The Mysterious Grotto, Through the Inferno,* and *Cave of the Witches.*

In his antecedent dispensation, *Hell Freezes Over,* the action, laid near the South Pole, was orchestrated to so much howling wind that one could at times hardly hear what the actors were saying — and no complaint from me. In addition to the wind, which blew audiences completely out of the theatre after a few nights, there was sufficient snow and ice to meet the purposes of two dozen *'Way Down East* companies, and such zero atmosphere throughout that the gesticulations of the actors in pretending to keep warm took on the aspect of a mass meeting of Zionists. In *The Willow and I* it is thunder, lightning, rain, and hail. One hasn't heard such a racket in a theatre since the 1907 days of *The Shulamite* when in the last act Lena Ashwell, apparently confusing her back yard with the Lounge of the old Waldorf-Astoria, ruminated placidly and without a hat, coat, or shawl on during such an electrical simoon as even Langdon McCormick in his prime never thought up.

Dealing with a young woman who goes insane on her wedding day after a death struggle with a sister who covets the bridegroom, Mr. Patrick calls in the aforementioned elements to accompany his heroine's prolonged effort to recapture her reason. For time on end the poor creature, now disclosed as an old woman, is made to stand or sit near a window grappling with the elusive past, whilst the heavy rumble and roll of thunder drums, the flash and crack of lightning flares, the squirting of the rain hose and the rattle of the hail beans play an obbligato to her silent agonies. In the end a boom of thunder and a bolt of lightning loud enough to have scared the wits out of George Jessel playing in the Broadhurst Theatre down in Forty-fourth Street somehow contrive to scare the wits back into her.

As an interesting dramatic psychiatrist Mr. Patrick would seem to be something less than a Pirandello. Or, to get down to more appropriate tacks, the author, whoever he was, of the melodrama called *Double Door*. It isn't that his research, including possibly even the effect wrought by thunder and lightning, may not be scientifically acceptable. It is rather that in his explorations of the psyches of his heroine and her evil sister he so makes himself up like a medicine-show pitchman and employs so many of the pitchman's sales tricks that what you get for your good money, theatrically speaking, is a bottle labeled *Psychoanalysis* but containing only an ounce of the stuff to a gallon of tincture of melodramatic potassium nitrate.

Mr. Patrick is also another of that large company of present-day playwrights who are firmly convinced of the desirability of having a play that has not said anything all evening make a big motion of saying it just as the final curtain is due to fall. In this case, doubtless appreciating that all that has gone before is more or less old-hat to those even remotely acquainted with fiction and drama, he breathlessly comes in at the stretch with a Deep Message. That his deep message not only has next to nothing to do with the play that has preceded it but, in view of the fact that, just fifteen minutes before, his old grandfather has proved from experience and the records that the world never much changes and always seeks the worst in itself, hasn't the slightest relevance or sense, doesn't seem to bother him in the least. His deep message — delivered with affecting solemnity by his representative of the younger generation — is the message, no less, of the late Dr. Munyon: *There is hope!* Only Mr. Patrick takes 729 words to say it.

THE THREE SISTERS. DECEMBER 21, 1942

A revival of the play by Anton Chekhov. Produced by Katharine Cornell and Guthrie McClintic.

PROGRAM

OLGA	*Judith Anderson*	AN ORDERLY	*Kirk Douglas*
MASHA	*Katharine Cornell*	COLONEL VERSHININ	*Dennis King*
IRINA	*Gertrude Musgrove*	ANDREY PROZOROV	*Eric Dressler*
A MAID	*Patricia Calvert*	KULIGIN	*Tom Powers*
BARON TUZENBACH	*Alexander Knox*	NATASHA	*Ruth Gordon*
CAPTAIN SOLYONY	*McKay Morris*	LIEUTENANT FEDOTIK	*Stanley Bell*
DOCTOR CHEBUTYKIN		LIEUTENANT RODDEY	
	Edmund Gwenn		*Tom McDermott*
NURSE	*Alice Belmore Cliffe*	ANOTHER OFFICER	*Walter Craig*
FERAPONT	*Arthur Chatterton*		

SYNOPSIS: Act I. Scene 1. *The home of the Prozorovs, a day in spring.* Scene 2. *The same, ten months later, evening.* Act II. *The bedroom of Olga and Irina, two years later, early morning.* Act III. *The garden of the Prozorov house, the following autumn.*

The action takes place in a Russian provincial town in the year 1900.

THERE ARE FOUR REASONS which may justify the revival of a modern play: (1) the play's authentic merit; (2) a notable improvement in the acting company over the antecedent company or companies; (3) the feeling that the play was not properly appreciated on its original production; and (4) the belief that a second view of the play may make things clearer to a person who had some difficulty in understanding it in the first place. Considering the recent revivals, only one — this *The Three Sisters* — meets the first reason and, at least in a locally relative degree, the second. And none, *The Three Sisters* included, meets either the third or fourth, since in the latter respect in particular anyone who could not readily comprehend its meaning on the first visit could not be expected to comprehend it on a second or even twentieth.

There is altogether too much claptrap about this last

business. Aside from maybe five or six plays in the whole range of drama, there is none — if we correctly dismiss from consideration such aberrant and confusedly worthless stuff as some of the early German Expressionistic drama, along with the deliriums of our Greenwich Village Dalis like Em Jo Basshe and Co. — that calls for any undue exercise in its assimilation and understanding. Yet the legend persists that a second view is often vital to the digestion of hypothetically baffling undertones, overtones, inbetweentones, and general cunning nuances. Since nine-tenths of the plays, one or two of the classics aside, which have been revived in the last ten years have no more such undertones, overtones, inbetweentones, and cunning nuances than "The Chattanooga Choo-Choo" or a philosophical treatise by Alfred Noyes, the person who cannot fully appreciate them at one gulp would be the kind who would resemble Mr. Robert Lawrence, ballet critic for the *New York Herald Tribune*. This Mr. Lawrence, it appears, is the reductio ad absurdum of the second look, as witness his review of a ballet called *Rodeo:*

> "Those who saw the première of Agnes De Mille's *Rodeo,* given at the Metropolitan Opera House last night by the Ballet Russe de Monte Carlo, cheered the cast and choreographer with real enthusiasm. A critical verdict in these columns will be deferred until Monday morning after I have attended the work a second time. In begging off again on the snap judgment of a new ballet, the writer feels like the boy who cried Wolf! Suspicion may arise as to equipment and ability. But there can be no point in condemning outright a première into which much hard work has gone and which a first-night audience admires, even if one does not share that admiration — nor, on the other hand, of vapidly praising a ballet because of high-voltage audience reaction — without absolute surety of mind and heart. Second sight is the best remedy for a case of indecision."

Since the ballet in question related the extravagantly simple story of a cowgirl unattractive in boots and trousers who proved more attractive and desirable to her swain when in skirts and since the choreography was as innocent of complexity as the story itself, the necessity for a second critical study of it in order to arrive at an opinion of its worth would seem to be as gratuitous as the necessity for a second critical look at such recent play revivals as Elmer Rice's *Counsellor-at-Law* and Karel Čapek's *R. U. R.* in order to determine, in turn, the simple fact that the former is merely a competent Broadway box-office play about a shyster lawyer from the Jewish East Side who marries into Park Avenue and finds to his grievous concern that the girl can't work up a proper taste for gefülte fish, and the second merely a precocious stunt about robots who kill off eight profoundly stupid human beings sequestered on a remote island and thus stupefyingly bring about the end of all civilization.

The Three Sisters is the least complex by far of Chekhov's better-known plays. The simple tale of three women condemned to the humdrum life of a Russian provincial town who are defeated in their dream of getting to Moscow, it presents even to a not particularly absorbent mind none of the possible perplexities of *The Cherry Orchard, The Sea Gull,* or even *Uncle Vanya.* While the play may seem theatrically to be somewhat dated under present world conditions, it still retains interest for the dramatic student and to the theatrical student on this occasion offered the diversion of contemplating an acting company which, while far from being uniformly competent, at any rate proudly gave its efforts to something better than the more usual revival fare about three mugs who frenziedly muss their hair and tear their neckties when the horse they have bet on threatens to lose a race.

Incidentally, *The Three Sisters* takes high place among the plays of the modern theatre in the matter of curtain lines. A curtain line, in the event you are unfamiliar with the term, is a line or passage of dialogue that marks the end of an act of a play, often the last. The passage in point, which concludes the present play in the original but which here for some inscrutable reason was senselessly cut, is as follows:

OLGA (*embracing both her sisters*). The music plays so gaily, bravely, and one wants to live. Oh, Lord! Time will pass and we shall be gone forever, they will forget us, they will forget our faces, voices, and how many of us there were, but our sufferings will turn into joy for those who will be living after us, happiness and peace will come on earth, and they will remember with some gentle word those who live now, and will bless them. Oh, dear sisters, our life isn't over yet. We shall live! The music plays so gaily, so joyously, and it looks as if a little more and we shall know why we live, why we suffer. . . . If we only knew, if we only knew!

(*The music plays always softer and softer; Kuligin, smiling and gay, brings the hat and cape; Andrey is pushing the baby-carriage with Bobik in it.*)

CHEBUTYKIN (*singing softly*). Ta-ra-ra-boom-de-ay . . , Sit on a curb I may. . . . (*reading the newspaper*) It's all the same! It's all the same!

OLGA. If we only knew, if we only knew.

I set down some other memorable curtain lines (a few may not be strictly curtain lines but they come close enough to the curtain's fall to be legitimately included) from the drama of our time.

A tag that persists in the recollection over many years is the fiendishly mordant last line of Hauptmann's famous labor drama, *The Weavers.* The starving workers finally revolt against their tyrannical oppressor, pillage his premises, are driven back, and the one old weaver who still steadfastly believes in the old order and refuses to leave his loom is shot down. His little granddaughter rushes into the room, grows frightened, notices that something has happened, puts her finger in her mouth, goes cautiously up to the dead man, and calls his name. Her aged grandmother, the weaver's wife, edges to her side, looks at old Hilse lying there, and speaks to him: "Come, husband, say something; you look as though you were afraid."

In that single word "afraid" there is more ironic poison than in all the other capital-and-labor dramas combined.

The comparatively recent *Rain from Heaven* of S. N. Behrman contains a curtain, or near-curtain, line that is one of the most piquing in modern polite comedy. Lady Violet Wyngate is hostess at her house near London to several Europeans and Americans. Among the former is a refugee music critic from Berlin, Hugo Willens, and among the latter the younger brother of a millionaire American publisher, Rand Eldridge. Eldridge in love with Lady Violet and, angered by her apparent interest in the German and unable to control his feelings, bursts out in the presence of the others with the sneer that Willens is a Jew. Whereupon Lady Violet takes the latter's hand in her own and very quietly and graciously observes to the stunned rival: "Remember — please — that Mr. Willens is not only my lover, he is also my guest."

In all the drama of Pinero, Jones, and the older like, that line would inevitably have been inversed.

One of the biggest laugh tags is that of the Hecht-MacArthur newspaper farce-comedy *The Front Page*. Hildy Johnson is a great reporter but constantly at odds with his brusque editor. He finally tells the latter, to his wrath at losing such a good man, that he is leaving the paper to get married. With a sudden pretense of warm affection, the editor gives him his watch as a parting gift, and Hildy is off on a train. The editor grabs the telephone, gets the chief of police on the wire, and instructs him to arrest the reporter immediately and bring him back. "The son-of-a-bitch stole my watch!" he yells.

In Yeats's *Cathleen ni Houlihan* an old and worried woman, Ireland personified, comes from afar to a peasant house. Strangers, she says, are in her own house and have taken her land and treasures from her. But there were those in other days who loved her and even died for her. One of the peasants, a miserly fellow, makes to give her a coin but she will have no such charity. "If any one would give me help, he must give me himself, he must give me all," she says. Michael, the young son of the household who is to be

married on the morrow, is fascinated by her, and, when she
leaves and when comes the news that the French are landing at Killala and that the boys are joining the invader
against the English, he breaks away from his protesting
bride and rushes out. The old woman's voice is heard singing. Michael's younger brother enters. His mother asks of
him: "Did you see an old woman going down the path?"
"I did not," replies the boy, "but I saw a young girl, and
she had the walk of a queen!"

The end of the fourth act of *The Doctor's Dilemma* is
Bernard Shaw at his most graceful and touching. Dubedat,
the artist, has just died. His proud and loving widow comes
to say goodbye to the doctors who have attended him,
among them one who has held him in small esteem, Sir
Colenso Ridgeon. "I felt," says Mrs. Dubedat, "that I must
shake hands with his friends once before we part today. We
have shared together a great privilege and a great happiness. I don't think we can ever think of ourselves as ordinary people again. We have had a wonderful experience;
and that gives us a common faith, a common ideal, that nobody else can quite have. Life will always be beautiful to
us; death will always be beautiful to us. May we shake
hands on that?" Sir Patrick, after briefly advising her on
certain legal matters, offers his hand and, thanking him,
she takes it. Sir Patrick goes. Walpole then shakes hands
with her and goes, and so, after tendering her his future
assistance, does Sir Ralph Bonington. Ridgeon now approaches her with "Goodbye" and offers his hand. Mrs.
Dubedat draws back with gentle majesty: "I said his friends,
Sir Colenso." He bows and goes out. She unfolds a great
piece of silk and goes into the recess to cover her dead.

There are, of course, those who prefer such celebrated
curtain lines as "And who are you?" — (*Removing his
whiskers*) "Hawkshaw, the detective!", which was a pretty
hot one at that, but there are others whose taste may perhaps be somewhat more inclined to the speech that ends the
Kaufman-Hart *You Can't Take It with You*. The Sycamore
family and its peculiar guests finally sit down to dinner
after all the hullabaloo that has driven the household crazy.

Grandpa taps on his plate. "Quiet! Everybody! Quiet!" Immediately the talk ceases and all heads are lowered as Grandpa starts to say grace: "Well, Sir, here we are again. We want to say thanks once more for everything You've done for us. Things seem to be going along fine. Alice is going to marry Tony, and it looks as if they're going to be very happy. Of course the fireworks blew up, but that was Mr. De Pinna's fault, not Yours. We've all got our health and as far as anything else is concerned, we'll leave it to You. Thank You."

Saroyan's *Hello Out There* offers a remarkably effective tag. A man is in a Texas jail cell awaiting his doom at the hands of a lynch mob. His incessant cry of "Hello out there!" — a plea for sympathy and understanding and help from the great outside world — reaches no ears in the vast emptiness save those of a little slavey around the prison. A blind, desperate love comes to the twain, a love of each other in all their futility, a love of possible freedom, a love for the future if a future there can be. The ceaseless supplication of the prisoner echoes still down the grim and unanswering corridor. The mob, headed by the husband of the ignoble woman the man is alleged to have assaulted and by the ignoble woman herself, smashes its way into the jail and makes for the man's cell. A shot rings out and the man crumples to his knees. The little slavey with a cry starts to rush toward him. The woman shouts at her: "Where do you think you're going, you damned slut?" and slaps her to the ground. The man is dead, and the gluttonish mob, along with the woman, leave. Slowly, painfully, the little slavey lifts herself half-way up from the floor, the while comes from her lips to the audience the choked and agonized and pleading whisper: "Hello out there! Hello out there!"

The final curtain of Laurence Housman's *Victoria Regina* is another one hard to forget. The occasion is Victoria's Diamond Jubilee. It is late in the day and the scene is a chamber in Buckingham Palace. In the room are gathered fifty or sixty of the Queen's direct descendants, along with representatives of the crowned heads of Europe. Without and below the balcony the great crowds are cheering. Presently Victoria enters, seated in her wheeled chair and flanked by her two sons. After the congratulations, Princess Beatrice, addressing the Queen, says: "Won't you go and rest now, Mamma?" "Not yet," replies the Queen. "That cheering that I heard means that my dear people are expecting to see me again. . . . I must try not to disappoint them." "It would be nice if you could, Mamma," replies the Princess. "Do you think that you can?"

Whereto, Victoria: "Yes. But I shall have to go as I am. I can't get up. It's very gratifying, very, to find — after all these years — that they do appreciate all that I have tried to do for them — for their good, and for this great country of ours. We have been so near together today — they and I; all my dear people of England, and Scotland, and Wales — *and* Ireland, and the dear Colonies, and India. . . . Everything so perfectly in order. Most gratifying! . . . So happy! As we were coming back — you were in front, Beatrice, so perhaps you didn't see — it was just by Hyde Park Corner, there was a great crowd there, and a lot of rough men . . . broke right through the lines of the police and troops guarding the route, and they ran alongside the carriage, shouting and cheering me. And I heard them say: 'Go it, Old Girl! You've done it well!' Of course, very unsuitable — the words; but so gratifying! And oh, I hope it's true. I hope it's true! I must go to them now. Have the windows opened. Hark! How they are cheering. Albert! Ah! if only *you* could have been here!"

The startling final curtain of W. W. Jacobs's *The Monkey's Paw,* with its family eagerly and nervously awaiting fate-hinging news from the world without, suddenly and at length hearing the knock on the door and opening it only to find no one there, is one of the most awesome wordless curtains in the whole of the modern drama, as the final curtain that arbitrarily and abruptly cuts off the excessively voluble central character of Tom Barry's *The Upstart* is one of the most humorously derisive. But in the way of the direct spoken line a shining example is to be had in the final curtain of the great Synge's noble tragedy

Riders to the Sea. The scene is one of the Aran islands. Maurya, now an old, old woman, has successively lost her husband, her father-in-law, and five sons to the merciless sea, and a sixth son, the last, is on the point of taking ship. Pleas are in vain and the boy leaves, only eventually to be brought back, his body covered with a shred of sail. From Maurya flow no tears, but only a sigh of deep relief: "They're all gone now, and there isn't anything more the sea can do to me. . . . It's a great rest I'll have now, and it's time surely. It's a great rest I'll have now, and great sleeping in the long nights after Samhain. . . . They're all together this time, and the end is come. Michael has a clean burial in the far north, by the grace of the Almighty God. Bartley will have a fine coffin out of the white boards, and a deep grave surely. What more can we want than that? No man at all can be living forever, and we must be satisfied."

Again, who that ever heard it can forget the heroic final curtain to Rostand's *Cyrano de Bergerac?* Thus the dying Cyrano: "One does not fight because there is hope of winning. No! It is finer to fight when it is no use. . . . What are all those? You are a thousand strong. Ah, I know you now — all my ancient enemies! Hypocrisy *(he strikes with his sword in the empty air)* — take this! Compromises, and Prejudices, and dastardly Expedients. *(He strikes again.)* That I should come to terms, I? Never, never! Yes, you have wrested from me everything, laurel as well as rose. . . . Work your wills! Spite of your worst, something will still be left me to take whither I go . . . and tonight when I enter God's house, in saluting, broadly will I sweep the azure threshold with what despite of all I carry forth unblemished and unbent . . . and that is . . . *(The sword falls from his hands, he staggers, and drops in the arms of his aides.)*

Roxanne bends over him, kisses his forehead: "And that is?" she repeats.

Cyrano opens his eyes, recognizes her, and says with a smile: "My plume!"

There's theatre for you, you present-day sissies!

As an example of the non-heroic final curtain line at its best, there is on the other hand that to Chekhov's *The Sea Gull*. The report of a pistol is heard off stage. Everyone starts. Madame Arcadina, alarmed, asks: "What's that?" Dorn nonchalantly replies: "It's all right. I expect something's burst in my medicine traveling-case. Don't be scared. (*He goes off and returns a moment later.*) As I thought. My ether bottle's burst. (*He sings, casually.*) Once more, once more before thee, love . . ."

Arcadina: "Good heavens, I was quite frightened. It reminded me of that time when . . . (*covers her face with her hands*) I felt quite faint."

Dorn picks up a magazine and idly turns the pages. Then to Trigorin: "There was an article in this magazine a month or so ago . . . a letter from America . . . and I wanted to ask you, among other things . . . (*puts his arm around Trigorin's waist and leads him down to the footlights*) . . . I'm very much interested in the question . . . (*in a low tone*) Get Irina Nikolayevna away from here. The fact is, Constantine has shot himself."

A further tasty example of the final curtain line is that in Anderson's and Stallings' *What Price Glory?*, wherein Sergeant Quirt ends the play with his gay shout to his captain returning to the front: "Hey, Flagg, wait for baby!" Another is that of Anderson's *Mary of Scotland* with Mary captive in a cell and challenging the Elizabeth who has put her there — the Elizabeth whose scheming has destroyed her as a monarch yet not as a woman — "But — still — I — win!" And another yet is the beautiful one of *The Green Pastures* with De Lawd saying to Gabriel: "Did he mean dat even God must suffer?" And the sound of a voice crying in the distance: "Oh, look at him! Oh, look, dey goin' to make him carry it up dat high hill! Dey goin' to nail him to it! Oh, dat's a terrible burden for one man to carry!"

Where, too, can you come upon a pleasanter tag than that of the otherwise negligible *Our Town*? The Stage Manager closes the curtains upon the play and its picture of the New England village. "Most everybody's asleep in Grover's Corners," he says. "There are a few lights on; Shorty Haw-

kins, down at the depot, has just watched the Albany train
go by. And at the livery stable somebody's setting up late
and talking. . . . There are the stars — doing their old,
old criss-cross journeys in the sky. Scholars haven't settled
the matter yet, but they seem to think there are no living
beings up there. They're just chalk — or fire. Only this one
is straining away, straining away all the time to make something of itself. The strain's so bad that every sixteen hours
everybody lies down and gets a rest. (*He winds his watch.*)
Hm. . . . Eleven o'clock in Grover's Corners. — You get
a good rest, too. Good-night."

Or, finally, upon a rarer one than that of *Family Portrait,* the play about the family of Christ? Christ has died on
the cross. Mary and Judah are on the stage alone. "If the
baby's a boy — what are you going to name him?" asks
Mary casually.

"We haven't decided."

"I wish — "

"What, Mother?"

"Will you do something for me, Judah?"

"Of course I will! What is it?"

"If it's a boy, will you name him after your brother —
after Jesus, I mean?"

"Why — why, yes, Mother. I'll talk to Deborah about
it — "

"It's a nice name," says Mary. "I'd like him not to be
forgotten."

NEW FACES OF 1943. December 22, 1942

A revue by John Lund, J. B. Rosenberg, and June Carroll, with tunes by Lee Wainer. Produced by Leonard Sillman.

Principals

Leonard Sillman, John Lund, Marie Lund, Laura Deane Dutton, Doris Dowling, Diane Davis, Irwin Corey, Tony Farrar, Ilsa Kevin, Ann Robinson, Dorothy Dennis, Hie Thompson, Robert Weil, Alice Pearce, Ralph Lewis, and Kent Edwards.

M<small>R. S<small>ILLMAN</small></small> is apparently of the persistent belief that what our musical shows and revues most need is new faces, and this exhibit was still another expression of that belief. Although I am far from disagreeing with him that new faces may not be welcome, it might not, however, be a bad idea to discover some that are supplemented by equally welcome new talents, and in this respect I fear that he was no Lorenzo. What he gathered together on this occasion were some countenances that previously had not been scanned by us, but the competences they offered were hardly of a novel sort to stimulate. They merchanted much the same old routine thing, and not one-hundredth so well as the old, established faces.

When it came to the generality of new faces seen on the musical or revue stage thus far in the season, as a matter of fact only four, despite the acceptable contours of some of the others', demonstrated anything at all in the way of talent: Constance Moore in *By Jupiter,* Susan Miller in *Beat the Band,* Lucille Norman in *Show Time,* and Marjorie Knapp in *Star and Garter.* (Nor was the dramatic stage even that rich in fresh dispensations. Save for Billy Koud in *Strip for Action* and the children Clare Foley and Alec Englander in *Janie* and *The Willow and I* respectively, nothing showed up of any particular interest.) So, for all the hospitality in the world, maybe we shall have to be content to get along for a while longer with musical shows populated by such familiar phizzes as those of Ed Wynn, Ray Bolger, Ethel Merman, Bobby Clark and the like, which after all isn't such a bad idea either.

Furthermore, when Mr. Sillman goes about his annual business of new faces, one could wish that, even if accompanying talent does not especially concern him, he might find some in the feminine department that are at least the equal of the already ascertained species. But he seems unable to have unearthed more than a single one, Diane Davis's, that is anywhere nearly so consoling as Nanette Fabray's, Carol Bruce's, Jane Ball's, the Mexican Rosario's, Mary Parker's, Joyce Beasley's, or any other such hitherto observed dainty's, whether white or black.

In this juncture, I hasten to his aid and rescue. If he is honest in his desire to give the theatregoing public some fresh physiognomy that it can contemplate with æsthetic pleasure, he might well scout the following, as yet unknown to the stage: Chao Ming Chu, a delicate Chinese-Javanese dancer with experience on the Continental stage; sloe-eyed Toni Battle, quondam cigarette vendeuse at the Stork Club (where Saroyan discovered Lillian McGuinnes and June Hayford for his *Across the Board on Tomorrow Morning* and *Talking to You* productions) ; Narita, the highly decorative Puerto Rican hummingbird late of the Monte Carlo; Fredericka, the French-Canadian beauty who has danced at Bertolotti's in Greenwich Village and other local inns; Helen Thomas, a bonny mavourneen who has played in the little summer theatres; Nina Orla, a lovely young Mexican who has sung in several New York night clubs and was momentarily in motion pictures; Beatrice Pearson, a cute sample who understudied Mary Anderson the season before in *Guest in the House* and who has talent in several pertinent directions; Betty Bacall, a decidedly attractive new face that producers seem to have overlooked; the pretty, Joen Arliss, who has played in the Woodstock, New York, summer theatre; the striking Brooklyn-Chinese singer, Beatrice Fung Oye; the colored dancing tootsy-wootsy, Jacqueline Lewis; and so on. Let Mr. Sillman give us such new faces and there will be a different story to tell.

FLARE PATH. December 23, 1942

Another English war grant, this one by Terence Rattigan.
Produced, of course, by Gilbert Miller.

Program

Peter Kyle	*Arthur Margetson*	Flight Lieutenant Graham	
Countess Skrczevinsky (Doris)		(Teddy)	*Alec Guinness*
	Doris Patston	Patricia Graham	*Nancy Kelly*
Mrs. Oakes	*Cynthia Latham*	Mrs. Miller (Maudie)	
Sergeant Miller (Dusty)			*Helena Pickard*
	Gerald Savory	Squadron-Leader Swanson	
Percy	*Bob White*		*Reynolds Denniston*
Flying Officer Count Skrcze-			
vinsky	*Alexander Ivo*		

SYNOPSIS: *Act I. Saturday evening, about 5.30 p.m. Act II. Scene 1. About four hours later. Scene 2. Sunday morning, about 5.30 a.m. Act III. Sunday noon.*

Action passes in the residents' lounge of the Falcon Hotel, Milchester, Lincs.

T HEY COME PRETTY BAD at times, these English imports that have achieved big success in London, but they do not often come quite so entirely bad as this. If the play has so much as even one-half of one redeeming feature, it has eluded this critical cunning. The author's purpose and intention is to pay tribute to the valor of the Royal Air Force; what he achieves, so trivial being his equipment, is something that rather puts that admirable body in a ridiculous light. And small wonder, considering the kind of plot into which he has incorporated it. Sniff:

Flight Lieutenant Teddy Graham's wife, Patricia, a former actress, has, unknown to him, enjoyed protracted premarital sexual experience with a moving-picture idol, Peter Kyle by name. Peter, now at forty-seven passé for screen purposes, pursues her to a provincial hotel where she is staying to be near her husband and tells her that he needs her now more than ever. Patricia, it is at once appar-

ent, still is amorously fetched by him but, interrupted only
by the periodic rushing in and out of R. A. F. fliers and
gunnery noises off stage, for the subsequent hour and a half
indulges in the elaborate repertoire of facial contortions
commonly employed under such circumstances to indicate,
seriatim, doubt, hesitation, gradual progress of decision,
and, finally, resolve. At ten-thirty she accordingly decides
that not only her heart but the rest of her anatomy and
physiology belong to Peter and is about to give him her all
when the door opens and in staggers Teddy just returned
from a bombing raid.

Teddy is broken. He senses what is up and confesses to
Patricia that he needs her even more than Peter does, since
he has lost his nerve and can no longer do his flying duty
unless he can lean on her love, rest on her faith, and know
when away that she will be waiting for him with receptive
arms. Taking a cue from Candida, Patricia concludes that
it is the weaker of the two men who needs her most, sends
Peter packing, and reinspires Teddy to new feats of derring-
do against the enemy.

The playwright's brilliant imagination does not, however, end here. Appreciating that there must be some humorous relief, he brings in a Polish flier who has enlisted
in the R. A. F. and permits him to induce ten or twelve
minutes of wild hilarity in the English characters by pronouncing *peasants* as *pheasants*. Appreciating also that
there should be at least one tender sentimental scene apart
from his triangle, he brings on Doris, the hotel barmaid
whom the Pole has married, and breaks her heart by having a letter from her husband, who is supposed to have
been killed in action, read to her by another character. The
reading of such letters, whether in war or peace plays, is
one of the favorite theoretical spontaneous combustibles of
playwrights good and bad, usually bad, and has been for
years on end. Once in a great while some playwright like
Anderson, in *The Eve of St. Mark,* contrives to get the desired audience reaction with a war-time letter written very
simply and without too much sentimental embroidery. And
once in a while lesser playwrights like the authors of *Let-*

ters to Lucerne manage the reaction moderately well. But more often the letters, generally, whether in war or peace drama, ending with "But know that whatever happens I shall love you always" — the kind vouchsafed by the Rattigans — so send up their moist signals in advance that the hoped-for effect dies before the envelopes are opened.

Mr. Rattigan's imagination, both humorous and sentimental, functions similarly in other directions, embracing his dry-lipped, caustic, flat-footed, elderly hotel mistress; his Squadron-Leader Swanson, whom the fliers allude to as Gloria; his war widow who difficultly affects an air of cheerfulness to hide her grief; his fliers, like Sergeant Miller, Dusty they call him, who come in sore and bedraggled from a hazardous raid, yet withal as smiling as if they had just returned from a week-end spent with George Robey; etc.

It's subversive.

PROOF THRO' THE NIGHT. December 25, 1942

An American war dividend, by Allan R. Kenward, originally named Cry Havoc. *Produced by Lee Shubert.*

Program

Cap	Ann Shoemaker	Andra	Helen Trenholme
Smitty	Katherine Emery	Nydia	Florence MacMichael
Flo	Florence Rice	Helen	Julie Stevens
Pat	Thelma Schnee	Grace	Muriel Hutchinson
Connie	Katherine Locke	Sadie	Ruth Conley
Steve	Carol Channing	Native Woman	Tevesa Teres
Sue	Margaret Phillips		

SYNOPSIS: Act I. Scene 1. *Afternoon.* Scene 2. *Four days later, 11.30 p.m.* Act II. *Late afternoon, several days later.* Act III. Scene 1. *Shortly before dawn, the following morning.* Scene 2. *Several hours later.*

Scene. *A converted gun emplacement adjacent to Bataan peninsula, early in 1942.*

I DON'T KNOW how you feel about it, but war plays on the average hardly constitute my idea of a grand evening in the theatre. There may be some whose notion of a gala time is sitting weekly for two and a half hours listening to the heart-rending agonies of people of various nations beset by the tragedies of war and watching them suffer the tortures of bomb raids, starvation, death, and all the other appurtenances of bloody conflict, but when it comes to me, I say no. And if you indignantly argue that that makes me out a rather trivial human being and a worse drama critic I quiet you by telling you that I get just as sick of listening to a similar succession of plays that have to do with women who for one reason or another quarrel with their husbands around a quarter to ten and then take until eleven o'clock to make up their minds that they love them willy-nilly and should considerately have allowed me to get to bed an hour and fifteen minutes earlier.

But about most of the war plays. After a man has spent the day immersed in distressing war news retailed by newspapers, the radio, and miscellaneous conversation, has laboriously figured out how he can buy more war bonds, has otherwise done his daily bit toward the national effort and has come home wishing to heaven that the Nazis, the Italians, and the Japs, to say nothing of what remains of Vichy, were all frying in hell, the prospect of an evening spent in a theatre listening to much the same stuff all over again is not what may precisely be called fascinating. Yet let such a man so much as drop a hint that he would much rather under the circumstances see Gypsy Rose Lee or hear some good jokes by George Jessel, and not only his wife but some of his other hypocritical acquaintances will promptly put him down for an ignominious lowbrow and an even more ignominious escapist, and will proclaim him a disgrace to decent society. All right, then I am an ignominious lowbrow, an even more ignominious escapist, and a disgrace to decent society, God bless me.

It isn't that once in a long spell some war play with symptoms of quality doesn't reward one for a visit. But in the case of the great majority the reward is akin to getting a dime for returning a lost purse containing a thousand dollars. You go, as in this season, to something like *The Morning Star, Yankee Point,* or *Lifeline;* you look at characters diving desperately under tables to avoid being smashed to bits by Nazi bombs, other characters black with despair over the prospect of things, and still others gasping their last breaths after being potted by enemy guns; and you are supposed to be having or to pretend to be having a wonderful time. Well, you can have it. I'll take Gypsy and George.

And in the case of something like this *Proof thro' the Night* I'll gladly settle for even Eugene Howard.

Containing an all-woman cast and purporting to deal with American nurses caught in the Bataan trap, the whole thing is so definitely Hollywood — the author is a movie scenarist — that what might have been an emotionally affecting play becomes before even the first twenty minutes are over a joke. For in that twenty minutes the author peoples his stage with an assortment of young females, announced to be volunteer nurses, who present the aspect of a stranded one-night-stand musical comedy company, who crack feeble witticisms about Hirohito's teeth and the like, and not one of whom would have been accepted as even a bed-pan chauffeuse in a Keely Cure. The heavy effort to type them by way of getting some variety, the common device of playwrights who are incapable of picturing character save externally, only adds to the musical comedy effect: the former burlesque queen, the former gum-chewing, wisecracking telephone-switchboard operator (in Thelma Schnee's impersonation made up to resemble Harpo Marx), the former hash-slinger, the drawling Southern nitwit, the tony Junior Leaguer, the girl who is man-crazy, the one who is pathetically sex-starved, the wild drug addict, etc. And the racket ever going on outside the shelter and the serio-comic charade ever going on inside only still further add to the impression that what one is looking at is less the tragic spectacle of nurses under the terror on Bataan Peninsula than a lot of heterogeneous cuties spending a few days' summer vacation in a shared Atlantic City Pacific Avenue hotel room during a boozy convention of Japanese rolling-ball game concessionaires.

Making matters still worse, the author, unable to imagine any internal action, lugs in a Hollywood spy story by desperate way of trying to sustain his audience's interest. Here he betrays an even smaller theatrical knowledge than in the other directions noted. First, he lodges all suspicion against his Harpo Marx female, forgetting that you cannot fool an audience into believing that the low comédienne is a villainous character and, secondly, that even if you could, the dramatic and tragic final effect hoped for would go for naught in the face of the antecedent laughter. He then commits the further theatrical mistake of turning up the actual spy in the person of a well-known Broadway actress (Katherine Locke) who has been given nothing to do for two whole acts but to sit silently in the background. You can never fool an audience that way either, not in this day. It knows from long experience that no well-known actress is going to sacrifice herself to a job which gives her no slightest opportunity to do anything for an entire evening and that, if she has nothing to do for two acts, she certainly will get her big chance in the last act or know the reason why. Accordingly, and despite all the suspicion thrown elsewhere, that the character played by Miss Locke was sure to turn out to be the spy — and a profusely declamatory one at that — was a foregone conclusion, and Mr. Kenward's mystery gesticulations thus not only failed to hold his audience's attention but relaxed it completely after it had surveyed Miss Locke's inactivity for even one act.

Just two more confidences. When the spy is at length brought to bay — she is an agent of the Bund, it is announced — she discharges a load of rhetorical fireworks denouncing democracy, whereupon the rest of the girls have at her with even more rhetorical set pieces in rebuttal, thus gratifying Mr. Kenward with the illusion that, for all he is of Hollywood, he is a serious dramatist with something to say. And, furthermore, it would take a playwright considerably more competent than Mr. Kenward sympathetically to interest anyone, for all the appropriate dramatic realism, in any stage occupied solely by slovenly, physically filthy, and repulsive females.

DOODLE DANDY OF THE U. S. A.
DECEMBER 26, 1942

A fantasy with music and dancing, designed for children of eight or over, by Saul Lancourt, with a score by Elie Siegmeister. Produced by Junior Programs, Inc.

PROGRAM

THE CLOCK	*Leon Kahn*	RUSH McNELTON	*Alfred Allegro*
BENJAMIN FRANKLIN	*Blake Ritter*	HUMPHREY DUMPHREY	*Leon Kahn*
THOMAS JEFFERSON	*Alfred Allegro*	ELIZABETH DRAKE	
JOEL BARLOW	*John Hurdle*		*Mary Whitis Bell*
ANNE HUTCHISON	*Mary Whitis Bell*	HENRY FIORO	*Blake Ritter*
DOODLE DANDY	*Sam Steen*	BENJAMIN FRANKLIN BUDD	
HIS LUCKY STAR	*Barbara Gaye*		*George Hoxie*
MICHAEL RIDGE	*Beman Lord*		

Most of the plays customarily designed for and purveyed to the young of the species so outrage their underrated capacities that it is all they can do politely to restrain themselves from assaulting the stages with especially juicy spitballs. Treating of their subjects, whether fanciful or realistic, with such arch condescension and with such a minimum of intelligence as would satisfy only adults given to an admiration of the art of the cinema, the plays are crammed down the throats of helpless youngsters who would give all the rights they owned in all the all-day suckers in the world to go instead to something like Rostand's *Chantecler* or *Tobacco Road,* and who would assimilate both with equal alacrity.

It is, in point of record, only once or twice in a dog's age that a play specifically wrought for children meets with their even half-way approval. One such is the exhibit under discussion. A patriotic fantasy in which Doodle Dandy, a celestial traveling salesman for Freedom, Inc., comes down to earth and brings about the downfall of an aspiring dictator named Humphrey Dumphrey, it is humorously maneuvered with some slight respect for children's too often overlooked mental faculties and amounts in the aggregate to considerably more intelligent entertainment than some such childish fantasy as Philip Barry's *Liberty Jones,* which it thematically resembles and which the Theatre Guild deemed food for adults.

SWEET CHARITY. December 28, 1942

A farce by Irving Brecher and Manuel Seff. Presented as a George Abbott production by Alfred Bloomingdale, it barely lasted out the week.

PROGRAM

MRS. PAT MITCHELL, Secretary	*Augusta Dabney*	HARRY TROTT	*Philip Loeb*
MRS. EVA INGERSOLL, President	*Viola Roache*	TRUMPET WILSON	*Dort Clark*
MISS BEULAH OGILVIE, Vice-President	*Jane Seymour*	BURTON SEDGEWICK	*John M. Kline*
MRS. LAURA BRINDLE, Treasurer	*Enid Markey*	MR. HOGARTH	*Leslie Litomy*
MYRON MITCHELL	*Whit Bissell*	MR. BEASLEY	*Hans Robert*
MRS. DIANE MARTINDALE, Ways & Means	*Mary Sargent*	MR. MERRITT	*John Adair*
JONATHAN BATES	*Harlan Briggs*	JOHN DEXTER	*John Kirk*
SHERIFF ANDREW BRINDLE	*Calvin Thomas*	SALVATION ARMY SOLDIER	*Clyde Waddell*
		THE FAMILY	*With Liselotte Krumschmidt*

SYNOPSIS: Act I. *Thursday afternoon.* Act II. *Friday morning.* Act III. *Saturday morning.* (*During Act III curtain will be lowered to denote a lapse of almost two hours.*)

Scene. *The entire action of the play takes place in main room of the "Friendly Hand" clubhouse, in a city several hundred miles from New York.*

SOME OF OUR producer-directors grow up, some grow down, and others just stand still. George Abbott appears to be in the last named category. One of the consequences is that we here once again got the Pithecanthropus farce about the three characters in mad quest of something or other, their increased frenzy when they do not seem to be able to get it, and, after two and a quarter hours, their fortuitous achievement of their goal. What the trio turbulently quest may be a secret tip on the races, as in *Three Men on a Horse,* funds with which to produce a play, as in *Room Service,* means whereby to hold a rich client, as in

See My Lawyer, or something else of the general sort. But
whatever it is — in *Sweet Charity* it is $2,500 to pay a swing
band for whose promised appearance clubwomen have sold
countless tickets in the cause of a children's home — it is
always essentially the same. Only in the case of *Sweet Charity* it is not merely the same but much worse.

Also as usual, Mr. Abbott relied upon his established
brand of grasshopper direction, jumping and scooting the
actors all over the stage, to invest his lifeless exhibit with
an aspect of inner vitality. Contributing further to the depression were the Piltdown scene wherein erstwhile staid
and formal females get drunk and unwontedly cut wild
capers (in this instance marijuana cigarettes, or reefers,
were substituted as a great novelty for the more customary
alcoholic liquor) ; the scene from the same epoch wherein
one man is elaborately mistaken for another; the assorted
kids suddenly brought on for a laugh at the final curtain;
the joke about vice presidents; the locking of an unwelcome character in the cellar until the deal at issue is safely
concluded; the theatrical agent who tears his hair for two
hours trying to get the money due him; the band leader
romantically known as King Cole whose real name is Gold-
stein; the comédienne who takes her shoes off; the second
comédienne who puts on a man's hat; the character who
persistently calls another by the wrong names; the sheriff
who appears on the scene just as everyone thinks everything
is nicely settled and knocks over the house of cards; etc.
The only relief was a single line of dialogue around
10.25 p.m. when, in retort to a harassed character's declara-
tion that he was going to join the Navy in order to forget
women, another, after scrutinizing him quizzically, in-
quired: "What navy?" If that's any relief.

There was a day when Mr. Abbott's rapid directorial timing was considered a quite remarkable theatrical achievement, and all his very own. But his means, to say nothing
of his later materials, now seem not only dated but all too
heavily transparent. It was, many forget, the late George
M. Cohan who first brought this quick-step species of direction into our theatre and who, long before Abbott,

brought it to perfection. One of Cohan's very earliest productions, it should be remembered, was called *Running for
Office,* and in it there was so much of the running that the
office itself didn't show up until the last minute. Abbott
is no Cohan. He manages the running well enough, but the
office doesn't show up at all.

THE RUSSIAN PEOPLE. December 29, 1942

A play by Konstantin Simonov, twenty-seven-year-old war correspondent for Krasnaia Zvezda, *the Red Army newspaper, in the American acting version by Clifford Odets. Produced for quick failure by the Theatre Guild.*

Program

Martha Safonova		Globa	*Luther Adler*
	Margaret Waller	Old Man	*Joseph Shattuck*
Maria Kharitonova		Second Old Man	*Jefferson Coates*
	Eleonora Mendelssohn	Rosenberg	*Rudolph Anders*
Kozlovsky	*Eduardo Franz*	Werner	*Harold Dyrenforth*
Valya	*Elisabeth Fraser*	Kharitonov	*E. A. Krumschmidt*
Morozov	*Robert Simon*	Red Army Man	*Ad Karns*
Safonov	*Leon Ames*	Captain Gavrilov	*Roger Beirne*
Borisov	*Randolph Echols*	Krause	*Walter Kohler*
Shura	*Anna Minot*	German Soldier	*David Koser*
Vasin	*Victor Varconi*	Semyonov	*Mark Schmeid*
Panin	*Herbert Berghof*	Major General Lukonin	
Lieut. Vasilyev	*Peter Hobbs*		*Robert Simon*

SYNOPSIS: Act I. Scene 1. *The home of Martha Safonova in the occupied part of town, evening.* Scene 2. *A railway station used as staff headquarters, the following day.* Scene 3. *The same, some days later.* Act II. Scene 1. *The Kharitonov home, late afternoon.* Scene 2. *The riverbank, that night.* Scene 3. *The headquarters, immediately after.* Act III. Scene 1. *The Kharitonov home, the next day.* Scene 2. *The riverbank, that evening.* Scene 3. *The Kharitonov home, later the same night.*

ALTHOUGH WE HAVE no exact means of knowing, it is a safe wager that the war plays currently being shown in Germany, Italy, and maybe even Japan are not materially different from most of those being shown in America, England, and Russia, and that the majority of them are just as bad. It is reasonable to assume that basically they are much the same, differing only in their points of view. Whereas our plays and those of our allies attest to the invincible spirit of the United Nations and the contemptible aspect of our enemies, the plays of the Germans, Italians, and

Japs unquestionably attest to the invincible spirit of the Axis nations and the contemptible aspect of ourselves.

This is readily understandable. The drama in times of peace, wherever you find it, consists largely in a people's self-criticism; in times of war it consists almost entirely in the criticism of other peoples. The drama of peace disparages its characters, or at least fills them with doubts and hesitations; the drama of war, with negligible exception, flatters them and rids them of all such doubts and hesitations. In short, when peace is upon a nation we say things about ourselves which in time of war would be subversive and actionable and which hence become the privilege of the enemy. Peace often makes dramatic cowards of heroes; war more often makes dramatic heroes of cowards.

It is easy to think of the Axis equivalents of many of the war plays that have been shown locally. Change the names of Mrs. Parrilow, Cliff Parrilow, and Sir Leo Alvers to Frau Pachner, Kurt Pachner, and Herr Doktor Leo Alpers, instead of London lay the scene in Cologne, and it does not take much imagination to see how, with a few other minor alterations, *The Morning Star* might become *Der Morgenstern* and portray the firm resolution of a German family under a British bombing raid. So, too, in a better play turn the Neil West family into the Niccolo Vespuccis, the Feller heroine into Filelfo, alter the scene from an American farming district to an Italian, and make other very slight changes in the text, and you would have an Italian counterpart of *The Eve of St. Mark:* the young boy going forth to war, his leave of his sweetheart, his experiences in camp, his eventual heroic death not in the fever-ridden Philippines but in fever-ridden Libya, his brothers sent by his family to follow in his footsteps, doubtless in their phrase also to make the world a safe place to live in — and all with intermittent appropriate sarcasms directed at us and our allies.

The Russian People calls for even less stretch of the imagination. An account of the Russians' indomitable bravery in battle with the Nazis, it is the easiest thing in the world to picture the Nazi paraphrase: the determination to crush the accursed enemy, the tremendous self-sacrifice to that end, the ignominy of the foe, the pursuit of a high ideal, etc. For every nation in war convinces itself, at least until the conviction is thoroughly beaten out of it, and sometimes even then, that it alone is in the right, that it alone is truly heroic, and that its enemies are a pack of rats.

That these Axis plays would be and undoubtedly are quite as poor as the majority of our own and our allies' plays — and in most cases, from our philosophical point of view, a damned sight worse and certainly more objectionable — needs little argument. But that most of our United Nations plays, for all their exalted and highly appealing sentiments, must suffer our own honest critical barbs no less, needs argument no more extended. This *The Russian People* is a case in point. For all its deservedly eloquent thematic testimonial to our gallant Slav brothers in arms, it amounts in strict appraisal to mere obvious, stenciled melodrama, as unimaginative in its dramatic devices as it is unimaginative in literary execution, and as cheaply hokum in the pursuit of its effects as such lesser distillations of the 10–20–30 dramaturgical moonshiners of our native youth as *The Boy Behind the Gun* of Charles E. Blaney.

Maneuvered for contemporary acceptance and patriotic audience reaction by making its characters Russians under the Nazi terror instead of, as in the old melodramas, Russians under the Czar's whip or Americans under the scalping knives of the Sioux Indians, Simonov's rampage similarly misses nothing that might contribute to meditative peace and quiet. The booming guns are there, both distant and near to hand. The "Take that, you cur-s!" with the resounding blows in the face are what may be termed in striking evidence. The "Into the cell with you-s!" accompanied by violent kicks are duly present. The Nazi tommy-guns pour their volleys into helpless innocents. Drinks are poisoned and Nazis "fall face forward on the floor and writhe in convulsions." Aged Russian mothers cry out to German officials: "Oh, I could choke you with these very hands!" and spit in their faces. People are hanged. Revolvers are quickly drawn when sounds are heard at doors.

Men fall across thresholds, their clothes drenched in blood. And machine guns play an obbligato to the evening.

The intrinsic dialogue is more or less what you would expect: "I was making my way . . . through enemy encirclement . . . they saw me . . . and then . . . My name is . . . water! Give me water!" Or again: "Why aren't you crying?" "I can't. I've seen everything there is to see. Things I'd never thought to see. And I can't cry. No more tears left." (*Slow curtain.*) Or still again: "I've never seen him before — that I know — but his voice seems familiar. Where could I have heard that voice before? I am certain I've heard it before. I am sure of it!" Or yet again: "Stalin. . . . You know, sometimes I don't believe one thing, and sometimes another thing. But I believe *him* — always and everywhere! When I heard his speech over the radio I was still suffering from the effects of shell-shock and the words sounded jumbled to my ears. But all the same the words I seemed to distinctly hear were, 'Stand firm, Safonov, and not a single step backward! Die, but stand firm! Fight on, but stand firm! Suffer ten wounds, but stand firm!'"

And surely and finally, at the last curtain fall: "But I very much want to live. To live on for a long time. To live on until with my very own eyes I shall have seen the very last one of those who did this (*grasping the list of Nazis' names from the Adjutant's hand*) lying dead! The very last one, *dead!* Right here, under my feet!"

Nor is another dodge characteristic of much of the modern Russian drama, whether war or not war, absent. I allude to the contrastedly soft singing of a song or strumming of a musical instrument in a tense and significant situation. (It is also not overlooked in Afinogenev's much discussed *Distant Point,* which will probably be along in due course.) In the Simonov play it makes its appearance like clockwork. You can sense it coming like a letter-carrier. "I've grown unaccustomed to sleeping," says the tortured Safonov. "But you try. I'll sing you a song," says Valya. "What song?" he asks. "One that they sing to children. A lullaby," she answers — and sings: "Sleep my infant, sleep my precious. . . ." Again, at the end of the act, as the soldier sleeps, she leans over him as though to waken him, conquers the desire, and sings, prophetically: "He will go to see thee off, and you will wave goodbye. . . ." Yet more, at the end of another scene, a character about to go forth to battle, when reaching the doorway, sings a sweet old Russian song: "Nightingale, nightingale, wee little bird . . ." whereupon another character: "Did you hear that or didn't you? Did you hear how *men of Russia go to their death!*"

In short, if such things affect and stir you, pay no attention to these critical sniffs. Revel, if you will, in such staple Slav sentimental passages as: "When everybody speaks of their motherland, their country, they probably imagine something huge and vast. But with me it's different. In Novo-Nikolaevak our little hut used to stand on the edge of the village near a stream with two birch trees on its banks. And I used to hang a swing on those trees. And when I hear people speak of their motherland, *I* always remember those two birch trees." Thrill, if you will, to the Russian who pretends he has gone over to the Nazis, who is treated with bitter contempt by his people, and who finally reveals himself a loyal soldier and a hero. Shout bravo, if you will, at some such old Drury Lane curtain speech as: "And tell the Captain that Major Vasin died at his post, died the death of the brave, having done all he could, and even more than he could. And also inform Captain Safonov that Panin, Chief of the S. D., has taken over command of the platoon. You may go now." Do all this, if you will, and more. As for me, though I surrender my deep admiration of the people of Russia in war to none, I still prefer my drama of the people of Russia in war to be something slightly superior.

Although Clifford Odets has, for the American acting version, edited some of the awkwardnesses out of the original manuscript and has changed the suspected-spy-turned-loyal-hero business, the exhibit stubbornly remains what it was in the first place, since you cannot basically improve a play merely by changing some of its phraseology.

In view of the complete trashiness of the play, it was critically dismaying to hear the late and once highly regarded Nemirovich-Danchenko, director of the equally highly regarded Moscow Art Theatre, observe: "In these stern days of war, it is difficult to over-rate the significance of *The Russian People* as art. . . . Tell the actors that the role of art has now matured as never before. Art cannot tolerate any compromise at this time. Art must teach the people to hate the dark and terrible forces of Fascism which threaten humanity and its culture."

So art is not art save it wear an Allied uniform and carry, with a curse on its lips, a gun in its hand!

Love, once the bread and butter of the drama, for the time being seems to be surrendering its thematic place to this hate. Where the delicate emotion once occupied the larger portion of drama, we now find its emotional opposite. Whereas the former drama was usually *for* something, the present is *against* something. The aforesaid Fascism and Nazism have been the forces motivating the change. The day may not be far off when the dramatic spectacle of a man tenderly kissing a woman will be as sensational as was the stage's first articulation of the term "son-of-a-bitch."

THE DOUGHGIRLS. December 30, 1942

A farce by Joseph Fields, co-author of the box-office hits
My Sister Eileen *and* Junior Miss. *Produced by Max Gordon.*

Program

Edna	*Virginia Field*	Natalia Chodorov	*Arlene Francis*
Julian Cadman	*King Calder*	A Stranger	*Harold Grau*
Mr. Jordan	*Sydney Grant*	Orderly	*Joseph Olney*
Colonel Harry Hallstead		Warren Buckley	
	Reed Brown, Jr.		*Edward H. Robins*
A Bellboy	*George Calvert*	Sylvia	*Natalie Schafer*
Vivian	*Arleen Whelan*	Chaplain Stevens	
A Porter	*Hugh Williamson*		*Reynolds Evans*
Waiter	*Walter Beck*	Admiral Owens	*Thomas F. Tracey*
Nan	*Doris Nolan*	Timothy Walsh	
Brigadier General Slade			*James MacDonald*
	William J. Kelly	Stephen Forbes	*Maurice Burke*
Tom Dillon	*Vinton Hayworth*	Father Nicholai	
Judge Honoria Blake			*Maxim Panteleieff*
	Ethel Wilson		

SYNOPSIS: Act I. *An August afternoon.* Act II. *Two weeks later.*
Act III. *Four weeks later, a Sunday morning.*
The scene is a Washington hotel suite.

I F YOU HAD TOLD theatregoers who only a few nights before had suffered in *Sweet Charity* the stale farce plot of the trio desperately in pursuit of something that they would encounter it again so soon and not only encounter it but find it to their taste, they would in all likelihood have put you down for a super-optimistic ass. Yet that is exactly what happened. For here again were the trio — this time three loose girls avidly stalking marriages with their lovers — tearing their hair for three acts until finally they got what they wanted. In other words a farce at bottom resembling not only the Abbott farces of the last half-dozen or more years but further and even more suggesting some such similar farce of the period considerably before as Zoë Akins's

The Greeks Had a Word for It, the only change being war-time Washington as the background.

But there was a difference that could not be overlooked and that difference was the remarkably adept editing, casting, and general stage direction of George S. Kaufman, the best man at such farcical business in the American theatre. Laying hold of materials that in their rough form would promptly have followed *Sweet Charity* to the theatrical graveyard, this virtuoso contrived to hornswoggle an indifferent script into hilariously rowdy entertainment. With perfect timing, expert calculation of gag effects, stage movement that, while plenty active, never seemed too greatly at variance with normal human conduct, and enormous shrewdness in handling smut as if it were the loving little sister of innocence, he managed to make an audience forget the hoary old plot in its hearty laughter at its incidentals.

Consider just one of the artfully maneuvered gag effects out of many. At the start of the first act, the lover of one of the girls, who hasn't enjoyed her company for quite a spell, tells her he will send a bottle of champagne up to her room and that later that night they will drink it before resuming their former happy relationship. Nothing more is heard of it until three-quarters of an hour later, when the audience has almost forgotten about it. Then a hotel houseboy casually delivers the bottle to the room, meanwhile overrun by a wild variety of characters. A general in the Army, who is among those present, puzzlingly accepts the bottle from the boy, who doesn't seem to know exactly for whom it is intended, and looks at the card attached to it. Who it is for, he pantomimes he doesn't know, but, anyway, he allows: "Very patriotic!" and reads off the inscription: "We did it before and we'll do it again." Curtain.

There was some critical reflection on the "bad taste" of the farce, since it spoofed not only the Army and Navy and the Administration, but also a character thinly disguised as Ludmilla Pavlichenko, the heroic Russian guerrilla fighter. Since when, one might have asked, has any good farce on any subject, whether in war time or time of peace, been precisely in good taste? And what does it matter? Whatever makes a representative and intelligent audience laugh justifies its taste, good or bad.

YOU'LL SEE STARS. December 31, 1942

A musical comedy biography of Gus Edwards; book and lyrics by Herman Timberg, music by Leo Edwards. Produced by Dave Kramer.

Program

Eddie Cantor	*Jackie Green*	Johnny Boston Beans	
George Jessel	*Jackie Michaels*		*Gordon King*
Gus Edwards	*Alan Lester*	Biff Dugan	*Jack Matis*
Walter Winchell		Pisha Pasha	*Maurice Dover*
	Irving Freeman	Georgie Price	*Buddy Simon*
Groucho Marx	*Lou Dahlman*	Mary	*Norma Shea*
Herman Timberg	*Fene Bayliss*	Hildegarde	*Patricia Bright*
Willie Hammerstein	*John Briter*	Lola Lane	*Reni Rochelle*
Harpo Marx	*George Lyons*	School Teacher	*Joan Barry*
Chico Marx	*Sal La Porta*	Cuddles	*Phyllis Baker*
Zeppo Marx	*Eugene Martin*		

SYNOPSIS: Act I. *School days at Hammerstein's.* Scene 1. *Gus Edwards Music Co.* Scene 2. *Hammerstein's stage door.* Scene 3. *Hammerstein's Victoria stage.* Scene 4. *Hammerstein's roof garden.* Scene 5. *Hammerstein's stage door.* Scene 6. *Hotel Astor.* Act II. Scene 1. *Walgreen's drug store.* Scene 2. *Madison Square Garden.* Scene 3. *Backstage Madison Square Garden.* Scene 4. *Finale at Madison Square Garden.*

LASTING FOR just four performances, which by unanimous agreement was just four too many, this achieved the low-water mark on the professional American revue stage, a position hitherto tenaciously held by the *London Follies,* unveiled some thirty-five years ago at the old Weber-Fields Music Hall, then for some time abandoned by the honorable gentlemen for whom it had been named. The authors' intention was a testimonial to Gus Edwards, long sentimentalized by denizens of Broadway for his great achievement in having once put on a vaudeville act called *School Days* and for having in it given initial impetus to the histrionic careers of such remarkable artists as Georgie Price, Lila Lee, Herman Timberg, and Zeppo Marx, not to mention such lesser lights as Zeppo's brothers Groucho, Harpo, and

Chico, George Jessel, Eddie Cantor, and Walter Winchell, the greatest actor of them all. The testimonial took the form of what the program, as indicated, termed a biography and was evidently inspired not only by the Catholic University of Washington's successful musical biographies of George M. Cohan and Joe Cook but by Hollywood's biographies of various such unknowns to the authors' Broadway as Zola, Pasteur, and Madame Curie. As a testimonial to the transcendent gifts of Mr. Edwards, however, it bore an ungrateful resemblance to that tombstone in an Ohio cemetery which is inscribed: "Here lies Joe Wozinski, thanks be to God."

The major portion of the testimonial consisted in impersonations and imitations, by an assortment of some rather terrible amateurs, of the geniuses whom Mr. Edwards had discovered. The impersonations and imitations were something to behold. One young man seemed to be under the impression that if you hopped up and down fifteen times, meanwhile loudly clapping your hands, Mrs. Cantor would forthwith be so convinced you were her loving son Eddie that she would promptly rush out and buy you a hundred dollars' worth of marinierte herring. Another appeared to imagine that if he stood stock still for three minutes and offered a broad grin, thereafter abruptly turning about and dashing frantically around the stage for another three minutes, the other Marx brothers would be unable to distinguish him from Harpo and would go out and buy him two hundred dollars' worth of marinierte herring. And still another enjoyed the hallucination that if he donned a very tight blue serge suit and so much as uttered the line: "Yes, mom, this is Georgie," it would be so impossible to differentiate between him and Jessel that the latter's former wives would conclude they had married identical twins and would be very much embarrassed.

When these rich impersonations and imitations were not holding the stage — I omitted to mention among others a young man who pulled his Fedora down over his eyes and thus became Winchell — voices were lifted in such lyrical masterpieces of the Edwards studio as "School days, school days, dear old golden rule days." And when the voices weren't being lifted, somebody billed as Willie Hammerstein would come up to the one billed as Mr. Edwards, would slap him a whack on the back, and would proclaim him a grand little guy and the salt of the earth.

There was no mention of Armida, the cute little Mexican dancer found and sponsored by Gus. An awfully pretty girl, little Armida. But doubtless the authors had too much affection for her memory to include her in their triumphant botch.

SOMETHING FOR THE BOYS. JANUARY 7, 1943

A musical comedy by Herbert and Dorothy Fields, with songs by Cole Porter. Produced by Michael Todd.

PROGRAM

CHIQUITA HART	*Paula Laurence*	MICHEALA	*Anita Alvarez*
ROGER CALHOUN	*Jed Prouty*	LT. COL. S. D. GRUBBS	
HARRY HART	*Allen Jenkins*		*Jack Hartley*
BLOSSOM HART	*Ethel Merman*	MR. TOBIAS TWITCH	*William Lynn*
STAFF SGT. ROCKY FULTON		CORP. BURNS	*Bill Callahan*
	Bill Johnson	SGT. CARTER	*Remi Martel*
SGT. LADDIE GREEN	*Stuart Langley*	MELANIE WALKER	*Frances Mercer*
MARY-FRANCIS	*Betty Garrett*	MRS. GRUBBS	*Madeleine Clive*
BETTY-JEAN	*Betty Bruce*		

SYNOPSIS: Prologue. Set 1. *Chiquita's dressing room in The Piccadilly Club, Kansas City.* Set 2. *6th Avenue at 50th Street, New York, N. Y.* Set 3. *An assembly line in a defense plant, Newark.* Act I. Scene 1. *Alamo Plaza, San Antonio, Texas.* Scene 2. *Near the P. X. at Kelly Field.* Scene 3. *The patio of the old Hart estate, near San Antonio.* (*Next morning.*) Scene 4. *A crossroads.* (*Night.*) Scene 5. *The patio of the new Hart estate.* (*Three weeks later.*) Act II. Scene 1. *The patio.* Scene 2. *The terrace of Col. Grubbs' home.* Scene 3. *The crossroads.* Scene 4. *The Cadet Club at the Texas Hotel, San Antonio.* Scene 5. *The corridor of the Texas Hotel.* Scene 6. *An Army plane.* (*Later that night.*) Scene 7. *The Cadet Club at the Texas Hotel.*

THE OFTEN REPEATED old saying that plays are not written but rewritten should have a little brother: that musical shows are not written but rebuilt. People outside the theatre, unlike those inside it, will in all likelihood regard this as just a tricky way to start off this chapter, since it is their long-standing conviction that a musical show is created by three simple processes: to wit, someone writes a book for it, someone else writes the music and lyrics, and someone then hires a scene designer, costumer, and company and says come on, let's go. It may have been that way once, but it is no longer that way, and it hasn't been for some time.

In the old days the chief concern of a musical-show producer came after the fact of actual production and consisted for the major part in keeping the comedian sober and the leading woman singer from running off with the leader of the orchestra, commonly a magnifico who used perfume on himself and esteemed himself accordingly a lady-killer. All but one of the comedians today are, if not exactly teetotalers, cautious boys when it comes to the bottle, none of the theatre orchestra leaders uses perfume, and all save one or two of the better-known leading women singers are either married or safely and prophylactically in love with slightly fat and hence emotionally trustworthy business men. So the producers need not worry unduly in that direction. Their worries are not over the actors in their shows but rather over the shows themselves, even before the actors are in them.

When *Let's Face It,* the previous Cole Porter success, was being shown in Boston before the New York opening, Vinton Freedley, its entrepreneur, found to his severe headache that several important numbers, in themselves satisfactory, were going for absolutely nothing. Summoning his official cabinet to meditate the situation, it was finally concluded that the costumes were of a color too similar to the scenery and that as a consequence the chorus of dancers and singers faded into zero. 'Raus mit 'em was the instant college yell; new costumes were ordered; and several days later all was balm. Except, that is, for some of Porter's lyrics.

Porter, as is sufficiently known, is generally a handy fellow at apt lyrics, but on at least one occasion he didn't in this instance seem to be up to snuff. So the long-distance telephone was put to an expensive buzzing and Porter at length came through with changes that evoked laughs where before there had been only grim silence. It thus, to give but one illustration, cost the producer something like sixty-eight dollars in phone calls to get the line rhyming the Duc di Verdura with manure-a, which proceeded to get one of the biggest howls of the evening, only hoping you don't ask me why.

There was, also, an exceptionally pretty girl in the front line of the chorus who presented the producer with something of a problem. It seems that while they were trying out the show this little peach-cake attracted so much enthusiastic and rapt attention from all the males in the audience that the song and dance numbers in which she figured didn't themselves get the proper degree of reaction, which from a business standpoint wasn't cologne. But on the other hand, a lulu like the little one was no slouch of an asset either. What to do? What to do by way of getting the numbers to register properly and not to lose the little lulu was to put her in the back row of the chorus. What to do was duly done — and came another load of balm.

But these are trivial cases in the great general music show dilemma. Ziegfeld several times threw away 25,000 dollars' worth of costumes and 30,000 dollars' worth of scenery before a show opened simply because he suddenly found he didn't like their looks or because the numbers they adorned slowed up the movement of the show. And when he discovered that one comedian didn't seem funny enough to keep his offering steadily amusing, he would rush out and hire a couple of extra ones. On one occasion, further, he went into rehearsal with a book commissioned from J. P. McEvoy, about which he was all excited, presently decided it wasn't right, and got McEvoy, who had spent three months on it, to go to his hotel room and write a completely new one in three days.

Producers, usually amateurs at the business, who still believe that shows are all right in the first place quickly learn their lesson. Early in the last season, one such — or rather three such in association — put on something called *Viva O'Brien* without bothering with any tinkering and lost their 85,000-dollar investment quicker than you could say whew. Realizing their mistake after the bad reviews were in and the customers out, they sought belatedly to engage Groucho Marx to liven up the comedy scenes. Groucho said he would accept if they would let him ad lib just one line. They wanted to know what it was. "I come on in the first act," Groucho apprised them, "and say: 'This is certainly one hell of a lousy show!' " The management decided to close the show instead.

When Ed Wynn's *Boys and Girls Together* was in the cocoon state, Ed lodged a hard gaze upon the chorus girls one afternoon and turned to one of his associates and remarked: "I'd have to be funnier than any six comedians rolled together to get by with a show with nothing better to look at than these babies. Let's make it a little easier for papa." Eight of the most beautiful models obtainable in New York were hired to counteract the looks of the chorus girls, and both Ed and the audiences thereafter got along fine.

The Marx brothers, in the preparation of their musical shows, were in the habit of trying out their jokes on personal friends, waiters, bootblacks, taxi-drivers, and suburban audiences to determine which to keep in the shows and which to cut out. They found the scheme enormously successful. Sometimes, however, producers discover that they have deleted the wrong things. A case in point was the cutting out of the song "Poor Butterfly" in a show being readied for the old Hippodrome. During rehearsals the song seemed to the producers to slow down the show. After the show opened and the song meanwhile had become a nation-wide hit the producers shamefacedly had to put it back where it originally was.

Little things suddenly discovered during the early stages of a show often help to insure success. The combination of Mary Martin and the song "My Heart Belongs to Daddy" — in Porter's *Leave It to Me* — might possibly, considering Miss Martin's coincidental strip-tease, have been sufficient to evoke the necessary audience reaction. But when someone casually offered the suggestion that it would all be much more amusing if the scene of the strip-tease were laid in icy Siberia, you could begin counting the profits in advance.

They tell the story of two not so young actresses who were failures in Hollywood and who were mercilessly bitter and mean-spirited about young actresses who had got on. The two were sitting together at a large party out there one night and commenting audibly on the young actresses who passed their table. This one, they were overheard to scoff, had false hair and a padded figure; that one had knock-knees and a nose with nostrils like a horse; that one was as skinny as a plucked chicken and had ears almost as big as Clark Gable's; and so on. Anita Louise was then seen approaching and a man standing near the women's table bent over in curiosity to eavesdrop the comment they would make. "Hm," sneered one of the witches to the other, "she's *too* beautiful!"

Some musical shows are less sarcastically and more soundly found to be too beautiful for their own good. One such was the 120,000-dollar Dennis King show, *She Had to Say Yes,* which was experimented with in Philadelphia two seasons ago. It proved to be so top-heavy in elaborately striking settings and costumes that the show within them could not compete with them. Subsequent failure was instantaneous.

It is not too generally known, but the out-of-New-York run of *The Dollar Princess,* with Lehar's esteemed score, was assisted no end by the sly incorporation into that score of a popular song by the American Jerome Kern called "They Didn't Believe Me." Nor is it generally known that one of the things that contributed to the great American success of the more recent *I Married an Angel* was the decision, after long debate, to modify the indelicacy of the important scene wherein the angel awakens the morning after the connubial night. Had that scene been left in the way it appeared in the Hungarian original, local audiences would unquestionably have been shocked to the point of disgust.

One of the most troublesome problems in whipping a show into shape is deciding just how much of the plot to leave in and how much to cut out. Many a show courts failure because of too much plot, since such plot clogs the flow and flattens an audience's interest. *Virginia,* the very costly Owen Davis and Laurence Stallings exhibit produced in the Rockefellers' Center Theatre, failed largely because the producers had not pruned it of its excess of plot. And there are all kinds of other examples. The Eddie Cantor show *Banjo Eyes,* based on the farce *Three Men on a Horse,* was found to be so overly crowded with plot and hence so dull that the try-out period had to be considerably extended in order to gain the time to do the necessary wholesale editing.

When the subsequently celebrated *Sunny* was being rehearsed some years ago, one of the worries was the manner of Marilyn Miller's first entrance. Miss Miller was the star lady in the proceedings and her entrance, naturally thought the producer, must be suited to her position. Half a dozen appropriately elaborate entrances were experimented with, but none seemed to be quite the thing. Miss Miller was no more pleased with them than the management and matters reached an impasse. Then one day just as everybody was about ready to give up trying to arrive at a solution, someone suggested that they dismiss the whole idea of a regulation star entrance and have Miss Miller come on hidden modestly in the chorus line. No sooner suggested than done — and when the show opened at the New Amsterdam it wasn't a moment before the audience delightedly and self-congratulatingly picked the star out in the line and rewarded her with twice the amount of applause she might have received from a more conventional circus entrance.

The comedian role is a stomach-ache de luxe for musical-show producers. After casting the role and warmly buying himself a drink in testimony to his great sagacity, the producer occasionally finds during rehearsals that the comedian he has selected isn't at all suited to the role and, what is more, the comedian himself usually finds it out at the same time. The producer is up a tree. The comedian who may be exactly right for the role is, he learns to his grief, either booked for some other show, refuses to leave Hollywood, demands fifty-five per cent of the gross in addition to his 2,000 dollars' weekly salary, or is in love with a night-club singer in Chicago and prefers to remain near his honeybunch. There remains only one thing to do. The role has to be completely rewritten to suit some comedian who *is* available. Thus when Ray Bolger suddenly found he didn't like the role in the late unlamented *The Lady Comes Across* for which he had been tentatively engaged, the management scoured around, finally hired Joe E. Lewis, and had to delay the opening for some weeks until the part could be revamped to fit Joe's entirely dissimilar talents.

Oscar Levant, who had written the best-seller *A Smattering of Ignorance,* met a friend on the street who said: "I didn't know you wrote a book, Oscar. Why didn't you tell me?" To which Levant replied: "Oh, that! What do you think I was doing all yesterday afternoon?" Nevertheless, a single afternoon in the changes of a musical-show book has sometimes been known to spell a lot of the difference between great success and abrupt failure.

Porter's and the Fields' latest offering, this *Something for the Boys,* is the popularly satisfactory show it is because of the extended careful editing to which it was subjected during its try-out period on the road. Here are just a few of the improvements out of many. A pranked-out reprise number, sung by the principals, which had been provided for the opening of the second act was found, for some inexplicable reason, to leave the audience cold. It was a good number even in repetition, but it got no response whatever. Various changes were made in the handling of it, but still the audiences declined to behave properly. So it was discarded in its entirety; Porter was rushed to work on a new ditty; it was given to a minor member of the company to sing; and, also for no explicable reason, the minor member succeeded in winning over the audience where the principals had failed. The new song, to make things even more difficult of understanding, was not nearly so good as the song for which it was substituted. Nor was its entrepreneuse one-tenth so talented as any of the principals. It sometimes, experiment eccentrically proves, happens that way.

A ballroom scene in the second act similarly failed to register until it was figured out that the cadets' khaki uniforms, worn throughout the earlier scenes, had doubtless become monotonous to the audience eye. The uniforms were changed to summer white — the scene was Texas —

and the scene promptly went over with a bang. One of Porter's songs, "Riddle Diddle Me This," which the producer predicted to himself would be one of the hits of the show, was unriddled on the fourth night of the Boston try-out to be possibly all right for some other show but a jarring note in this particular one and, to the producer's private tears, had to be thrown out. A fast barn dance, placed early in the proceedings, was discovered to be so lively that what followed suffered, and was accordingly moved toward the end of the act. And although it had not been planned, when the show was being concocted, to include the mechanical effect of an Army bomber flying directly at the audience, the necessity of incorporating some such effect by way of building excitement into the finale was subsequently determined.

Thus what in less hard-working hands might have been a moderate success was converted into a box-office smash.

As for critical rather than merely popular appraisal, the show's book, treating of three assorted characters who inherit a Texas ranch, find it to be adjacent to an Army flying field, and, turning the ranch house into a residence for officers' wives, are dumfounded when it is mistaken for a sporting house, holds up amusingly in the first act but goes to pieces in the second. The effort to switch from the ribald idea to a discovery by one of the heirs that carborundum rubbed on teeth fillings gives one radio-receiving potentialities — a discovery which causes the military authorities to absolve the heirs from guilt in connection with the house — too greatly complicates an initial plot that might have been better had it been allowed to continue on its own legs. Among the more tuneful of Porter's songs are "Something for the Boys" (somewhat reminiscent of "I'm Always Chasing Rainbows"), "Hey, Good Lookin'," "Could It Be You?" and "He's a Right Guy" (lyric humor borrowed from W. S. Gilbert). Ethel Merman disclosed herself to be a constantly improving comédienne, and in Bill Johnson, who resembles a cross between a younger Maxie Baer and Toots Shor, the producer presented a romantic hero who was a God-sent relief from the usual pretty waxwork.

NINE GIRLS. JANUARY 13, 1943

A murder melodrama by Wilfred H. Pettitt. Produced by A. H. Woods.

PROGRAM

JANE	*Maxine Stuart*	SHIRLEY	*Marilyn Erskine*
FRIEDA	*Ruth K. Hill*	BETTY (TENNESSEE)	
ALICE	*Barbara Bel Geddes*		*Kayo Copeland*
EVE	*K. T. Stevens*	STELLA (SHOT-PUT)	*Irene Dailey*
SHARON (GLAMOR PANTS)		MARY	*Adele Longmire*
	Mary McCormack		

SYNOPSIS: Act I. Scene 1. *Saturday evening.* Scene 2. *Late the same night.* Act II. Scene 1. *Sunday morning.* Scene 2. *Sunday night.*

The entire action takes place in the front room of a sorority club-house in California's Sierra Nevada mountains.

THIS MARKED THE RETURN to the theatre of Al Woods, the melodrama and hayloft king of other days. But only for a brief five-day stopover. Seeking to combine the elements of such of his past box-office hits as the melodramatic *Secret Service Sam,* the murderous *The Trial of Mary Dugan,* and the hayloft *Up in Mabel's Room* and *Parlor, Bedroom and Bath,* his purchased script, while it duly contained the elements, contained them so miscellaneously and ineffectually that those critics who love the old boy (there never was a more likable theatrical figure) couldn't help wishing he had come back, a chip on his shoulder, with a joint and simultaneously played revival of two of his earlier masterpieces like *Queen of the White Slaves* and *Getting Gertie's Garter.* Not only would it have been much more fun, but the combination would certainly have constituted a better play, however also slightly eccentric, than this one.

A glance at the program will, with only an additional hint, tell you all you need to know about the Pettitt revelation. Take the nine girls, make one of them a killer, have the unkilled residuum cumbrously track her down, and interlard the whole with a heavy dose of cheap smut, and you know the worst. Well, not quite. There is also a bit in which one of the girls, an amateur actress, comes down the stairs reciting Lady Macbeth's sleep-walking scene, which so unnerves the killer that she is brought near to confession. So if you didn't know the worst before, you know it now.

DARK EYES. JANUARY 14, 1943

A comedy by Elena Miramova, in collaboration with Eugenie Leontovich. Produced by Jed Harris.

PROGRAM

LARRY FIELD	*Carl Gose*	NATASHA RAPAKOVITCH	
WILLOUGHBY	*Oscar Polk*		*Eugenie Leontovich*
GRANDMOTHER FIELD		TONIA KARPOVA	*Elena Miramova*
	Minnie Dupree	OLGA SHMILEVSKAYA	
PEARL	*Maude Russell*		*Ludmilla Toretzka*
HELEN FIELD	*Anne Burr*	JOHN FIELD	*Jay Fassett*
PRINCE NICOLAI TORADJE			
	Geza Korvin		

SYNOPSIS: Act I. Scene 1. *The living-room, late afternoon of a summer's day in 1942.* Scene 2. *The same, after dinner the following evening.* Act II. Scene 1. *A bedroom, later that evening.* Scene 2. *The same, next morning.*

The entire action of the play takes place in the Fields' family home on Long Island.

Time. *The present.*

T HIS ONE, in order, marked the return to the theatre of Jed Harris, once known as the Broadway Wunderkind. His producing career began with a succession of notable hits like *Broadway, The Front Page, Coquette,* and *The Royal Family,* but a subsequent prolonged period of failures like *The Wiser They Are, Wonder Boy, The Fatal Alibi, The Lake, Life's Too Short,* and *Spring Dance,* interrupted only by *The Green Bay Tree* and *Our Town,* conspired to induce the one-time prodigy to seek refuge in Hollywood. In that remote slum, by way of sustaining his self-esteem the ex-wizard for a subsequent stretch of four years busied himself giving out interviews loftily avowing that he was altogether too good for the theatre, that the theatre and its audiences had become too uncivilized and degraded for a genius like himself, that the playwrights, even the best of them, had all gone to pot and could no longer write anything faintly worthy of his cultured perusal, and that the critics, including first and foremost the present commentator, were a congress of morons whose mean capacities were far from sufficient to appreciate a man of his great and subtle gifts. But these voluptuous dicta somehow didn't seem to convince anyone, including the ex-Wunderkind himself and, peculiarly enough, the movie colony, and nothing else was heard of him, even so far as the films were concerned, until after the four years in question he eased himself back into New York and, after a spell and hiding his indignation between his legs, announced that he was about to make up again to his old love.

Under the circumstances, it was more or less logical, or at least human, that the announcement should be greeted on many sides, and on the critics' in particular, with politely suppressed grins. Axes were mentally sharpened; Roget was combed for synonyms for *decline, collapse, awful,* and *terrible;* and "Back to Hollywood!" was appetizingly rolled on the aggregate tongue. Came the night of the prodigal's stage return. The curtain rose and for the first fifteen minutes you could hear the I-told-you-so's throughout the theatre, for here was conventional stuff ordinarily handled. Then — bang! — something happened. Suddenly the stage came to life; suddenly Harris's old, early exceptional talent in direction became manifest; and for the rest of the evening the house was the redeemed chanticleer's own.

The whisperers have it that the original script of this *Dark Eyes* wasn't especially amusing and that Harris, serving as editor-producer, brought in several outside humorists to improve it. Whatever the facts, as finally disclosed it presents itself as a minor but original and freshly diverting comedy, at times highlighted by a pretty wit, and for the most part directed and acted with uncommon proficiency. The story is of three Russian women, down and out in New York, who through peculiar circumstances find themselves spending a week-end in the house of a Long Island tycoon and who proceed to go to work on him. But it is the embroidery and not the story that stimulates the evening: the travesty of Russian soulfulness; the comical fortissimo colloquies on Tchaikovsky, Lermontov, Dostoievsky, and other Slav magnificoes; the hilarious scene in which the tycoon, wholly indifferent to the sex attraction of one of the women, is third-degreed by another as to his evil concupiscent intentions; the dead-pan Negro butler who, when two of the women are supposedly dying of poison, shuffles to the door of the bathroom wherein they are agonizedly giving up their all and calls out: "I want to take this opportunity to thank you ladies for the lovely necktie you gave me"; etc.

In short, save for the inert beginning noted, an amateurish overindulgence in profanity, a Long Island heiress in the acting person of Anne Burr who rather suggests Long Beach, a juvenile in the person of Carl Gose who comports himself in the early portion of the play like Della Fox, and the usually circumspect Stewart Chaney's settings, which suggest a Long Island house considerably less than, in the first act's living-room, a fraternity house at a Midwestern college and, in the second act's bedroom, an annex to the Monte Carlo night club — save for these lapses, which may be overlooked in the interrupting laughter, the exhibit makes for intelligently entertaining playgoing and is a token that the Wunderkind has salvaged his prestige and long-lost cunning.

The laughing success of the show, unlike that of *The Doughgirls,* is unquestionably to be credited in large part to the incorporation into it during the experimental period of situations and gags that were not in the original script. The laughing success of *The Doughgirls* on the other hand is to be credited to the deletion of situations and gags that were in the original script and that during the try-out period were discovered to be so funny that they paradoxically got in the way of other funny gags and situations. Too many laughs are often as bad for a play as too few, since the timing must be spaced lest the effect of one kill another. Eugene O'Neill, as I have recorded in the past, thus found it necessary to blue-pencil fully twenty minutes of grand humor out of *Ah, Wilderness!* not only because it slowed down the action but because it minimized the force of the rest of the humor. In *The Doughgirls,* on a much lower dramatic level, Joseph Fields had to cut out at least half a dozen juicy comic morsels for the same reason, even one that, while the play was being tried out in Washington, had the audience roaring: to wit, a situation wherein two of the loose females discussed the possibility of becoming mothers.

"I could have a baby at the drop of a hat!" declared one.

"Why don't you, then?" ironically retorted the other.

"My husband went to Australia."

"And took his hat with him, I suppose?"

That Negro butler gag, which as delivered by Oscar Polk sets an audience howling, was, I understand, inserted into *Dark Eyes* at the last minute. As some years ago the biggest laugh of its season: to wit, "She comes from one of the first families of Pittsburgh — as you enter the city," was said to have been reworked into a Channing Pollock comedy by the author just one minute before the curtain was due to go up on the first performance.

THE PATRIOTS. January 29, 1943

A dramatic document on the birth of American democracy, by Sidney Kingsley. Winner of the New York Drama Critics' Circle award for 1942–3. Also the Theatre Club, Inc., Prize and the Newspaper Guild's Drama Prize. Produced by the Playwrights' Company in association with Rowland Stebbins.

PROGRAM

CAPTAIN	Byron Russell	NED	George Mitchell
THOMAS JEFFERSON		MAT	Philip White
	Raymond Edward Johnson	JAMES MONROE	Judson Laire
PATSY	Madge Evans	MRS. HAMILTON	Peg La Centra
MARTHA	Frances Reid	HENRY KNOX	Henry Mowbray
DOCTOR	Ross Matthew	MR. FENNO	Roland Alexander
JAMES MADISON	John Souther	JUPITER	Doe Doe Green
ALEXANDER HAMILTON		MRS. CONRAD	Leslie Bingham
	House Jameson	FRONTIERSMAN	John Stephen
GEORGE WASHINGTON		THOMAS JEFFERSON RANDOLPH	
	Cecil Humphreys		Billy Nevard
SERGEANT	Victor Southwick	ANNE RANDOLPH	Hope Lange
COLONEL HUMPHREY		GEORGE WASHINGTON LAFAYETTE	
	Francis Compton		Jack Lloyd
JACOB	Thomas Dillon		

SYNOPSIS: Prologue. *1790. The deck of a schooner.* Act I. *New York — 1790.* Scene 1. *The presidential mansion.* Scene 2. *The smithy of an inn on the outskirts of New York.* Act II. *Philadelphia — 1791–1793.* Scene 1. *Hamilton's home.* Scene 2. *Jefferson's rooms.* Scene 3. *The same, a few days later.* Act III. *Washington — 1800.* Scene 1. *Jefferson's rooms at Conrad's boarding house.* Scene 2. *The interior of the capitol.*

THIS PLAY REPRESENTS almost everything for which I normally have no critical appetite, yet in my opinion it is nevertheless the year's relatively worthiest exhibit. Its disfigurements are numerous, beginning with its very title, which, unlike the instances in which such playwrights as Ashley Dukes and Lennox Robinson have employed it either in the singular or plural to satiric end, in this case

pokes the flag right up our noses. It relies for its final fillip
upon Jefferson's eloquent inaugural address, much as Sherwood relied upon Lincoln's ringing words to excite the
Pulitzer Prize committee into the conviction that Sherwood had probably also ghosted the Gettysburg Address.
It somewhat unwarrantedly by way of theatricalizing the
ideological conflict between Jefferson and Alexander Hamilton makes the latter now and again indistinguishable
from the conventional melodramatic stage villain, and it
at times so stacks the cards that one momentarily expects
Hermann the Great to be revealed as a member of Washington's cabinet. It goes in heavily for my pet aversion:
analogies and parallels between the past and present. Its
dream passage involving Jefferson and his wife is of stage
valentine lace all compact, and its scene wherein Hamilton's
wife learns of his infidelity is pop out of the Henry Arthur
Jones bottle. And it suggests fleetingly the "there's an ugly
rumor about" species of historical drama.

It is all this, and more. Yet so honest is it at bottom, so
unostentatious in its deeper dramatic current, so intelligently handled in general, and so genuinely stirring in its
overtones and after-image that it amounts in sum not only
to the most critically acceptable full-length offering of the
season but to one of the most skillful historical-biographical plays our American theatre has disclosed. If it has its
blemishes, statistical and otherwise, they are to be forgiven
in the play's final driving effect.

Treating of the ten years in Jefferson's life just preceding
his election to the Presidency, the drama concerns itself
with his vision of the true democracy, with the plutocratic
forces arrayed in all sincerity against him, and with his battle to achieve the security of the young nation and its people. With negligible rant, with some gratifying humor, and
with passion brewed from cold intelligence, the play, for
all its red-white-and-blue title, never descends to mere patriotic benzedrine, seldom falters on its dignified course,
and always, save in a rather cinema prologue and some of
that Hamilton business, maintains its inner probity.

Yet though I thus pay my critical respects to the play, it

would be an even more acceptable one to me if Kingsley were not quite so fetched by the noted business of parallels. In this he is, however, not alone. Nothing so surprises and excites an American playwright as his discovery that some celebrated figure of the past entertained views on some subject or other not unlike the present views on the same subject. And nothing so satisfies his Nostradamus complex as to imply from the coincidence that the present views must therefore and accordingly be sound, or at least applaudable. If you were to say to him that it does not in strict logic necessarily follow that, because Jefferson anticipated certain philosophies currently believed in by Sidney Kingsley and George Jean Nathan, Kingsley's and Nathan's concurrence in them not only makes Jefferson something of a clairvoyant phenomenon but justifies Kingsley and Nathan in esteeming themselves minds of the first karat, he would reply that flippancy is the last recourse of a shallowpate. Yet this stratagem of converting the Washingtons, Jeffersons, Franklins, Lincolns, and other such past greats into mere fortune-tellers by way of flattering audiences into an ideological identity with them has become altogether too miscellaneous.

It is an old theatrical saw that one of the highest hurdles an historical-biographical play has to leap is the difficulty of the actors in approximating the looks and physical deportment of the magnificoes under consideration. There is much sarcasm about unruly wigs, padded legs, and the like, along with a general implication that the actors have apparently just stepped out of a Madame Tussaud fire-sale and constitute an affront to the illustrious men they seek to impersonate. That this is sometimes true, I would be the last to deny. But that every now and then the actors pass very well in both looks and deportment for the heroes they depict, I would be the first to affirm. What is more, they often in such cases probably look a lot more like and comport themselves a lot more like the greats than our ill-founded imaginations allow.

That Washington and Jefferson, for example, had just as much trouble keeping their wigs and hair-ribbons straight

as the actors Humphreys and Johnson, who impersonate
them in this play, is doubtless the family fact. That Humphreys actually looks a great deal more like Washington,
and Johnson considerably more like Jefferson, than the
Gilbert Stuart paintings which flattered the former and
the nickel and postage stamp, to say nothing of the famous
Trumbull portrait, which ziegfeld the latter is not hard to
believe. And that both estimable gentlemen frequently
looked and comported themselves less like the historical
matinée idols we have come to think than like maybe Albert Lasker and Bernie Baruch in short breeches, perukes,
and peculiar haberdashery is a good bet for anybody's
money. Although Kingsley's exhibit does not abandon all
the august paralysis in the instance of its personages, it at
least gestures very satisfactorily in that direction. Which is
a credit to his extensive research.

The critical school of which on occasion I have been a
member in high standing will undoubtedly have ready
rebukes for your renegade. They will smilingly banter that
I so contradict myself and my former point of view that
there is no longer any way of telling whether I am standing
on my head or my feet. My answer here can only be my
old answer: that the craft of criticism grows out of contradictions, both self-imposed and otherwise. They will
further argue that patriotism is often the first refuge of a
meagre playwright,.even though in time of war they themselves often not only politely blink the fact but even generally endorse the playwright. Yet the moment the guns
are silenced they have at him again with the old sardonic
recriminations, the old loud cries of hokum. Why is it that
they isolate playwrights in this respect from other artists?
Why don't they, if consistent, I ask them, similarly deride
Verdi for his *Hymn of the Nations,* Tchaikovsky for his
1812, Brahms for his *German Requiem,* Prokofiev for his
Alexander Nevsky, Sibelius for his Finnish testimonials?
Why don't they deride Meissonier for his Napoleon cycle,
or Pradier, Cortot, Rude, and Étex for their Arc de Tri-

omphe de l'Étoile or, above all, Shakespeare for his *Richard II?*

Continuing, these critics will affirm that truly creative dramaturgy consists in independent writing and not in relying for effect upon the recorded eloquence of the past notabilities it may deal with, and there is often, as I have agreed in an earlier chapter, something to be said for their affirmation. But the affirmation may be carried too far, as, for example, in reflections upon creative writing in general by my colleague John Mason Brown in the antecedent season.

Properly taking John Steinbeck to task for falling back upon a sizable quotation from Socrates to give point to an important situation in his *The Moon Is Down,* Mr. Brown had this further to say: "Historians, essayists, preachers, scholars . . . yes, even dramatic critics, are at liberty to call in the classics to help them out. They are not creative writers. But Mr. Steinbeck," etc.

What we engaged here was once again the old arbitrary derogation of certain classes of writers as non-creative and the flattering implication that any other sort of literatus who so much as imagines Gwendolyn St. Clair's reaction to Rupert St. Albans in the moonlight is ipso facto of the creative elect. If ever a definition called for drastic reappraisal and revaluation it is that which concerns itself with this general business. The theory that a dramatist, novelist, or poet, however bad, is deserving of the tribute *creative* and that any other species of writer, however good, belongs down at the end of the line with the plumbers and hod-carriers has too long enjoyed its punditical day. It is time to get rid of it. If the historian Gibbon with his *Decline and Fall,* the essayist Dryden with his *Dramatic Poesy,* the preacher Newman with his *Apologia,* the scholar Hume with his *Human Understanding* . . . yes, even the dramatic critic Hazlitt with his *On Wit and Humor* — if such as these are not creative writers, hair-splitting has assisting need of a new and powerful microscope.

The notion that writers like, say, George Santayana and

Julian Huxley are not creative because they merely invent ideas instead of characters without them is nonsensical in precise ratio to its popularity. It is a peculiar mind that esteems a novel like *Frenchman's Creek* as a work of creation and disesteems something like Hogben's *Mathematics for the Million* as not one. With very few exceptions, we hadn't in America in the year Mr. Brown was writing a single dramatist, novelist, or poet who, when it came to pure creativeness, matched the authentic creativeness — any sound way you looked at it — of even W. T. Stace's *The Destiny of Western Man.* And confining ourselves to relative creativeness in drama and elsewhere, I'll exchange Rice's *American Landscape,* the Barkers' *American Holiday,* George O'Neil's *American Dream,* Robert Middlemass's *Americans All,* George M. Cohan's *American Born,* Dreiser's and Kearney's *An American Tragedy,* Kaufman's and Hart's *The American Way,* and Marcy's and Weiser's *American Dictator,* and throw in a case of beer, for Mencken's *The American Language.*

Finally, and in a slightly different direction, I give you a critical morsel which will undoubtedly impel you sympathetically to rush out with Mr. Kingsley and shoot at least one critic on sight: to wit, the hitherto numbered Burton Rascoe. Thus Mr. Rascoe: *"There would appear to be little excuse for presenting such a play as Mr. Kingsley has contrived at this time unless his intention was that it should be a contribution to the war effort."*

The italics, I hope, are yours.

A BARBER HAD TWO SONS. February 1, 1943

More boom-boom drama by Thomas Duggan and James Hogan, both inmates of Hollywood. Produced by one Jesse Smith, also from out there.

Program

Mrs. Alta Hjalmer *Edit Angold*	Johann Mathieson *Walter Brooke*
Lunke Hjalmer *Walter Soderling*	Major Bowmann *Alfred Zeisler*
"Ma" (Mrs. Mathieson)	Sergeant Brunnemann
Blanche Yurka	*Richard O'Connor*
Hilda *Anita Vengay*	Corporal Heimer *James Darrell*
Rudolph Bjorin Nilsen	Lars Tugar *Wolfgang Zilzer*
J. Arthur Young	Colonel Schmidt *Eddy Fields*
Karen Borson *Tutta Rolf*	Captain Ulmer *James Bass*
Christian Mathieson	Carl Nagel *Fairfax Burgher*
Richard Powers	

SYNOPSIS: Act I. *April 1940.* Act II. *Two years later.* Act III. *The same, later that night.*

Place. *The village of Aalesund.*

The entire action of the play takes place in the barber shop of "Ma" Mathieson.

Hollywood screen artisans who venture into the theatre and are subjected to rough treatment by the critics are given to shrugging their shoulders and saying that the latter arbitrarily have it in for them. Save for the adverb, they are right. And for a good reason. Nine-tenths of them who try their hands at playwriting are, as they constantly prove, of no slightest merit whatsoever. They may now and then conceivably confect a good gag or two, but beyond that polar achievement they customarily show themselves to be hacks suited only to high office in the film industry.

The authors of this spasm are still another case in point. What they have written is a grade-P paraphrase of *The Moon Is Down,* embellished with an act-curtain which they unquestionably believed would knock a New York audience out of its seats: to wit, a Nazi Gestapo officer who, during the occupation of Norway, comes into a barber shop for a shave and, strapped to the chair, unwittingly gives himself into the hands of a razor-wielder whose wife he has seduced. That essentially the same scene, minus only the seduction, figured in the gangster melodrama of the season before, *Brooklyn, U. S. A.*, and did not materially ruffle an audience, they were doubtless too busy writing similar old Grand Guignol junk for the movies to learn.

Leading up to this, their great moment, are two acts loaded to the muzzle with Norwegians who are the epitome of everything high, wide, and handsome and, oppugnantly, Nazis who are the epitome of everything somebody forgot to drop down the sewer. The heroics take the pulpish literary form of "I know that when a man is willing to die for something bigger than himself, he has earned his right to live!" The comedy relief takes the form of the nervous husband who says he is going to have a baby any minute. The melodrama takes the form of dropping murdered Nazis down a trapdoor that leads to the sea, having characters ooze around an upstairs door and eavesdrop the hatching of the loyal Norwegians' plots, and seizing revolvers and shoving the daylights through traitors. And the acting took the form of standing defiantly nose-to-nose with the Nazi villain on the part of the hero, of gazing glass-eyed at the audience and absent-mindedly fondling the hair of her beloved son on the part of the mother-heroine, and of pushing out her left cheek with her tongue to imply her cognizant foxiness on the part of the flirtatious, scheming ingénue.

But it all, mercifully, didn't last long.

COUNTERATTACK. February 3, 1943

Yet more boom-boom, by Janet and Philip Stevenson. Derived from a Russian play by Ilya Vershinin and Mikhail Ruderman. Presented as "A Margaret Webster Production" by Lee Sabinson.

Program

First German Soldier	Philip Pine	Huebsch	John Thomas
Second German Soldier		Stillmann	Martin Wolfson
	Douglas Hubbard	Ernemann	Rudolph Anders
Third German Soldier		Krafft	John Ireland
	Richard Rudi	Kulkov	Morris Carnovsky
German Sergeant	Harold Stone	Kirichenko	Sam Wanamaker
Emma Dahlgren	Barbara O'Neil	Lieutenant Petrov	
Weiler	Richard Basehart		Donald Cameron
Giltzparer	Karl Malden	Barsky	Orin Jannings
Mueller	Richard Sanders	Generalov	Bert Freed

SYNOPSIS: Act I. *Late afternoon.* Act II. *Dawn of the following day.* Act III. *A day later, 6 a.m.*

Scene. *The cellar of a house on the eastern front, autumn, 1942.*

THOSE CRITICS who maintain that plays which do not concern themselves with contemporary events are out of place in our present theatre have certainly been getting their wish's bellyful, and it serves them right. Since it is obviously the war they have in mind, they thus far in the season were ironically brought to eat most of their words (though they made a fine show of concealing their gulps) under the pressure of no less than ten successive war dramas, four war comedies, three plays replete in war analogies, one other overlaid with war embroidery, three musical shows and revues with a war background, several vaudeville shows which intermittently touched on the subject, three sidestreet semi-amateur dispensations that dealt with it, and even one dog act that didn't miss the trick.

This punishment, furthermore, got under nice way in the season just before with thirteen war dramas, ten plays more or less touching either directly or analogically upon the war, three musical shows that did not permit themselves to overlook it, etc., etc.

The answer the critics in point probably make is that their argument is perfectly sound and that the wretched quality of most of the plays does not invalidate it. I regret to believe, however, that it does. Immediate events are most often the property of journalism, not of art. Art, for all the self-ignitionists, is the result of analysis and meditation; journalism is the instantaneous shutter of a camera. The drama of war is mostly like that shutter: the record of the moment, and as evanescent. Only time can touch up the crude picture, bring out its hidden lights and shadows, and lend it some value and beauty and permanence. For one exception, there are a hundred mere transient snapshots. Furthermore, although the remark may seem superficially ill-placed, will not the critics agree that the love of man for woman, the glory of aloof art, the search of mankind for values far above any immediate worldly conflict — will they not agree that such things are every bit as part of contemporary life as the thunder of the war guns? They will, of course, not.

Under the circumstances, I therefore quote to them the words of William Butler Yeats which, set down forty years ago, spoke his attitude on the question of contemporary alarm and propaganda:

"We have to write or find plays that will make the theatre a place of intellectual excitement, a place where the mind goes to be liberated, as it was liberated by the theatres of Greece and England and France at certain great moments in their history. . . . If we are to do this we must learn that beauty and truth are always justified of themselves and that their creation is a greater service to our country than writing that compromises either in the seeming service of a cause. We will doubtless come more easily to truth and beauty because we love some cause with all our heart, but we must remember when truth and beauty open their mouths to speak all other mouths should be silent. Truth and beauty judge and are above judgment. They justify and have no need of justification."

The play under present consideration only added to the discomfiture of those critics who violently disagree with Yeats. A machine-made Grand Guignol melodrama showing a group of Nazis caught in a cellar with two Russian soldiers during a shelling on the eastern front which has blocked the sole exit, it followed the usual pattern of depicting the Nazis as devils incarnate and the Russians as angels of the purest ray. At such times as the Nazis were not spitting out their hateful doctrines and the Russians benignly countering with their bravo-evoking own, the action steadily busied itself with the machinations of the Nazis to get possession of their captors' firearms and to make away with them. At eleven o'clock, just as things looked blackest for the audience's heroes, the Marines duly arrived in the form of a Russian rescue party and the curtain came down on the triumphant singing of the Slav national anthem. All very noble, obviously, but none the less dramatic tripe, a sufficient key to which is to be had in such sample rhetoric as: "After all, human nature is in the hands of mothers. They mustn't be Fascists. With mothers we can make a whole new world, full of love!"

The exhibit, as noted, once again employed that favorite device of imaginatively sterile playwrights: the isolation of a set of characters in quarters from which there is no prospect of immediate escape and the betrayal of their fundamental human emotions and philosophies under the increasing strain. Once in a great while, as in the instance of some play like *The Deluge,* the stencil may be maneuvered into fairly interesting drama. But more regularly all we get is a succession of obstreperous cuckoo-clocks like *Glory, Hallelujah, The Strings, My Lord, Are False, Brother Cain, Cry Havoc,* and this *Counterattack.*

ASK MY FRIEND SANDY. February 4, 1943

A farce-comedy by Stanley Young. Produced by Alfred De Liagre, Jr., and quickly storehoused.

Program

Harold Jackson	*Roland Young*	Mary (Squeegee) O'Donnell
Jane Brennan	*Kay Loring*	*Phyllis Avery*
Minnie Mae	*Anna P. Franklin*	Li *Joseph Tso Shih*
Mrs. Jackson	*Mary Sargent*	Christopher Dickson
Sandy	*Norman Lloyd*	*Franklyn Fox*

SYNOPSIS: Act I. *The present.* Act II. Scene 1. *The following morning.* Scene 2. *Several weeks later.* Act III. *A few hours later.*
Scene. *The New York apartment of Mr. and Mrs. Jackson.*

IT IS ALLEGED that one of the most deplorable aspects of contemporary play-reviewing is its habit of either condemning a presentation outright and with no modifications or eulogizing it to the skies, also with no modifications. Something, in short, is either totally excellent or totally awful. By way of giving some further support to the allegation, which hasn't much basis in fact, let me say, with no reservations whatever, that this farce-comedy of Mr. Young's is totally awful. If it has one redeeming feature, a close two-hour scrutiny of it did not succeed in revealing it to me.

To pass muster, a farce, which the exhibit essentially is meant to be, must, as everyone knows, be possessed of a modicum of human possibility. The greatest playwright living could not contrive an acceptable one based upon the idea that a man with both his legs amputated might win a prize as a champion cross-country runner or that a movie actor might have a mind the equal of Socrates' or of even a Hollywood barrister's. This Young attempt proceeds from an idea so impossibly silly that, even were the playwright a ten times more competent hand than he is, an audience's compliance would be alienated. What that audience is asked to believe is that a highly intelligent book publisher meeting casually with a scatter-brained young soldier is instantaneously persuaded by him to part with every cent he has in the world in order to forestall a possible government confiscation of all property. What it is further asked to accept is the idea that the publisher thereafter finds himself entirely without funds, although he has exchanged part of his fortune for redeemable war bonds, that though he is and has long been a copious and sound drinker he will get so stupidly tipsy on two rye highballs that he will not know what he is doing, and that, finally, he can recoup his fortune through a small book of obviously not more than a hundred pages which becomes a best seller and which, at the normal royalty scale on a dollar-and-a-half book, could not, even if it sold 100,000 copies, bring him more than enough to run his elaborate household for a single year — in addition to which he would have to wait nine months after publication to get most of the money due him.

The general imagination, writing, and staging of the humorless affair were of a piece with its generic scheme. The scene showing the morning-after hangover, that staple of bad farce, was duly in evidence. The pseudo-comical Negro servant girl, the Chinese manservant rocky from the effect of unaccustomed alcoholic liquor, the middle-aged wife with a flirtatious eye for the boys who indignantly packs her bag and leaves her husband after a quarrel, the sympathetic female secretary, the pet dog lugged into the proceedings to evoke an audience's oh-isn't-he-cute, the ancient gag about telephoning out for some Scotch, with someone else ringing the doorbell a second later and the remark: "What service!", the drunk who unsteadily tries to walk a straight line, the brash young hussy named Squeegee with her staccato insults — all also were again set to doing their routine tricks.

Incidentally, the war flavor of the whole, what with the endless talk about Hitler, the Army, the financing of the war, the war's aftermath, the economic aspects of the peace, etc., provided the critics mentioned in the foregoing chapter with still another severe dose of their own contemporary medicine.

FOR YOUR PLEASURE. February 5, 1943

A vaudeville bill [original title Dansation*] cooked up by the dancers Veloz and Yolanda. Produced in the name of George M. Gatts.*

Principals

Veloz and Yolanda *naturellement,* Susan Miller, Jerry Shelton, the Golden Gate Quartet, Bill Gary, Al and Lee Reiser, and Vincent Gomez.

Veloz and Yolanda are a pair of hotel-restaurant and night-club dancers of the ballroom species who, apparently yearning for kudos in a loftier quarter, went out, gathered together the several performers listed above to serve as a stage frame, and thereupon offered their talents to the inspection of the theatre critics, evidently under the impression that men who have hastily wolfed a hamburger and a cup of coffee must inevitably be more astute connoisseurs of the art of the dance than persons who have dined leisurely off a terrine, a consommé, a pheasant, a choice salad, a tutti-frutti pudding, and a bottle of vintage Bollinger. To say nothing of under the supplementary impression that men the majority of whose terpsichorean taste runs firmly to Buck and Bubbles and Ann Pennington and whose idea of the dancing art at its apogee is a swan ballet in a Shubert musical show may possibly provide laudatory notices that will be of great assistance to an artistic career.

Although I surely do not mean to present myself as an exceptional authority on ballroom dancers, I have scrutinized so wholesale a dose of them since the distant era of the Castles and Maurice and Walton that I may perhaps be tolerated as an empirical opinionater. In that capacity it is my notion that this Veloz and Yolanda team is merely of the current average skill, not nearly so good as the De Marcos, that is, if it is Renée and not the present Sally who serves as Tony's partner, yet somewhat better than some of the couples publicized in the floor shows. Veloz looks more like a good, healthy barkeep than the usual plastered black-haired, sallow-cheeked, and emaciated male. Madame Yolanda, on the other hand, with black hair glued to skull, face chalked into a corpse's pallor, mouth aflame with lip rouge, and eyes etched with lamp-black, is in the more regulation sultry, quasi-Latin pattern. The team's specialty, as in the case of most of its ilk, consists in the man's seizing the woman around the waist every few minutes and rapidly twirling her around in the air.

For some reason that I am unable to make out, this elementary and facile business nevertheless seems always to draw enthusiastic applause from an audience, even though the audience has seen it negotiated by dancing couples for the last full thirty-five years. In the same way, and for a reason I similarly can't make out, an audience will invariably applaud a tap dancer who periodically crosses one foot behind the other during his act, a guitar-player who, while strumming the instrument, occasionally drums with his left-hand fingers on the wooden part of same, and a dog act in which the smallest of the canines hops off the stage in an erect position. The tap dancer and the guitar-player duly entered into their respective tricks in this show and were again duly rewarded with the audience's bravos. The tap dancer was a poor copy of Paul Draper, although — despite the finger-drumming business — the guitar-player, Vincent Gomez, proved himself something of a virtuoso.

The bill, which might have provided a serviceable floor show and been fairly acceptable with eight or nine rounds of drinks, was out of place in a theatre and, lacking all humor and lively variety, quickly by reason of its repetitiousness and monotony laid its spectators against the backs of their chairs. Following Al and Lee Reiser, who played two pianos in concert and opened the show, issued forth Veloz and Yolanda in three numbers: "Moonlight Madonna," in which Yolanda, held at some distance by M. Veloz, closed her eyes dreamily and permitted herself some languid swaying around the stage; "Darktown Strutters' Ball," in which the couple in evening dress capered the old coonshow standby; and "Carnival," which they announced was their impression of two people who had just stepped off a prolonged merry-go-round ride. Bill Gary, the before-mentioned tap dancer, next obliged, with set grin. He was succeeded by Gomez, the guitarist, and again out glided Veloz and Yolanda for three more numbers: "Caprice," which like their first three numbers consisted mainly in Yolanda being swung around in the air; a Rhumba, or more accurately Son, too familiar to call for description; and something called "Dance of Mistakes," in which M. Veloz coyly pretended to be unable to dance and in which Yolanda guided him out of his errors.

Now a quartet of Negroes clustered around a microphone and harmonized a pair of songs about Adam and his rib and a number which, they confided, they had composed especially for the occasion. Its title, "Stalin Wasn't Stallin'." And then again Veloz and Yolanda in a familiar Mexican folk dance, the audience being instructed, as per custom, to clap its hands in accompaniment upon M. Veloz's signals.

After an intermission, during which a third of the opening-night customers went home, the Reiser boys proceeded to bang at the two pianos anew; the tap dancer tapped out a gypsy and a Spanish number which were largely indistinguishable from his first number, which was neither gypsy nor Spanish; and then yet again Veloz and Yolanda in three numbers: "The Blue Danube," heaven spare us!; the "Maxixe," which one thought had gone out with Reisenweber's; and a travesty of the minuet, which one thought had gone out with Francis Wilson in the time of *Erminie*. Susan Miller followed with several popular songs, but unfortunately permitted herself to sing them into a mike amplifier which gave her otherwise agreeable voice the sound of an auctioneer selling a foghorn. Then one Jerry Shelton, who manipulated an accordion. And then, for a finale, Veloz and Yolanda in *four* numbers: "Three Easy Lessons" (the title provides a sufficient clue to the heavy attempt at humor); "Alexander's Ragtime Band," a dance number which one thought had gone out with Bustanoby's Domino Room; and a Samba and a Tango, both in the floor-show tradition. And, of course, the twirls in the air.

THE MOON VINE. February 11, 1943

A Dixie cup by Patricia Coleman. Produced by Jack Kirkland, who made all that money out of Tobacco Road.

Program

Mrs. Meade ("Miss Eloise")		Zack Meade	Richard Tyler
	Vera Allen	Mattie	Ruth Anderson
Strother Meade	Grace Coppin	Ovid Carter	Philip Bourneuf
Miss Lucy Telfair		Mariah Meade	Haila Stoddard
("Aunt Lullah")		Ellen Hatfield	Mary Lou Taylor
	Kate McComb	Danny Hatfield	Arthur Franz
Mrs. Sylvaine ("Miss Bessie")		Porter	Robert Crawley
	Agnes Scott Yost	Fane	Michael Road
Larkin	Robert W. Albury	Andre	Youl Bryner
Drop Dead	Drop Dead	Brother Walt Littlejohn	
Miss Francie Taylor	Phyllis Tyler		A. Winfield Hoeny
Uncle Yancey Sylvaine		Rev. Dr. Randolph Hatfield	
	Will Geer		John McKee

SYNOPSIS: Act I. *The side veranda, late afternoon.* Act II. Scene 1. *The same, two weeks later, early evening.* Scene 2. *A section of the revival tent, the following night.* Act III. *Same as Act I, two weeks later, late afternoon.*

Place. *The Meade house, Mansfield, Louisiana.*
Time. *June 1905.*

THE one and only mitigating attribute of this exhibit was the presence in its case of Miss Haila Stoddard, in private life the wife of Mr. Kirkland, the producer. Not by virtue of any considerable histrionic virtuosity on her part, but because in both look and manner she wistfully reminded almost every other man in the audience of all the six or seven first girls he was in love with in his boyhood. Miss Coleman, the playwright of the evening, on the other hand only reminded the men of the less wistful fact that, when it comes to plays about Dixie, whether the Dixie of actors in costume or of a later day, no really good one seems yet to have been written for our stage. (If you wish to come up with *Uncle Tom's Cabin,* that's your fault.)

Writing to the hereinbefore embalmed Burton Rascoe, temporarily substituting as the *World-Telegram's* connoisseur of dramatic art for John Mason Brown, who is in war service, one James Street, author of several novels about the South, had this to say: "When will some of your learned brethren learn that a book or play about Southern whites can be quite authentic without mansions that look like a state capitol, peopled by woolly-haired old retainers, ladies in crinoline who talk about 'damyanks' in a Southern accent never before heard on land or sea, colonels who look like old posters of Bill Cody, and tall young men who kiss ladies' hands every five minutes?"

Instead of reflecting upon the learned brethren, Mr. Street, if he had only waited to send in his communiqué a day later, might better specifically have asked the question of Miss Coleman, since her play includes the house, if smaller, with the white porch columns, the ladies who talk about the "damyanks" in a Southern accent never before heard on land or sea, the character who looks like an old poster of Bill Cody, and at least one tall young man who enters into the hand-kissing business. It also includes the regulation profuse flowers and blooming vines on the porch columns, the still smouldering feeling about the Civil War, the coy and fluttering Southern maidens, and many of the other routine appurtenances of drama of the species. It is further written in such a mixture of moods — farcical, straight comedy, dramatic, melodramatic, and tragic — that it is next to impossible to figure out its author's dramaturgical intention, although it is easy to figure out that she knows nothing of dramatic construction. And it was still further so confusedly directed by Mr. John Cromwell that one didn't know whether one was supposed to laugh at the characters or cry one's heart out over them.

To make bad matters worse, there was the plot, and a lot of it. A Dixie belle at the turn of the century finds herself engaged to a missionary in Australia whom she doesn't love, meets a young actor from a stranded *Ten Nights in a Barroom* troupe whom she loves at first sight, concocts a letter announcing that her missionary fiancé and his entire retinue have died of the plague, thereupon learns that the young actor has been in a New Orleans fancy house playing the balcony scene from *Romeo and Juliet* with one of the inmates (who is an authority on Shakespeare), during which recital an important Louisiana political figure has been murdered, gets caught with the young actor in a mutual web of lies, hears the young actor confess at a revival meeting that he was in the sporting house at the time of the murder, lets on that she is no longer in love with him, and otherwise does all kinds of things, including a monologue about playing some day with E. H. Sothern in Julia Marlowe's place (she is stage-struck) and a soft-shoe dance, until she and the young ham make up and run away to get married and join a Cincinnati, Ohio, stock company.

The before-mentioned Mr. Rascoe nevertheless proclaimed that the chowder "has every bit as much psychological depth and realistic differentiations of character as have Chekhov's *The Cherry Orchard* or *The Three Sisters.*" It is this same Mr. Rascoe who further entertained the town no end with his indignations over his elders' reactions to the Cajuns as revealed in *The Great Big Doorstep*. The Cajuns, he stoutly affirmed, are none of them the people his elders described. They are, he declared, to the contrary "if anything prettier, handsomer, cleaner, neater, tidier than the play represented them." All Cajun ditchdiggers invariably "require a clean shirt every day." All the Cajuns "have beautiful, even teeth." They all dress up in "lovely and colorful dresses" and they all "have beautiful hair-does." Etc. In other words, not the beggarly folk at least one of his elders, in company with the late Sherwood Anderson, found them in their habitat to be, but just a whole lot of Vanderbilts.

THIS ROCK. February 18, 1943

The boom-boom drama again, this time by Walter Livingston Faust. Produced for no good reason, and badly, by the hitherto meritorious Eddie Dowling.

Program

CHILDREN: Suzanne Johnson, Lois Volkman, Joyce Van Patten, Buddy Millard, Dickie Millard, Harlan Stone.

DANNIE	Walter Kelly
MARY	Joan Patsy Flicker
JOANNIE	Joan Shepard
DOUGLAS MACMASTERS	Zachary Scott
JOHNNY MACMASTERS	Alastair Kyle
PATTON	Roland Hogue
MARGARET STANLEY	Jane Sterling
CECILY STANLEY	Billie Burke
MALCOLM STANLEY	Nicholas Joy
ROBERT DUNCAN	Everett Ripley
CUTHIE	Ethel Morrison
ANGUS	Malcolm Dunn
MR. HIGGINS	John Farrell
MR. HARLEY	Gene Lyons
MRS. PROUDIE	Mabel Taylor
MR. PROUDIE	Victor Beecroft
LITTLE DAISY	Lorna Lynn
LITTLE 'ARRY	Gerald Matthews

SYNOPSIS: The action of the play takes place in a room in the Stanley home on the River Tyne, England. Act I. Scene 1. An early evening, October 1939. Scene 2. The same, Christmas eve, 1939. Act II. The same, an April afternoon, 1941. Act III. The same, a late summer afternoon, 1942.

MULTIPLY THE CHARACTER of Peg o' My Heart by ten, introduce the ten assorted brats into the same kind of rural English household, lay the time during the Nazi air blitz, go on from there, and you have *This Rock,* only in this instance you have it not ten but fifty times worse than the old Hartley Manners play. Peg — in this case the ten poor youngsters from the East End of London who have been evacuated to one of Watson Barratt's high-toned interior sets peopled by women who change from one elaborate Valentina frock to another at the height of the bombing and are waited on by a super-Manners butler — is hostilely accepted at the beginning but gradually through her arch and winning ways worms herself into her opulent benefactors' hearts, as per Manners, aye Fauntleroy, schedule.

Mixed up into all of this is the John Howard Lawson young male character who snarls about class distinctions, spits in the rich young Lawson heroine's eye, and, following the Lawson principle, of course thus naturally in the end so captivates her that she marries him. This, Mr. Faust apparently believes, is a notable contribution to the science of sociology.

The writing throughout is an amalgam of purple plush and small-time vaudeville. The old gardener (he has been with the family for four generations) comes in when the garden has been bombed and delivers himself of this sample: "Ah, Mum, 'twas one of the oldest gardens in all of England, but it doesn't matter. Flowers can be replaced. But if it had hit the house 'twould have taken flowers only God could replace." "Dear old Angus!" thereupon shortly afterward exclaims one of the household; "I don't know what we would do without him!" As for the vaudeville odor, the brash East End father of one of the children, several times commanded to take his hat off in the drawing-room, each time obediently removes it and then immediately claps it onto his head again. And as for the movie flavor — it is there in extra-heavy measure — the final curtain duly comes down on the embrace of the young lovers with three of the other characters pleasedly peering around the corner of the door and with the grinning little boy ejaculating "Cripes!" The whole is stuffed further with copious tributes to the invincibility of dear old England, the contemporary practice of Americans who once stayed at the Savoy for a few days and had the honor of meeting Lord Moochbanks and lending him ten dollars.

Every once in a while some business man, otherwise a commendable figure in the community, feels it incumbent upon him, by way of proving to the world that his soul aspires to loftier heights, to write a play. Yet though the records reveal the productions of numerous such opera they do not reveal one that has been any good — and why should they? To ask of some such business man as this Mr. Faust, who is vice president of a big and successful petroleum company, that he should also and at the same time be a competent playwright would be like asking me, in addition to my present job, to be a competent vice president of a big and successful petroleum company. Beside my achievement in any such office Mr. Faust's play, dreadful as it is, would take on the relative quality of *Hamlet*. The petroleum business is just as respectable in its way as the theatre. Let Mr. Faust and others like him who yearn to be O'Neills or even Sam Shipmans ponder the fact.

Yet it is doubtful if they will. And the inevitable, understandable, and under the circumstances even forgivable result will be still more grossly amateur concoctions of this species and of the species that one of the banking Rothschilds contributed to the Paris stage, that such oil men as Davis wrote in *The Ladder*, that such brewery executives as Edwin B. Self wrote in *The Distant City*, and that other men successful on the Stock Exchange, in the glue-factory business, the manufacture of ladies' underwear and bathroom fixtures, and even the law have written in a wide variety of plays like *Wall Street* and *His Name on the Door*.

HARRIET. MARCH 3, 1943

A biographical flageolet, the author of Uncle Tom's Cabin *its subject, by Florence Ryerson and Colin Clements. Produced, no new English war testimonial apparently being available at the moment, by Gilbert Miller.*

PROGRAM

AUNTIE ZEB	*Alberta Perkins*	DR. LYMAN BEECHER	
HENRY WARD BEECHER			*Robert Harrison*
	Sydney Smith	MR. TUTTLE	*Harrison Dowd*
CATHARINE BEECHER	*Jane Seymour*	MR. WYCHERLY	*Victor Franz*
HARRIET BEECHER STOWE		CELESTINE	*Mildred Taswell*
	Helen Hayes	MRS. HOBBS	*Helen Carew*
CALVIN STOWE	*Rhys Williams*	FREDDIE STOWE	*Jack Manning*
WILLIAM BEECHER	*Guy Sorel*	GEORGIE STOWE	*Joan Tetzel*
EDWARD BEECHER	*Geoffrey Lumb*	HATTY STOWE	*Betty Wade*
MARY BEECHER PERKINS		ELIZA STOWE	*Lenore Wade*
	Carmen Mathews	JERUSHA PANTRY	*Seth Arnold*
CHARLES BEECHER	*Hugh Franklin*	LOWELL DENTON	
THOMAS BEECHER	*Gaylord Mason*		*William Woodson*
ISABELLA BEECHER		SUKEY	*Edna Thomas*
	Harda Klaveness	HALEY	*Benedict MacQuarrie*
JAMES BEECHER	*Ronald Reiss*		

SYNOPSIS: Act I. *Cincinnati, Ohio — the 1830's and 1840's.* Scene 1. *The Stowe cottage, January, 1836.* Scene 2. *Some years later, July.* Act II. *Brunswick, Maine — the 1850's.* Scene 1. *The Stowe house, more years have passed.* Scene 2. *The following December.* Scene 3. *Some months later.* Act III. *Andover, Massachusetts — the 1860's.* Scene 1. *The Stowe mansion, April 1861.* Scene 2. *July 1863.* Scene 3. *Two weeks later.*

THE AUTHORS are a team of Hollywood literati whose directly previous contribution to dramatic glory was a delicacy about a ravishingly handsome movie actor called *Glamour Preferred.* It was just what you guess it was and it was junked, by public demand, after eleven performances. Their latest contribution, treating of the life and times of Harriet Beecher Stowe, is similarly just what you guess it is, which is high-school biographical drama, but since the box-office favorite Helen Hayes occupied the stellar role its success was infinitely greater.

The general dramaturgical complexion of the play may be gleaned, first, from such warmed-over humorous cold-cuts as the young Stowe daughter feigning a sprained ankle by way of getting her young swain's arms about her, the swain unable to tell the Stowe twins apart and persistently calling them by the wrong names, Calvin Stowe atop a ladder and decorating a Christmas tree loftily allowing that he is fully sufficient unto the job and thereupon promptly dropping everything in his hands, the articulation of the word "leg" and the quick hushing of it in favor of "limb," and such period jocosities as "You shouldn't play rough games like croquet."

Secondly, the dramatic ingenuity may be appreciated from such devices as the old female Negro fugitive kneeling before Harriet and tearfully beseeching her to intercede for her, the while the bebooted slave-trader stands to one side snarling his sneers; Harriet seated at a desk and writing with rapt intensity amidst the household's turmoil; Harriet, her entranced family gathered about her, reading aloud from her finished book; gushing references on the part of the family to the laudatory letters sent to her by Dickens and Thackeray; Calvin Stowe's burlesque absent-mindedness, which takes such forms as removing his slipper and putting it into his pocket; the cook's howling indignation when one of the Beechers messes around in the kitchen and her packing up in a huff to leave; and Harriet at the final curtain backed by American flags and addressing the assembled populace with irrelevant rhetoric in denunciation of tyrants.

Thirdly, the biographical value of the contraption may be measured by the conversion of Henry Ward Beecher into a comic-strip granpappy, of the witty Calvin Stowe into an addle-pated oaf, and of Harriet herself into little more, despite her occasional abolitionist outbursts, than a Maggie Wylie playing a decrepit paraphrase of *What Every Woman Knows* to her husband Calvin's John Shand.

It was generally agreed by the reviewers, who never saw

Harriet Beecher Stowe, that Helen Hayes looked and comported herself like her to the life. Maybe she did, maybe she didn't; I wouldn't know since, like the reviewers who were positive in the matter, I never laid eyes on Harriet either. Miss Hayes gave a performance which persuaded me, for right or wrong, that her physical portrayal was accurate, so that is all that mattered so far as I was concerned. As I have intimated in connection with *The Patriots,* this whole business of stage portraiture of famous figures of the past is frequently fraught with critical sophistry. Let some actor appear as, say, Stephen A. Douglas or some actress as, say, Nancy Hanks, and a corps of pundits are sure to arise and loudly protest that neither looks in the least like what either of the celebrities looks like in the pundits' purely conjectural imagination. While perfectly satisfied to accept as exact likenesses the heroes and heroines of classic Greek historical drama and the kings, queens, and princes of Shakespearean chronicle drama, the pundits belabor the air if some figure closer to the present is played by an actor who so much as weighs ten pounds less than the figure or by an actress whose hair is a shade redder or browner or what not. Such double-entry critical book-keeping must occasionally lead to subsequent self-embarrassment, as in the case of Wolcott Gibbs, who in his appraisal of *The Patriots* delivered himself thus: "A modern actor almost invariably looks jocose when made up to represent a celebrated figure out of the past. The darky butler comes in and announces 'General George Washington,' but what enters is just a man of customary stature," etc. For the fact is that what enters is an actor (Cecil Humphreys) who, far from being a man of the customary stature, is to the very quarter-inch the recorded considerable altitude of Washington.

Far from looking invariably jocose in the roles of celebrated historical figures, modern actors four times out of five picture them very satisfactorily. Any number of actors from the hams in the old Hal Reid drama to Frank McGlynn in the Drinkwater and Raymond Massey in the Sherwood have looked as much like Lincoln as Lincoln himself. Arliss's Disraeli, Berton Churchill's President Harding,

Albert Phillips' General Grant, William Corbett's Robert
E. Lee, Helen Hayes's Queen Victoria, Thais Lawton's
Queen Elizabeth, Maurice Evans's Napoleon, Edward
Trevor's Lafayette, Charles Trexler's Byron — all kinds of
such actors and actresses, good, bad, and even here and
there pretty terrible, have notwithstanding realistically re-
suscitated the dead.

In short, the belief that, when an actor in the majority
of cases comes out on a stage in the guise of an illustrious
personage of yesterday, the audience starts derisively laughing its head off remains largely a critic-fostered legend. The
truth is that it is not actual persons who are difficult of histrionic portrayal but, paradoxically, purely fanciful ones.
Although actors and actresses have sufficiently pictured
everyone from Oliver Cromwell to Teddy Roosevelt and
from Nell Gwyn to Carry Nation, there has not been one
who has managed even remotely to suggest such creatures
of the imagination as, among numerous others, Maeter-
linck's Lancéor or Rostand's far-away princess Melissinde.

This *Harriet* once again and furthermore proves that
fine plays, contrary to the popular opinion, are not and seldom have been the prime essential of and greatest contribution to an important histrionic career. It is often rubbish
that has elevated an actor or actress to eminence in the profession. *Camille* has done more for certain actresses than
any of the considerably more worthy plays they have appeared in, as has such unholy claptrap as *David Garrick,
The Bells,* and *The Corsican Brothers* for certain male
idols. Bernhardt and Duse built their careers largely on
second- and third-rate drama; Irving, Tree, and the elder
Guitry ditto. And so in the case of many others.

Miss Hayes, who occupies a foremost position among our
American actresses, has surely not attained to that kudos
by virtue of the consistent quality of her plays. For one
reputable one like *Cæsar and Cleopatra* or even *Victoria
Regina* she has appeared in at least half a dozen like *Ladies
and Gentlemen, Petticoat Influence, The Good Fairy, Coquette, Mr. Gilhooley,* and *Young Blood.* For one actor
like Maurice Evans who has made name and fame princi-

pally out of Shakespeare, you will have small difficulty in finding another like, say, David Warfield who had them removing the horses and pulling his carriage uptown on the score of his performances in such ghastly flubdub as *The Auctioneer, The Music Master, The Return of Peter Grimm,* and *A Grand Army Man.*

MEN IN SHADOW. March 10, 1943

Again, a war melodrama, this number by Mary Hayley Bell. Produced by Max Gordon.

Program

Moy	*Joseph De Santis*	Lew	*Roy Hargrave*
German Captain		Mordan	*Dean Harens*
	Peter von Zerneck	Enshaw	*Ernest Graves*
German Lieutenant	*Peter Knego*	German Sergeant	*Martin Brandt*
Cherie	*Michelette Burani*	German Corporal	
Kenny	*Everett Sloane*		*Michael Ingram*
Polly	*Francis De Sales*	German Soldier	*Wesley Adams*

SYNOPSIS: Act I. *Wednesday, late afternoon.* Act II. *Thursday night, around 11.30.* Act III. *Friday morning, dawn.*

The entire action of the play takes place in the loft of an old, unused mill, adjoining a farmhouse somewhere on the French coast.

The time is the present.

OUTSIDE THE THEATRE the lofts of old, unused mills are simply the lofts of old, unused mills, tenanted solely by spiders, rats, and an occasional hoot-owl. In the theatre, however, the lofts of old, unused mills peculiarly take on a volume of human activity that often makes them kin to Times Square on election night. If it isn't a gang of counterfeiters who have quarters there, it is either real or spurious ghosts, and if it isn't ghosts it is likely to be an old miser stalked by a posse of greedy relatives, including a nephew who has fallen under the influence of a trio of scheming crooks from the city. In war time it is spies or fugitives of one sort or another. In this particular loft of an old, unused mill it is, accordingly, not only spies and fugitives but, inclusively, French peasant underground agents, American and British saboteurs, grounded Allied aviators, a French female handy at surgery, and assorted Nazi snoopers, among them a Gestapo chief. Only the Tiller girls are missing.

Of English origin, the exhibit, at least in its Americanized form by Joseph Fields, meets every fondest desire of rough-tough melodrama addicts save adept melodramatic playwriting. The beautiful elementals are all present, and in abundance: the broken, bleeding legs of a crashed flier are set in full view of the audience, and to the accompaniment of appropriate howls of anguish on the part of the victim; the American saboteur jiu-jitsus the Gestapo bully to the floor, twists his arm until it cracks in two, and then for good measure breaks his spine to the accompaniment of a concealed sound-device which gives off a realistic loud click-snap; a Nazi officer has a long knife ground into his back up to the hilt; the American saboteur seizes a rope, swings himself with knife held aloft over a staircase, drops upon a Nazi mounting the stairs, and plunges the blade deep into him; and more. But the gaps between these fetching delicatessen are filled with so much idle, time-killing talk that when the big moments come a great deal of their effect goes for little.

What the author further has not learned in the way of such Grand Guignol horror stuff is that it cannot prosperously be stretched over too great a space of time. Max Maurey and his Guignol playwrights appreciated that horror is most impressive when dealt out in a small, compact dose and that, if it be unduly piled upon itself, not only is the effect diminished but an audience's unwelcome levity frequently the result. So far as I know — and I attended no less than seventy or eighty such exhibits during the long life of the famous little theatre up the Paris alley — the most successful specimens of the art were regularly in the form of one-act or at most two-very-short-act plays, never under any circumstances full three-acters. And it was thus that such affecting spectacles as the pouring of vitriol drop by drop on a faithless mistress's or amorous interloper's face, the infecting of an enemy water-supply with cholera-morbus germs, or the driving of a villain insane by strapping him to a chair and slowly dripping water on his head so worked up the audiences' hysteria that for some years medical assistance was held in readiness in the lobby.

In *Men in Shadow* the repetition of horrors induces the

same reaction as a revolver several times suddenly shot off behind one. The first time you jump; the second time you only twitch; the third time you laugh.

The general writing of the play, as intimated, contributes further to the diminution of proper melodramatic response. The stencils crowd each other: I-know-I've-seen-you-somewhere-before-but-where?,   Remember-that-little-Danish-girl-we-had-together-in-Shanghai?,   But-what's-in-the-*back*-of-that-wallet?,   *Now*-I-remember-I-saw-you-at-the-German-Legation-in-Hongkong!,   The-Nazis-are-due-here-any-minute-now!, etc. And all orchestrated to the inevitable bombing planes, whistling signals in the dead of night, tread of enemy soldiers without, and periodically doused lights.

In the end all the heroes escape through a trapdoor in the roof of the old, unused mill, theoretically making good their get-away though the mill at the moment happens to be completely surrounded by a regiment of Germans.

KISS AND TELL. March 17, 1943

Another one about adolescents, by F. Hugh Herbert. Produced by George Abbott.

Program

Mr. Willard	*James Lane*	Lieut. Lenny Archer	
Louise	*Frances Bavier*		*Richard Widmark*
Corliss Archer	*Joan Caulfield*	Mary Franklin	*Paula Trueman*
Raymond Pringle	*Tommy Lewis*	Bill Franklin	*Calvin Thomas*
Mildred Pringle	*Judith Parrish*	Dorothy Pringle	
Dexter Franklin	*Robert White*		*Lulu Mae Hubbard*
Janet Archer	*Jessie Royce Landis*	Uncle George	*Walter Davis*
Harry Archer	*Robert Keith*	Robert Pringle	*Robert Lynn*
Private Earhart	*John Harvey*		

SYNOPSIS: Act I. Scene 1. *About five in the afternoon on a summer's day.* Scene 2. *An hour and a half later.* Act II. Scene 1. *Late afternoon of the next day.* Scene 2. *Saturday morning, two months later.* Act III. *Several hours later.*

The entire action of the play takes place on the back porch of the Archers' home.

THIS PRESENTATION REPRESENTS the other of the two strings to Producer Abbott's bow. The first, as hereinbefore indicated, is the farce about the trio furiously bent on achieving something or other. The second is the minnow-drama, or the play about youngsters. *Kiss and Tell,* like Abbott's previous *Brother Rat* and *What a Life!,* to say nothing of his musicals like *Too Many Girls* and *Best Foot Forward,* thus expresses again his fondness for theatrical versions of the old *Our Gang* film comedies. Although the output of a writer who has consecrated himself to the crocheting of Hollywood movie scenarios and radio plays, it is curiously not without its periods of acceptable light amusement and even occasionally suggests that its author has in his career surprisingly observed other children than Mickey Rooney, Freddie Bartholomew, Jane Withers, Gloria Jean, and the counterfeit kind.

Critically a weak distillation of Booth Tarkington, the play manages its entertainment not in terms of sound character-drawing, wherein it is frequently overstrained and bogus, but rather in its dialogic turns, some of which, despite the mouths they are placed in, are very funny. Having to do with a fifteen-year-old female household-wrecker, or chicken-pox, whose culminating contribution to the household's agony is a confession that she is with child (she is shielding the secret marriage of a girl friend whom she has been accompanying to an obstetrician), the action involves a Montague-Capulet feud between the two neighboring families and further does not overlook the opportunity once again to dress up its juveniles in soldiers' uniforms by way of persuading the audience that it is thoroughly contemporary. The characters, as intimated, are largely the stock figures: the flapper pretending she is considerably older than she is to impress the veteran of twenty-four on whom she has a sudden crush; the small boy given to a superior attitude toward life and his elders, and expressing it in hypothetically humorous polysyllables; the father who is seized with histrionic apoplexy whenever things happen to annoy him; the contrasting wise, patient, and tolerant mother; the dumb, red-headed gawk of a boy from next door whose sole repartee is "Holy cow!" etc. Nor is all the humor of a piece; it sometimes descends to such levels as an attempt to brew comedy from naming a dog Marmaduke, the distressed avowal of a young miss that she thinks she'll enter a monastery, and the articulation of *fragrant* where *flagrant* was intended. And while the comic melodrama culled from the chicken-pox's artless admission that she is enceinte is momentarily amusing, it misses by virtue of blacksmith writing the considerably more sustained amusement negotiated in a fundamentally similar dramaturgical situation by André Birabeau in his *Dame Nature,* shown locally several seasons ago.

In short, a successful Broadway box-office show not without some humorous merit, but less an authentic comedy of youngsterhood than an artfully maneuvered comic strip.

In an earlier chapter I animadverted on the usual play-

ers of adolescent roles and allowed that I preferred them
to be played not by the over-bubbling pop bottles who customarily play them but by boys and girls somewhat older
who, directors here and there notwithstanding, might
bring some little critical discernment to their interpretation. I see no reason to contradict myself in the case of
Joan Caulfield, who has the role of the fifteen-year-old in
this exhibit and who, with Mr. Abbott's help, contributes
to it a first-rate, intelligent performance. Miss Caulfield, I
am informed, is no fifteen-year-old but happily in her twen-
ties, as is the married Gwen Anderson of *Janie* and as was
the married Mary Anderson of last season's *Guest in the
House*. (Don't forget such wonderful kids of the past as the
completely adult Maude Adams of *Peter Pan*, Marguerite
Clark of *Prunella*, Anna Laughlin of *The Wizard of Oz*,
and the like, and, above all, the forty-year-old famous
Lotta as the Little Nell of *The Old Curiosity Shop*.) The
droll little fat boy, Tommy Lewis, who here repeats the
comical impression he made in *All in Favor* the season before, is, like the two small youngsters mentioned in a foregoing chapter, an exception to the theory I have often
shared with H. L. Mencken: that the general run of child
actors should be painted on the scenery and their lines read
from behind the scenes by someone like Alfred Lunt or
Billie Burke.

THE PLAYBOY OF NEWARK. MARCH 19, 1943

A comedy by Ben K. Simkhovitch. Produced down in the old Provincetown Playhouse by the American Actors' Company.

PROGRAM

SAM DUPREE	*Dwight Marfield*	HELEN DUPREE	*Peggy Meredith*
EDDIE VENUTTI	*Tony Manino*	ELLA HAYROTH	*Jane Ross*
MINERVA DUPREE	*Donna Keath*	BANCROFT BINKS	*Russell Collins*
GEORGE UPTON	*Ad Karns*	ILOMAY PIERSON	*Lillian Little*
LINKS BINKS	*Will Hare*	JAN	*Norman Brown*

SYNOPSIS: *The Dupree house situated along the railroad tracks in Huntington, L. I. Time. Autumn, 1940. Act I. A morning in September. Act II. Late afternoon, three weeks later. Act III. Morning, next day.*

Another RANDOM EXAMPLE of the activities of the amateur experimental groups, it re-established the lamentable fact that these present groups are a far cry from those which a score and more years ago contributed so handsomely to the advancement of the American stage and its drama. The plays they put on are generally either plays that the Broadway producers have wisely rejected as being worthless or plays written by hopeless amateurs hopeful of bringing them to the attention of the aforesaid producers, who shrewdly never go around to see them and who, if they did, would even more wisely have nothing further to do with them. So far as true experiment goes, the current gestures of the groups amount to little more than a finding out for themselves that a play is not necessarily and inevitably a meritorious one simply because it has been turned down by five or six professional theatre men.

The Playboy of Newark, which was held for a time by various such producers and in turn abandoned by them, is a case in point. In it the author gives evidence that he has either seen too many plays of other writers or too few. That he has seen too many appears from the circumstance that

he has absorbed, among other things, the central character of Erskine Caldwell's *Journeyman,* the philosophy of
Evreinoff's *The Chief Thing,* the holy hokum of Jerome's
The Passing of the Third Floor Back, the bawdiness of
Robert Buckner's and Walter Hart's *The Primrose Path,*
and the romantic optimism of Saroyan's *Love's Old Sweet
Song.* That he has seen too few is on the other hand to be
suspected from the circumstance that he appears to believe
he has been the first to think up all of these. His play, as
a result and furthered by dramaturgic incompetence, presents the aspect of a cracked mosaic.

APOLOGY. March 22, 1943

A little number by Charles Schnee. Produced by Lee Stras-berg.

Program

The Lecturer	*Elissa Landi*	Laura	*Thelma Schnee*
Albert Warner		Bingham	*James Todd*
	Theodore Newton	Janitor	*Harold J. Stone*
Florrie	*Thelma Schnee*	Mr. Downing	*Clay Clement*
Paul Vannon	*Ben Smith*	Shoplifter	*Merle Maddern*
Fortune Teller	*Harold J. Stone*	Manny	*Lewis Charles*
Fraulein	*Merle Maddern*	Lester Ballantine	*James Todd*
William McCready	*Ben Smith*	Evelyn	*Peggy Allardice*
Betty	*Erin O'Brien-Moore*	Weber	*Robert Simon*
Mr. Warner	*Clay Clement*	E. B.	*Clay Clement*

Mr. Schnee is still another novice playwright apparently determined, come hell or high water, to be novel. His conception of novelty, however, suffers seriously from stage statistics. He may not have known it, but his play is technically little more than a paraphrase of Thornton Wilder's *Our Town,* which in turn was technically little more than a paraphrase of Andreyev's *The Life of Man,* which in further turn was technically little more than the old morality *Everyman.* All he has done is to convert Wilder's male commentator into a female, to add a few touches from Wilder's *The Skin of Our Teeth,* and then to write forty or fifty times less ably than Wilder.

In the way of dramatic induction he is even less original. After his commentator has opened up things by talking aimlessly for twenty-odd minutes about the origin of species and throwing some screwy lantern slides on the wall illustrating nothing in particular, he introduces, as German comedy-writers of thirty years ago and as Italian playwrights have since done, his actors in propria persona and then sets them to playing his characters. His ensuing plot is still less novel, since it deals, in the character of a man willing to sacrifice everything for success and finding eventual apology and solace only in God (here peculiarly symbolized by enlistment in the armed forces), with our ancient thematic friend: mankind's eternal search for the answer to life's mystery and the reason for its existence. And his production devices are yet more familiar, relying as they do upon lights, shadows, stereopticon slides, and small sliding platforms containing a table, a chair, or a papier-mâché rock to embroider his otherwise bare stage.

Mr. Schnee further seems to be persuaded that drama may be written not so much with a pen as with a migratory baby spotlight. When the baby spotlight accordingly isn't in action, which is rarely, his personal contribution to dramatic literature consists chiefly in causing his commentator to step to the footlights, pontifically to inquire: "What is Truth?" and thereupon to indulge in a succession of women's-club addresses on the Persian Empire, Napoleon Bonaparte, etc., that have no slightest connection with the feeler.

Every once in so often a playwright like Mr. Schnee or a producer like Mr. Strasberg concludes that the public is fed up on plays like *Life with Father* and such, which nevertheless have a stubborn way of running on and on and making all kinds of money, and would enthusiastically welcome something in the way of a novelty. A novelty, to both their minds, is not a play of unusual imagination, profound philosophy, beautiful prose, or anything else of that sort, but rather something of a merely freakish theatrical nature. And the consequence of their conclusion is hence a series of exhibits that most often have nothing more to recommend them than a two-headed cow or a bearded lady has to recommend it or her, in turn, to the circus trade.

Although an occasional freak play may find favor with the public, the records prove overwhelmingly that it is the more conventional species of drama that finds itself in the chips. The list of the greatest popular successes in the modern American theatre includes potentially only one single solitary play that may be termed a novelty in the sense that the playwright and producers in point customarily use the word: to wit, Wilder's before-mentioned *The Skin of Our Teeth*. *The Green Pastures* may be held an exception by some, but even that is open to some doubt under the strict definition; and no other play in the list is open to any doubt. And of the longest-run musicals, only *Hellza-poppin'* and its derivative, *Sons o' Fun,* fall into the freak category.

Of all the many abnormal plays produced in our theatre in the last twenty-five or thirty years, the only ones I can at the moment recall that commercially got even a relative distance were *On Trial,* a melodrama played backwards; *Seven Keys to Baldpate,* which fooled an audience with tricky dramaturgy; *The Tavern,* a lunatic roughhouse travesty; *The Unknown Purple,* in which the vengeful hero made himself invisible and, represented by a purple glow, moved about among the other characters and raised the devil with them; *Processional,* a paraphrase of German Expressionist drama; and *The Night of January 16,* with members of the audience sitting in a stage jury box and nightly passing the verdict on the guilt or innocence of the accused. All the others that come to mind either got absolutely nowhere or only a short and very unprofitable distance.

Mr. Schnee's numero managed but a few performances.

RICHARD III. March 26, 1943

The tragedy by William Shakespeare. Produced by Theatre Productions, Inc.

Program

QUEEN MARGARET		EARLE RIVERS	*Norman Rose*
	Mildred Dunnock	LORD GREY	*James Ganon*
KING HENRY VI	*Harry Irvine*	DUKE OF BUCKINGHAM	
RICHARD, DUKE OF GLOUCESTER			*Philip Bourneuf*
	George Coulouris	LORD STANLEY	*Stuart Casey*
KING EDWARD IV	*Tom Rutherford*	MARQUIS OF DORSET	
QUEEN ELIZABETH			*Eugene Struckmann*
	Norma Chambers	CATESBY	*Ralph Clanton*
EDWARD, PRINCE OF WALES		LORD MAYOR OF LONDON	
	Larry Robinson		*Harry Irvine*
GEORGE, DUKE OF CLARENCE		RICHARD, DUKE OF YORK	
	Harold Young		*Michael Artist*
SIR RICHARD RATCLIFF		SIR JAMES TYRREL	*Herbert Ratner*
	John Parrish	SIR JAMES BLUNT	*John Ford*
LORD HASTINGS		DUKE OF NORFOLK	
	Anthony Kemble-Cooper		*Randolph Echols*
LADY ANNE	*Helen Warren*		

The entire action of the play is laid in England from 1471 to 1485.

To the multiplicity of the play's murders, Mr. Coulouris and his company added another: that of the play itself. Under the species of acting which they visited upon it, Shakespeare's tragedy was for the most part transformed into something vaguely resembling *Dr. Jekyll and Mr. Hyde,* without Jekyll. In the role of the bloody, Machiavellian Richard, Coulouris dismissed from consideration the faintest implication that the character had a mind and projected it, save for a fleeting moment or two, in terms of a screen Bela Lugosi crossed with a grand-opera Quasimodo. The picture was of peanut-gallery, ranting villainy all compact, unrelieved by any trace of cerebral guile, introspection, witty hypocrisy, or diplomatic cunning. A highly serviceable actor in other plays, the star of the evening was here tinsel.

The hunchback who was to rule England has received various peculiar histrionic treatments since the play was first produced in New York at the Nassau Street Theatre in the February of 1750. Coming down to the period within the ken of the present reviewer, Robert B. Mantell's interpretation most closely resembled Coulouris's, for if ever there lived an actor to whom a role was all externals it was this Mantell. His conception of mentality lay primarily in forehead-creasing, tightened lips, and eyes fixedly scrutinizing the nowhere. His subtlety consisted in dropping his voice, slowly walking around his vis-à-vis, and surveying him quizzically out of the corner of an eye. And inner strength, as in the cases of Robert Downing, Melbourne MacDowell, and other such bulls of the epoch, was in his estimation best to be suggested by a tensing of biceps, the depression of the neck as far down into the collar of a costume as it would go, a compression of the mouth that turned the lips white, and a grinding of teeth that threatened to break at least half of them.

Richard Mansfield's hunchback was an American drawing-room version of Mantell's, the essentials remaining much the same. Henry Irving's was a Bloomsbury parlor version of Mansfield's American drawing-room version and in the portrayal there was even less finesse than in his performance in *The Bells,* which was minimum minus. Fritz Leiber in more recent times, though full of all the Shakespearean stock tricks, given to considerable bellowing and periodically an orator rather than an actor, at least here and there provided some hint of the character's intellectual foxiness. Walter Hampden, as in all his many parts save Cyrano, remained the college professor lecturing the role rather than playing it. Of them all, only John Barrymore handled the character much as the critical student of the tragedy and the role would have it. In Barrymore's grip Richard became no mere rusher of the historic growler, no mere stereotyped deep-dyed melodrama knave with mind filled with visions of complementary railroad express tracks, buzz-saws, and dizzy cliffs, no mere classical Jake Dalton sneering and snarling his way to his ends, but one whose shrewd and devious head had in it not achievement of some such minor goal as "the papers" but the great throne of England, and who comported his histrionic approach in keeping.

Not all of Barrymore's performance was of a piece; there were lapses. But, on the whole, it better than any of the others noted suggested the evil fascination, the workable hypocrisy, the pragmatic irony, the human being within the shell of viciousness, and the possibility of future ruler-ship that in sum convincingly constitutes the character.

Coulouris and his troupe, acting out the tragedy on a two-level set, either growled the lines so ferociously that the stage frequently became of a piece with a zoo or read them at such breakneck speed that it in turn became one with an Indianapolis automobile race. The manifold kill-ings, either in report or performance, were staged in such wise that the play now and then took on the flavor of some gangster melodrama like *Brooklyn, U. S. A.* played for sub-urban audiences who had to catch the train back to Mor-ristown at 10.45. And the two-level stage with its flights of stairs, hopefully employed to give the presentation a sem-blance of fluid action, gave it instead, under the kind of direction imposed upon it, the appearance of the circus act in which a troupe of trained dogs for no reason at all first run up the steps, pausing only momentarily to jump through a hoop on the top platform, and then run down them, thereafter, still for no good reason, repeating the same thing three or four times over.

The text arrangement deferred the famous opening soliloquy in favor of an inclusion of the third part of *Henry VI,* showing the murder, and omitted the ghost scenes, the touching departure of the little princes to their death, and the admirable Queen Elizabeth scene in the final act. While the elimination of the ghost scenes was perhaps forgivable, the aforesaid embellishment and dele-tions were in the nature of impudent editorial assistance to the greatest of dramatists.

THE FAMILY. March 30, 1943

More bombazine, based on the Atlantic Monthly *prize-winning novel of the same title by Nina Fedorova, by Victor Wolfson. Produced by Oscar Serlin.*

Program

KAHN	*Joseph Tso Shih*	PETER	*Nicholas Conte*
PHILIP STOWNE	*Lowell Gilmore*	MRS. PARRISH	*Carol Goodner*
DIMA	*Alec Englander*	AMAH	*June Kim*
GRANNY	*Lucile Watson*	DR. ISAACS	*Boris Tumarin*
MME. MILITZA	*Evelyn Varden*	WAH GAY	*Kaie Deei*
PROFESSOR CHERNOV	*Arnold Korff*	CHINESE GENTLEMAN NEXT DOOR	
MR. SUNG	*Yung Ying Hsu*		*Ping Yuen Zi*
LIDA	*Elisabeth Fraser*		*Takashi Ohta*
TANIA	*Marion Evensen*	JAPANESE	*Nelson Kawate*
ANNA PETROVNA CHERNOV		LODGERS	*Henry Takeuchi*
	Katherine Squire		*P. C. Arenal*
JIMMY BENNETT	*Bill Lipton*		*George Yamashige*

SYNOPSIS: Act I. Scene 1. *May 1937, morning.* Scene 2. *Later that afternoon.* Act II. Scene 1. *A month later.* Scene 2. *Several weeks later.* Act III. *An hour later.*

The living-room of number 11 Long Street in the British concession, Tientsin, China.

Iꜰ ᴛʜᴇ ᴍᴏᴠɪᴇꜱ always more or less bastardize the plays they film, the theatre often more or less bastardizes the novels it dramatizes. Here is another instance. The novel, dealing with an impoverished family of White Russian exiles living in the British concession of Tientsin, China, just before the Japanese attack in 1937, is the gentle story of a matriarch grandmother who through her orthodox Christian faith holds together her household and comforts and guides it in the evil swirl of life about it. The play deals only superficially with this material and reduces it to vulgarity by the inclusion of elements that would do credit to the imagination of a Hollywood screen director. The net result is an exhibit that starts somewhere, gets nowhere, and in the gradual getting introduces enough Japanese spies, self-sacrificing Chinese, irrelevant girl-swim-ming-contest and slow-awakening-of-love business to tire out even Mr. Samuel Goldwyn, if possible.

When the play was tried in Boston, it was announced to be a dramatization of the Fedorova novel. Lambasted by the critics there who had taken the trouble to read the latter, Mr. Wolfson took the precaution at the New York opening to specify that his play was merely based on it. He should have taken the further precaution to announce that his play, though it does its share of borrowing, was based on it in the sense that a bomber that flies to Cologne is based remotely on England, and that his play's load was equally effective in blasting the novel to pieces.

As it emerges on the stage, the book's story of family character triumphant under adversity becomes largely the old theatrical stencil of the tranquil household invaded by the evil female and of the turmoil that results. Sometimes, as in Strindberg, the she-devil is already there when the curtain goes up and the ructions proceed from her patho-logical conviction that her husband, to say nothing of any-one else in trousers, is her natural enemy and, besides, is in comparison with the female sex such a mental and emo-tional weakling that he should be got rid of as soon as pos-sible. Sometimes, in the more modern playwrights, the bitch is simply a born trouble-maker and cannot help her-self, or a superficially guileless creature who exercises her sex appeal against both the husband of her hostess and the young fiancé of her hostess's daughter and thus raises hob with the family until she is either conveniently burned to death in a mysterious fire in the barn on the estate or is denounced and packed off.

At still other times, as in Ibsen, she is a compound of complexes whose belief that she has been frustrated in life leads her to take it out on everyone in sight and, in the end, on herself. Other versions include the considerably milder one in which the intruder is a Little Miss Fixit who artlessly embroils the household in all kinds of difficulties, and the one in which the visiting fireman unvolitionally through the sheer puissance of her animal magnetism, subtle charm, and expensive perfume gets the menfolk where they live but who finally, after all the hearts and chinaware in the house have been broken, puts matters to right by suddenly announcing her intention to marry the rich bachelor next door — or, in the extremely sophisticated plays, the family's chauffeur.

In this instance she is the Mrs. Parrish of the novel, a dipsomaniac who seeks to take out her disappointment in life on the household and who, in the doing, adds to its already harassed existence. To make matters duller, the playwright has incorporated a series of scenes between her and the young man of the family in which both constantly hurl vicious insults at each other, thus, as in *This Rock,* quaintly paving the way for a deep love and, through it, the woman's redemption.

Further items: (1) The hokum Jewish doctor exiled by Hitler and accepted warmly into the bosom of the Christian household. (2) The white-bearded old Russian who writes advice to Mussolini, Hitler, and Roosevelt and who goes about moaning: "This is a mad, mad world!" (3) The ingénue who comes down the stairs in a new white dress and throws the family into raptures over her loveliness. (4) The persistently grinning, bowing Chinese houseboy. (5) The small boy who stands on an empty stage and prays cutely to God for a pet dog. (6) The speech about the needlessness of war, since all men ask for "is to be allowed to live their lives in peace and good-will." (7) The loud bombing effects.

Bretaigne Windust's direction permitted a number of the actors so to shout their lines that the aforesaid expensive bombing effects were lost in the din. His stage manipulation took the further form of such incessant and furious running about that it seemed Tientsin was invaded not by the Japs but by George Abbott, the only relief being periodic, momentary stills wherein Grandma alternately and affectionately embraced one character or another.

OKLAHOMA! MARCH 31, 1943

A musical comedy, based on Lynn Riggs's play Green Grow the Lilacs. *Music by Richard Rodgers; book and lyrics by Oscar Hammerstein II. Produced by the Theatre Guild.*

PROGRAM

AUNT ELLER	*Betty Garde*	ALI HAKIM	*Joseph Buloff*
CURLY	*Alfred Drake*	GERTIE CUMMINGS	*Jane Lawrence*
LAUREY	*Joan Roberts*	ELLEN	*Ellen Love*
IKE SKIDMORE	*Barry Kelley*	ANDREW CARNES	*Ralph Riggs*
FRED	*Edwin Clay*	CORD ELAM	*Owen Martin*
SLIM	*Herbert Rissman*	MIKE	*Paul Schierz*
WILL PARKER	*Lee Dixon*	JOE	*George Irving*
JUD FRY	*Howard da Silva*	SAM	*Hayes Gordon*
ADO ANNIE CARNES	*Celeste Holm*		

SYNOPSIS: Act I. Scene 1. *Laurey's farmhouse.* Scene 2. *The smoke house.* Scene 3. *A grove on Laurey's farm.* Act II. Scene 1. *The Skidmore ranch.* Scene 2. *A meadow.* Scene 3. *Stable shed.* Scene 4. *Laurey's farm.*

Time. *Just after the turn of the century.*

Place. *Indian Territory, Oklahoma.*

T HE THEATRE GUILD's entrance into the musical-comedy field, conventional scare-mark in title and all, has been considerably more successful than its later-day attempted entrance into drama. Save for the inclusion in the exhibit of an excessive amount of Agnes de Mille choreography, which leans rather too much to the arty, some visible economy in the matter of its leading players, and the talented Rouben Mamoulian's anticlimacteric staging of its second act (after the rousing *Oklahoma!* number the extension of the action loses the audience) , the evening constitutes agreeable entertainment.

When it comes to the average folk play, it is better to have it with music, which is the case with Mr. Riggs's specimen. Whereas in its dramatic form the play was on the languid side, in the musical it gains the measure of life it

earlier lacked. Rodgers's score, one of his best, does wonders for the script, and if Riggs's plot doings still lag when
mouths speak them instead of singing them the improvement is nevertheless immense.

The so-called folk play as we have commonly experi-
enced it on the more modern local stage has needed a
Rodgers, if not a de Mille, badly. From *Bunty Pulls the
Strings,* which was nothing but the same old Little Miss
Fixit plot in Scotch dialect, to such recent outgivings as
Papa Is All with its gun figuring climactically in a Men-
nonite community that notoriously forbids the presence
of all firearms, and from Lula Vollmer's *Trigger* and *The
Hill Between* with their dated themes concealed in Southern mountaineer accents to the later *The First Crocus* with
its Scandinavian-Americans comporting themselves like so
many Winchell Smiths in a James A. Herne makeup, eight
out of ten of the plays have been largely sophisticated and
bogus affairs. Only those emanating from Ireland, and now
and then Spain, have had any authenticity and, at that,
several of the Irish seem occasionally to have confused
Seumas O'Mulligan, the illiterate village drunk, with
W. B. Yeats, as several of the Spanish appear to have mixed
up the genealogical charts of their peasants with those of
Sardou and Al Woods.

It is thus, to repeat, that while many such folk plays fail
as drama they offer likely material for the song and dance
stage. There the dubious plots and characters they contain
do not much matter, since gay melodies, lovely costumes,
fancy scenery, and pretty legs make one oblivious of their
deficiencies and reconstitute their materials into something that, at least superficially, seems to have more body
to it than the usual Broadway musical-comedy book.

ZIEGFELD FOLLIES. April 1, 1943

A revue by Jack Yellen, Ray Henderson, et al. Produced by the Shuberts in association with the Messrs. Bloomingdale and Walters.

Principals

Milton Berle, Ilona Massey, Arthur Treacher, Jack Cole, Sue Ryan, Nadine Gae, Tommy Wonder, Imogene Carpenter, Dean Murphy, et al.

THAT THE LATE Florenz Ziegfeld's *Follies* were the great successes they invariably were solely on the score of the looks of their girls is a theatrical legend with no more foundation in fact than such extra-theatrical popular beliefs as the relentlessly permanent epidemic of athlete's foot and the cerebral brio of Harry Emerson Fosdick. It is perfectly true that Ziegfeld's girls were more symphonious than those on any of his competitors' stages, and it is also true that they were a factor in making his shows the successes they were. But they were no more singly responsible for that success than George Lederer's earlier stunners were for the success of his shows. In the whole history of the last one hundred years' musical stage only one show's prosperity has been attributable first and last to its girls, at the time somewhat eccentrically esteemed as lallapaloosæ. That show was *The Black Crook.*

It is generally forgotten that Ziegfeld's exhibits contained numerous sterling box-office lures in addition to the feminine department. Exceptional comedians like Eddie Cantor, Ed Wynn, Will Rogers, Bert Williams, Fannie Brice, Ina Claire, W. C. Fields, and such were one of the additional aces. Skits by Ring Lardner and other, if lesser but still satisfactory, humorists were another. (One of the best things Lardner ever wrote was a baseball sketch for one of the *Follies.*) Tunes by Victor Herbert, Jerome Kern, Victor Jacobi, Irving Berlin, et al., were still another. Amusing stage novelties such as Mae Murray seen

rushing down a street from afar on a movie screen and
popping through the screen in person just as she reached
the near end of it were yet another. And settings and costumes the beauty of which the local stage had not before approached added the final fillip.

And there was still something else which contributed
perhaps even more than any of these to the *Follies* estate.
That was the romantic air with which Ziegfeld and the
public invested them. They represented then, as linger-
ingly in memory they do still, all that the term "glamorous"
meant before Hollywood aborted it to ridicule in connection with sweatered mammary glands, toupéed brunet
mimes with ophthalmoplegia, and quondam drive-in waitresses languishing seductively on chaises-longues with one
leg raised to God. They represented in the theatre what
Sherry's and Delmonico's, what hansom cabs (the driver
and maybe Richard Harding Davis or Robert Collier and
a toast of the town inside them and with Finley Peter
Dunne perched spirituously on the box), and what gal-
loping sleigh races to McGowan's in Central Park for the
champagne trophy represented out of it. Their opening
nights were the occasion of the season, with regiments of
police clearing the path to the New Amsterdam for the cars
of notabilities in the world of society, public affairs, finance,
and the arts. And when the curtain fell, the infection of
their stages permeated for long hours into the dawn the
gay parties at Rector's, Jimmy Europe's dancing band at
the Sans Souci, the tinkling palm court of the Plaza, and
the brilliant Rose and Gold Rooms at the Beaux Arts.

'The *Follies* constituted their own theatrical epoch. It
was the epoch of American chorus girls the pictorial equiva-
lent of those in George Edwardes's equally famous London
Gaiety shows, of Ann Pennington's patella dimples, Bert
Williams's droll poker pantomime, W. C. Fields's grand
clowning, Marilyn Miller's blond loveliness, 25,000-dollar
three-minute spectacular numbers, and a general lavishness
that New York hitherto had not sniffed elsewhere since
the fashionable orgies engineered by Dominick Lynch, in
the late Ward McAllister's phrase "the greatest swell and

beau that New York had ever known." It was the era of
"A Pretty Girl Is Like a Melody" and "Hello, Frisco,
Hello," of Will Rogers's allusions to Mr. Ziegfield (he
could never get the boss's name straight), Ben Ali Haggin's
sumptuous "living pictures," Kay Laurell atop a huge spin-
ning globe in the approximate altogether, Ray Dooley
squealing hilariously in a baby-carriage, Diamond Jim
Brady's bijouterie outdazzling the stage from the front row,
Jimmy Walker coming down the aisle at nine o'clock and
stealing the audience's applause from the opening number, and Billie Burke, the boss's wife, all decked out in
fluffy white, raptly beaming her approval on the whole
works from an upper right-hand stage box.

The full moon seemed always to be making a special
welcoming appearance over Forty-second Street when a
Follies opened; enough cops, hoping to catch an intermittent earful of the stage doings, crowded the New Amsterdam's inner lobby to give the place the aspect of a Police-
men's Annual Ball; and the mob of curiosity-seekers — not
autograph fiends, since that was before their birth — made
the thoroughfare outside take on the look of a D. W. Grif-
fith Babylonian epic. And inside and on the stage you'd
see the delicately lovely young Fairbanks twins in Urban's
settings of purple night, and the girls in soft light blue
swinging out over the audience, and a wonderful kid stage
trick that with the aid of passed around red and green cel-
luloid spectacles made a gigantic hand seem to reach out
over the footlights and muss up your hair, and John Steel
ruffling the ladies' emotions with songs of love, and Andrew
Tombes making uproarious faces, and Justine Johnstone,
Olive Thomas, Lillian Lorraine, Martha Mansfield, and
that overpowering of all Powers models yet to come, the
celebrated, stately, and regal Dolores. Not forgetting, surely
not forgetting, Ziggy himself, surveying the scene from the
back of the house and, amid all the ermine, sable, mink,
and white ties, super-resplendent in a lavender shirt, pea-
green cravat, and maroon socks.

The Shubert *Follies* (they have purchased the right to
use Ziegfeld's name in connection with them), while not

without a flicker of entertainment, are a very far cry from the master's. Milton Berle is not in the comedian class with Ziggy's gala old crowd; the girls, aside from Ilona Massey and a little dancing blonde named Ganley, will not materially sadden the middle years of Marion Davies, Gladys Glad, Annette Bade, Mary Eaton, Jessie Reed, and all those other super-stimuli; the Winter Garden is not the New Amsterdam; and the old Ziegfeld New York and its atmosphere have passed into the far shadows. But even New York as it is deserves a rather handsomer wreath to Ziegfeld's memory than this Shubert tissue immortelle with its repeated wheezes on rationing, its rewritten sketches from George White's *Scandals* and the revue called *Who's Who*, its old Ed Wynn acrobatic-act travesty, its tired Ray Henderson songs, its monotonously repeated dance routines, and its facetiæ about Boris Karloff and Tommy Manville. The only things in it that Ziegfeld would probably have approved are the looks of the two girls previously noted, some of Miles White's costume color, Nadine Gae's dancing, Christine Ayers's shapely figure, and the presence once again on the opening night and in a right-hand stage box of his still loyal and lovely widow, Billie Burke.

TOMORROW THE WORLD. April 14, 1943

More Naziphobe drama, by James Gow and Arnaud d'Usseau. Produced by Theron Bamberger.

Program

Patricia Frame	*Nancy Nugent*	Emil Bruckner	*Skippy Homeier*
Jessie Frame	*Kathryn Givney*	Fred Miller	*Richard Taber*
Frieda	*Edit Angold*	Dennis	*Walter Kelly*
Michael Frame	*Ralph Bellamy*	Butler	*Richard Tyler*
Leona Richards	*Shirley Booth*	Tommy	*Paul Porter, Jr.*

SYNOPSIS: Act I. *A Saturday morning in early autumn, 1942.* Act II. *An afternoon, ten days later.* Act III. *Early the next morning.*

The Scene. *The living-room of Professor Michael Frame's home in a large university town in the Middle West.*

The familiar dramatic device (*vide The Family*) of the wanton intruder into the benign household and the disorganization induced by the character again serves the present playwrights. On this occasion, however, the rococo artifice is given a contemporary fillip by constituting the interloper a German youth who has been inculcated with the Nazi doctrine and who, the nephew of a Middle Western college professor, is imported into the latter's home following his father's and mother's death. The drama lies in the youngster-automaton's persistent adherence to and practice of the Hitler dogma, the manner in which he devastates the household, and his ultimate persuasion to the fact that the American way of life may be the better after all.

Compounded of obvious melodrama and even more obvious sentimentality, the play rests for audience response solely on the spontaneous combustible under present circumstances inherent in its theme, since the writing is without trace of subtlety and since the expedients employed to further the theme involve such valetudinarian stage business as the youth's slashing of the oil painting of a hated one, his utilization of a bronze book-end murderously to strike another hated one on the head, his machinations against the fiancée of the hero (in this case, of course, Jewish), his supplemental machinations to steal the key to the hero's chemical research laboratory and have a copy of it made without the latter's discovery, his tearful break-down following the ancient orphan-drama question: "Was my mother beautiful?", with the tender assurance that she was, and his eventual sudden and somewhat incomprehensible redemption when, after a brief ten days, a little American girl babytalks her forgiveness of his trespasses and gives him a watch for his birthday.

Add to this the kind of dramaturgy that consists almost entirely in bringing on the characters in pairs, thus bequeathing to the stage a seemingly endless succession of duologues; the character of the hero's bitter old-maid sister who opposes his marriage since it will give the house which she has long supervised into the hands of a stranger; the laboratory janitor who is disclosed to be a scheming member of the Bund; the kindly old German servant who is proud of her American citizenship; the lovable American child in contrast to the obnoxious Nazi child; and so on — and it becomes doubly plain that only the natural force of the theme stands between successful audience reaction and audience lethargy.

The idea of oppugnant philosophies in the instance of the intruder-into-a-peaceful-household dramatic scheme is quite as old as the scheme itself. In the last thirty years it has served time and again, as in such exhibits, among countless others both native and foreign, as *A Strange Woman,* wherein it took the form of contrasting the point of view of a worldly woman with that of a provincial social morality, and as in *Pagan Lady,* wherein it argued for freedom from inhibitions in terms of a South Pacific island woman and a hidebound New England family. In such plays the final curtain customarily descends either, as in the first case, upon the central character's inability to bring the others to her way of thinking and her decision to throw up the impracticable job and go forth again into the world or, as in the second, on the character's triumph, ending with her acceptance by the family and marriage to its young son. In still other plays, as in the one under present consideration, the rehabilitation of the household guest by bringing the character into concordance with whatever point of view is popular with an audience at the moment is relied upon for a satisfactory conclusion. It is thus, to repeat, that the sure-fire implicit in beating down a disciple of Nazism into concurrence with an audience's prejudice accounts for the play's automatic effect.

Whatever reflections on child actors have appeared in the antecedent chapters are again uncomfortably contradicted by the success in the immediate exhibit of a youngster named Skippy Homeier, drafted from the radio studios and making his first appearance on the stage. Save for a too strident and hence intermittently monotonous speech (the fault of his director), here was for one so tender in years a quite remarkable demonstration of acting. Holding every second of the audience's rapt attention, the youngster took hold of the one-tone and difficult role of the little Nazi and with thorough inner understanding, admirable stage comportment, adroit pantomime, and an emotional equipment, as testified to in the preliminary and final break-down scenes, that was, to put it mildly, unusual, provided the season with one of its most fascinating performances.

If such embarrassing surprises continue, the day is possibly not far off when I may also have to eat my words about the histrionic ability of even Walter Hampden.

This success of young Homeier, however, is at least in part to be attributed, if not to his often canny director, to the nature of his role, since, all things considered, one of the surest ways for a player to make an impression upon the public as well as the critics is to get hold of the role of an odious and detestable character. In the theatre of the last thirty seasons and more there is small record of any actor or actress, young or old, who has failed in such a role, provided only it was sufficiently despicable. From the day Jameson Lee Finney, after years of getting nowhere, found himself, in *The Deep Purple,* in the part of a character without a single redeeming trait and was forthwith acclaimed an actor of size to the more recent success of such novices as Mary Anderson as the young viper in *Guest in the House* and this Homeier youngster, the statistics seem to be eccentrically on the side of anti-sweetness-and-light. Moreover, it has often been that way in the farther past. More mediocre actresses have got by as Hedda than ever good ones have prospered as Nora.

Katherine Kaelred was a nonentity until she appeared as the Kipling vampire in *A Fool There Was.* Chrystal Herne waited for her real chance until *Craig's Wife* came along. Florence McGee has been lost since she floored audiences as the vicious brat in *The Children's Hour.* Charles Laughton in *Payment Deferred,* Henry Daniell in *Kind Lady,* Mary Morris in *Double Door,* Flora Robson in *Ladies in Retirement,* Edward G. Robinson in *A Man with Red Hair,* Otto Preminger in *Margin for Error,* Joseph Spurin-Calleia in *Small Miracle,* Vincent Price in *Angel Street,* and dozens in other such roles — whether the plays or they themselves have been meritorious or not — have come off with flying colors.

Just as there is no truth in the old facetia that nobody loves a fat man, as the success on the stage of all sorts of meatballs like Maclyn Arbuckle, Frank McIntyre, Sydney Greenstreet, et al., have attested, so there seems to be little truth in the belief that audiences invariably cotton most greatly to characters possessed of honor and nobility.

In thematic conclusion. An indication of what we may possibly expect in one phase of the post-war drama is to be gleaned from the play under immediate scrutiny. It is the conviction of its authors, as has been intimated, that only by kindness, chivalry and tender consideration, along with maybe a bit of dialectics on the superiority of the democratic way of life, may the twelve million youngsters who have been indoctrinated with Nazism be redeemed into comfortable world citizens and members of society. That more of this faith-hope-and-charity philosophy in regard to the Germans will permeate our stages once the war is over and that forgive-and-let-live will take the place of the present hate-and-kill doctrine seems, if the record of the past be taken into consideration, more or less likely.

It is generally the way of the theatre, save only the French, to become so generous to an enemy after a war that the previous boiling attitude toward him takes on an aspect of having been not only bounderish but slightly ridiculous. After our own Civil War there issued forth all kinds of Northern plays with Dixie heroines so magnolia-fair and lovable and Southern soldiers so valorous and handsome that the Yankee characters seemed nigh deep-dyed villains in comparison. After the last war with the Hun, Boche, Baby-Eater or whatever he was called during it, there was so much sentimental vocalizing of "Heidelberg, Dear Heidelberg" in one form or another that the stage sometimes metaphorically appeared to regard our own Harvard as a foul concentration camp and our own Yale and Princeton as relative smallpox quarantines. And the quondam detested German, when he showed up dramatically or musically at all, showed up as either an old professor so adorable you could hardly stand him or a children's nurse so sweet you could taste her for days afterward. And when it wasn't the old professor or the nurse it was either a naturalized old German who threw kisses every ten minutes to the picture of Lincoln over the mantel or a plump female household servant who exuded enough homely charm to fascinate a boa constrictor.

In the case of other past wars between other nations it has frequently operated likewise. A short time after the last battle has been fought, their stages have treated the bloody matter as little more than an ordinary barroom fight, with both boozers affectionately wrapping their arms around each other's necks, buying each other a drink, and singing "Sweet Adeline" at the tops of their lungs.

Whether the authors of *Tomorrow the World* are correct in their assumption, I would not know. Whether someone like Dr. Richard M. Brickner in his *Is Germany Curable?* is in turn correct in his slightly less positive recipe for paranoid rehabilitation, I also would not know. And whether the all-out realists, sterilizationists, mass-killers, and such are correct in their therapeutics, I similarly would not know. But when it comes to the drama I do know that such love-cures-all ideological exhibits as this *Tomorrow the World* and others like it which are unquestionably due to befall us once the war is done stubbornly and idiotically take on the air of the innumerable old reform-school and prison plays in which the kindly ministrations of some small-town Aunt Minnie in the first instance transformed the erstwhile little bastard Gus into an angel a week after his release and by the simple saying of grace before meals and the reading of the Scriptures after the apple pie in the second completely regenerated all the escaped convicts who, in the guise of long-lost nephews, came to rob the old widow of her life's savings.

What is more, I hardly think that ingrained Nazis, young or old, are to be turned, whether in life or in reputable drama, into cherubim closely resembling Hartley Manners and Catherine Chisholm Cushing by any Manners or Cushing psychology.

THE FIRST MILLION. APRIL 28, 1943

A something by Irving Elman. Produced by one Jimmy Elliott, a youthful member of the cast of Junior Miss, and withdrawn after four nights' exposure.

PROGRAM

"MAW" BOONE	*Dorrit Kelton*	SHERIFF	*Russell Collins*
HOKE BOONE	*Wendell Corey*	TOM BOONE	*Henry Barnard*
MINK BOONE	*Dort Clark*	MR. FAIRWEATHER	*John Souther*
SANK BOONE	*George Cotton*	LUCIUS J. BEASEL	*Harlan Briggs*
EMMY LOU	*Lois Hall*	PIDGIE	*Louise Larabee*

SYNOPSIS: Act I. *Late afternoon in early summer.* Act II. *That night.* Act III. *Later that night.*

Time. 1940.

Place. *A cabin in the Ozarks.*

IT SEEMS RAPIDLY to be becoming a tradition that each year at this late period in a season some usually hitherto unknown producer will enter the lists with a play that needs only two dray-horses attached to it to fulfill its destiny. In the season of 1929–30 the play was *Spook House;* in 1930–1 it was *Unexpected Husband;* in 1931–2 it was *Back Fire,* along with *The Boy Friend* for extra good measure; in 1932–3 it was *$25 an Hour;* in 1933–4, *Furnished Rooms;* in 1934–5, *Them's the Reporters;* in 1935–6, *Pre-Honeymoon,* to say nothing of *A Private Affair;* in 1936–7, *Without Warning,* along with *Curtain Call;* in 1937–8, *The Man from Cairo;* in 1938–9 *Clean Beds;* in 1939–40, *Russian Bank;* in 1940–1, *Your Loving Son* and, above all, *Snookie;* in 1941–2, *Comes the Revelation;* and in 1942–3, this *The First Million.*

Like the producer, the author is a sapling, and this exposition marked his initial gesture toward the drama. That dramaturgy, however, is still an occult science to him is evident from the inner confusion of his maiden effort, since whether it is intended as comedy, melodrama, or satire is something an audience cannot possibly determine. His fable is of the mother of three hillbilly bank-robbers whom she persuades to follow in their late bank-robber father's footsteps, whom she coaches in the acquisition of a little short of one million dollars, only to have it indignantly burned by a more moral member of the household, and whom she thereupon determinedly starts toward the goal of another million. As revealed on the stage, the fable lacks the humor to constitute it comedy, the suspensive lift to constitute it melodrama, and the faintest symptom of ironic wit to constitute it even milk-mild satire.

Youth in the theatre is to be encouraged — when it shows so much as a modicum of ability and promise. But a great deal of the overly ambitious youth currently exercising itself in that department of the arts and crafts should be constructively urged to return to school and learn the famous lesson of Darius Green and his flying machine.

THE CORN IS GREEN. May 3, 1943

A return engagement of the Emlyn Williams play. Produced by Herman Shumlin.

Program

JOHN GORONWY JONES		MISS MOFFAT	*Ethel Barrymore*
	Tom E. Williams	ROBBART ROBBATCH	
MISS RONBERRY	*Esther Mitchell*		*Patrick O'Connor*
IDWAL MORRIS	*Kenneth Clarke*	MORGAN EVANS	*Richard Waring*
SARAH PUGH	*Gwyneth Hughes*	GLYN THOMAS	*Gene Ross*
A GROOM	*George Bleasdale*	JOHN OWEN	*Peter Harris*
THE SQUIRE	*Lewis L. Russell*	WILL HUGHES	*Bert Kalmar, Jr.*
MRS. WATTY	*Eva Leonard-Boyne*	OLD TOM	*J. P. Wilson*
BESSIE WATTY	*Perry Wilson*		

SYNOPSIS: Act I. Scene 1. An afternoon in June. Scene 2. A night in August, six weeks later. Act II. Scene 1. An early evening in August, two years later. Scene 2. A morning in November, three months later. Act III. An afternoon in July, seven months later.

The action of the play takes place in the living-room of a house in Glansarno, a small village in a remote Welsh countryside.

The time is the latter part of the last century, and covers a period of three years.

PRODUCED IN NEW YORK originally in the November of 1940 and running for 470 performances, and meanwhile having toured the nation, the play on a revisit substantiates this reviewer's first opinion of it. That opinion has been expressed in a foregoing chapter and calls for no qualification or extension. As for the performance of the returned company, which included a number of newcomers, it indicated, save in the case of the experienced Ethel Barrymore and one or two others, the seeming persistence of the histrionic conviction that everybody outside New York is stone-deaf and that it is accordingly necessary for actors so to lift their voices that all that is needed to give the scene a convincingly relevant atmosphere is two goal posts and a football.

This is of course due to the suddenly varying sizes of

the auditoriums before which a traveling theatrical troupe
is called upon to play. Since for every normal-size house
such a troupe finds itself acting to two or three auditoriums
each large enough to hold a couple of three-ring circuses
and Hendrik Willem Van Loon, it is not unnatural that
vocal disposition and pitch should become so confused that
adjustment is difficult.

Miss Barrymore's performance was as thoroughly right
as on the occasion of the play's première. Several of the newcomers, however, and Lewis L. Russell, substituting for
Edmond Breon, in particular, appeared to supplement
their belief in the deafness of out-of-town audiences with
a belief that New York theatregoers who wait for revivals
at cut-rate prices cannot, being possessed of only modest
incomes, appreciate honest character interpretation as well-
to-do first-night audiences invariably are able to, but must
be condescended to with a heavy leaven of caricature so
that the poor, ignorant souls may be provided with some
relieving laughs.

SONS AND SOLDIERS. May 4, 1943

A play by Irwin Shaw. Produced by Max Reinhardt, Norman Bel Geddes, and Richard Myers.

PROGRAM

JOHN TADLOCK	*Herbert Rudley*	LINCOLN GRAVES	*Leonard Sues*
VICTOR CARNRICK	*Millard Mitchell*	ERNEST TADLOCK	*Kenneth Tobey*
REBECCA TADLOCK		MATTHEW GRAVES	*Karl Malden*
	Geraldine Fitzgerald	MARIE	*Sara Lee Harris*
ANDREW TADLOCK	*Gregory Peck*	ANTHONY	*Roderick Maybee*
ANDREW TADLOCK, as a Child		MISS GILLESPIE	*Martha Greenhouse*
	Jack Willett	MR. LEVERHOOK	*William Beach*
DORA APPLEGATE, as a Child		MARK LOWRY	*Edward Forbes*
	Joan McSweeney	DORA APPLEGATE	*Audrey Long*
LINCOLN GRAVES, as a Child		CATHERINE CARNRICK	*Stella Adler*
	Bobbie Schenck	THE MAILMAN	*Edward Nannery*
ERNEST TADLOCK, as a Child		THE SALESMAN	*Jesse White*
	Ted Donaldson	MINISTER	*Royal Dana Tracy*

The play is in three acts, the action taking place in a small American city, starting in 1916.

Aᴛ sᴜᴘᴇʀғɪᴄɪᴀʟ preliminary glance, this seemed to hold promise of a rather interesting theatrical evening. First, there was Irwin Shaw, who, though his previous attempts at playwriting were not very successful, is not only a short-story writer materially above the average but a man with an eager and observant mind. Second, there was Max Reinhardt in charge of the staging. Third, there was Norman Bel Geddes, one of the theatre's most imaginative designers of stage settings. Fourth, there was Geraldine Fitzgerald, who on her only previous appearance in New York in the Orson Welles production of *Heartbreak House* in 1938 hinted at the possibility of a developing talent. And fifth, it had been announced that the Metro-Goldwyn-Mayer picture company had put up handsome monies to let the producers go the whole hog in every direction. But that superficial preliminary glance proved to be as inexpedient

as superficial preliminary glances commonly are. The occasion rivaled the flatness of the simile-honored pancake.

In all the plays he has contrived before, and in the present one in particular, Mr. Shaw indicates himself to be a
writer of isolated likely scenes with no likely play as their
foundation. His drama therefore regularly takes on the
comparative appearance of a number of independent and
distinct short-story episodes, some of them not without
merit, unblushingly thrown together between covers and
labeled a novel. His scattered dramaturgy thus further
gives the impression of a succession of such arbitrary and
stenciled chapter endings as "But the next day was to de-
cide!", "Yet was it?" and "Nevertheless, she could not help
wondering" — with the turn of the page each time cheating the reader with small progression and much static.
What is worse, the measure of inventiveness and originality
he has here and there demonstrated in sections of his antecedent plays is nowhere evident in this, his latest effort.

His story is of a woman of 1916 who is told that if she
gives birth to a child she will die and who in her hysterical
subconscious sees visions of a born son and all the agonies
of life, including endless wars, that he and she will have to
suffer, but who nevertheless at the final curtain decides to
go through with childbirth come what will. This story
Shaw tells in the most commonplace manner imaginable.
His characters are the old paper stage dolls, ranging from
the cynically epigrammatic doctor to the sophisticated married woman who seduces the youthful hero and from the
sweet girl next door he will ultimately marry to the small
boy who rebels at piano practice, the girl-chasing college
boys, the minister who coughs as a reminder that he has
not yet been paid for performing the wedding ceremony,
the brashly intruding salesman of vacuum cleaners, etc.
And his scenes are often of a piece: the harlot cruelly dis-
illusioning the youth who believes she loves him, the
birthday party at which paterfamilias awkwardly reads a
poem he has composed for the occasion and at which the
hitherto abstemious materfamilias gets gayly tipsy, the
young Lothario's account of his conquests by way of lord-

ing it over his shy boy friends, the mother's bravely hidden tear when her son goes off to war, the inevitable tacked-on last-act speech by the father intended to give the play a contemporary war-philosophy flavor, and so on. And all, save a single comedy-relief scene and a restrained handling of a sentimental passage in the concluding act, written so pretentiously, what with its numerous allusions to Beethoven, Bach, Keats, César Franck, etc., that the whole sounds much like a rewrite of a Samuel Shipman play by the late Augustus Thomas.

We turn to Reinhardt. There was a period, subsequent to the advent of Hitler, when one of the hoped-for silver linings of the grim central and eastern European clouds was the emigration to this country of many of the celebrated stage directors of the war lands. These refugees, it was thought, would bring to the American theatre talents it might profitably avail itself of and so add to its stature and acclaim. What the arrivals on these shores may conceivably do in the future only the future can tell, but the regrettable fact persists that thus far they have made a very dismal showing.

This Reinhardt, the best known of them all and the forerunner of the general exodus, has in the years he has been operating on American soil given us as the chief token of his theatrical skill the production of *The Eternal Road,* which, as all who saw it will recall, represented approximately a half-million dollars consecrated to stupefying tedium. Add to this a candy-box reproduction of his old *A Midsummer Night's Dream* in the Hollywood Bowl and in a few Middle Western cities, a supremely sluggish motion-picture version of the same play, the consistently obvious staging of a Thornton Wilder adaptation called *The Merchant of Yonkers,* and the staging of *Sons and Soldiers,* and you have a picture of his principal achievements hereabout.

This, his latest job, was nothing for even a second-rate Broadway director to be proud of. Furthering the pretentiousness of the script, he not only loaded it with an overdose of off-stage piano-playing that at times suggested the

exhibit belonged in Town Hall (on an amateur night) ;
with so much overacting, notably in the instance of Miss
Fitzgerald, whom he coached so to exercise her throat mus-
cles in loud declamation that the poor woman's blood
vessels seemed imminently on the verge of bursting; and
with such an exit scampering, particularly in the case of
Herbert Rudley in the sedate father's role, that what he
apparently hoped would provide an atmosphere of dramatic movement provided rather a suggestion that the
characters were bent without delay on achieving an off-
stage lavatory; but with so steadily portentous a reading of
the simplest speeches that the actors all seemed to be close
relatives of the Rev. Charles Rann Kennedy.

And what of Mr. Reinhardt's principal European colleagues since they joined him over here? Leopold Jessner,
who did some very fine things in Germany, especially his
production of *Julius Cæsar,* has been languishing in Hollywood and tinkering now and then with minor pictures.
Otto Preminger, the Austrian, has fooled around with the
purely commercial drama and has delivered nothing but
the staging of a court-room melodrama, *Libel!,* a murder
mystery, *Margin for Error,* and a revival of *Outward
Bound.* He has managed these trivial tasks well enough,
but there are any number of American directors who could
have done them fully as well, if not better. Erik Charell,
once famous for his Berlin musical-show productions, has
restaged his old *White Horse Inn,* which brought nothing
new in the way of stagecraft, and an overnight failure in
the form of a jazzed production of a show based on *A Midsummer Night's Dream* called *Swingin' the Dream.* Yet the
story of none of these has been quite so gloomy as that of
Erwin Piscator. Among the several plays he has botched
down in the little Studio Theatre in West Twelfth Street,
a typical example is to be had in *King Lear.* With it he
proved himself at once not only the most preposterous
hand at Shakespeare the American theatre has seen in many
a year but one of the most thoroughly incompetent, irrelevant, and immaterial of all the refugee directors.

This *Lear* of his, filtered through his directorial vanity, self-assertion, and mental obfuscation, amounted to atrocious and offensive burlesque. Setting it upon a stage that resembled a revolving Tower of Pisa topped by a Lilly Daché hat and utilizing loud speakers and enough reverberating movie sound effects to engender a Hollywood earthquake — and further indicating an ignorance of important elements in the drama's text — his contribution to American theatrical art was so ridiculous that even the most sympathetic and hospitable reviewer could not believe his eyes and ears. From his absurd induction showing Cain and Abel symbolically licking the daylights out of each other to his incorporation of a group of eccentric dancers and from his four-level turn-table platform that arbitrarily converted his poor actors into acrobats and ski-jumpers to his projection of the dramatic action into the laps of the audience and his Broadway night-club lighting, the enterprise in its entirety indicated not only a throwback to the old German production antics at their worst but also that, like him, most of his fellow-countrymen refugees, God bless them otherwise, are not worth a farthing to the American theatre.

As for the Russians, Michael Chekhov's initial production in English, *The Possessed,* drew such a volume of derision and so few customers that it went to the storehouse in quick order. And the same with his *Twelfth Night.* Ilya Mottyleff's staging of *Empress of Destiny* suffered a similar reception and a similar fate. Andrius Jilinsky's production of Strindberg's *The Bridal Crown* was so bad in every particular that the management closed it overnight. Leo Bulgakov, who has been over here for a much longer time, has exercised himself with such trash as *Close Quarters* and *Don't Throw Glass Houses* and has not perceptibly improved it. And there is still another Slav, well known to himself, if not to the rest of us, as Vadim Uraneff, who has occupied himself solely in staging the garbage called *Clean Beds.*

The pre-war encomiums on the part of American travelers which some of these gentlemen enjoyed were understandable. The stages of England, France, and America during that period were conducted so unimaginatively that what the voyagers saw on the German, to say nothing of the Russian, stages, albeit occasionally erratic to the point of lunacy, naturally made a deep impression upon them. For here at least was a valiant attempt to break away from the flat, fanciless, and dull staging that for years had made the English, French, and American dramatic platforms pictorially indistinguishable from so many displays in Siegel and Cooper's shop-windows and the musical almost equally indistinguishable from those in Schwarz's at Christmastime. To a people fed up on such bleak routine the German directors seemed veritable geniuses. For they had contemptuously thrown aside all the old conventional décor and all the old stereotyped direction and had substituted for it something that, for all its periodic daft quality, seemed to inject into drama and the stage in general a new throb and vitality and color.

Some of them did some good work and deserved not only the public but the critical regard that was liberally meted out to them. One or two of them, indeed, now and then did excellent work. But even at their best these and the others always indicated their belief that they, the directors, were infinitely more important than the dramatists they served. And this fact, together with the circumstance that, as the years passed, their staging became in its expressionistic, constructivist, and similar departures as conventional and routine as the manner and methods they had cast aside, conspired gradually to put them in turn into the discard.

In conclusion, and in direct relation to *Sons and Soldiers*, there was Mr. Geddes. A designer of much true imagination, he is nevertheless more at home in spectacle than in the more intimate form of drama. Some of his larger productions have been admirably contrived, even though now and again top-heavy with needless embellishment. But when he has applied himself to settings for the normal drama that same needless over-elaboration has frequently conspired to drown the drama itself in them. His capital realistic setting for *Dead End* was an exception. Yet here in the case of *Sons and Soldiers* his small-town expansive drawing-room with its Roxy staircase and his beflowered and becolumned set-in dream scenes only helped to make a play that was not there in the first place seem even more absent than it was.

THREE'S A FAMILY. MAY 5, 1943

A farce-comedy by Phoebe and Henry Ephron, previously known as The Wife Takes a Child, Three-Cornered Pants, *and* The Home Front. *Produced by John Golden in association with the Messrs. Pollock and Siegel.*

PROGRAM

SAM WHITAKER	*Robert Burton*	EUGENE MITCHELL	
IRMA DALRYMPLE	*Ethel Owen*		*Francis De Sales*
ADELAIDE	*Doro Merande*	ANOTHER MAID	*Gee Gee James*
KITTY MITCHELL	*Katharine Bard*	A GIRL	*Jean Bellows*
ARCHIE WHITAKER	*Edwin Philips*	DR. BARTELL	*William Wadsworth*
HAZEL	*Dorothy Gilchrist*	JOE FRANKLIN	*Richard Midgley*
FRANCES WHITAKER	*Ruth Weston*	MARION FRANKLIN	*Virginia Vass*

SYNOPSIS: Act I. Scene 1. Late afternoon, September. Scene 2. Later the same night. Act II. Scene 1. Two months later, Thanksgiving Day. Scene 2. An hour later. Act III. An hour later.

The action takes place in the living-room of Sam and Frances Whitaker's apartment on West 110th Street in New York.

AFTER A START that had the audience reaching for its hats, involving as it did a succession of such Gay Nineties sallies as "One doesn't have to be a hen to know a bad egg," Mr. and Mrs. Ephron's farce-comedy (the designation always desperately tacked onto a farce that has been found to move not so quickly as it should) progressed turtle-wise into faintly better entertainment. Having read in the papers that there were a quarter of a million more births in the United States during 1942 than in the previous year, that out of a total of 180,000 medicos in the land more than 50,000 are in military service and unavailable to the civilian trade, that there are some 30,000 fewer nurses than heretofore, and that the maternity hospitals are overcrowded, the authors evolved the idea that it would be very funny to show a household and its visiting relatives giving birth to such an untoward number of babies that there remained no means to handle the situation. That the idea would be very funny if dramatized as skillfully as Margaret Mayo dramatized an essentially not altogether dissimilar fancy in her prosperous farce of many years ago called *Baby Mine* is more than possible. But that skill is here lacking and what sporadic amusement there is springs from the largely extrinsic introduction of an octogenarian obstetrician who is both deaf and almost blind and who picks out the wrong women, including a crabbed spinster, as the objects of his professional ministrations, along with a female Negro servant whose repartee consists for the most part in stretching her mouth open in such a grin as threatens the security of her very ears.

These two incidental characters and the vaudeville comportment induced in them go a long way toward alleviating such staples as the difficulty in holding servants, the young husband who has the usual comical jitters while his wife is giving birth to a child, the old maid who sits to one side of the stage and peddles the customary ironic remarks, the hypothetical humor of a person trying to adjust himself to a folding bed, the spinster in the old-fashioned, long white nightgown who does her exercises before retiring and indulges in the familiar supposedly convulsing deep breathing at the open window, the comedy servant girl who purloins the whisky and becomes intoxicated, the quarrels between the young married pair, the women in war work, etc.

Any such farce theme that depends for its humor on unavoidably repeated situations — in this instance, as noted, the plethora of baby deliveries — demands a doubled dramaturgical virtuosity and a high comic ingenuity. If they are not present, the repetition becomes monotonous. This is the case with the Ephrons' script. After their first baby, the succeeding babies, whether born or imminent, become as increasingly unamusing as the reiterated joke about effeminacy in *By Jupiter*, which opened the season of 1942–3 as this exhibit closed it.

Especially Interesting Performances

BY JUPITER
Ray Bolger
Nanette Fabray (successor to Constance Moore)

LAUGH, TOWN, LAUGH
Ed Wynn
Smith and Dale

STAR AND GARTER
Bobby Clark

THE MERRY WIDOW
Wilbur Evans

THE NEW MOON
Wilbur Evans

I KILLED THE COUNT
Clarence Derwent

SHOW TIME
George Jessel

HELLO OUT THERE
Eddie Dowling
Julie Haydon

STRIP FOR ACTION
Billy Koud

THE EVE OF ST. MARK
Eddie O'Shea
Mary Rolfe

BEAT THE BAND
Susan Miller

THE DAMASK CHEEK
Flora Robson (except for that resolute charm-smile)
Margaret Douglass

NATIVE SON
Canada Lee

ROSALINDA
Oscar Karlweis

THE SKIN OF OUR TEETH
Tallulah Bankhead

COUNSELLOR–AT–LAW
Jennie Moscowitz

THE PIRATE
Alfred Lunt
Lynn Fontanne

LIFELINE
Whitford Kane

THE WILLOW AND I
Barbara O'Neil

THE THREE SISTERS
Judith Anderson
Katharine Cornell
Edmund Gwenn

FLARE PATH
Doris Patston

THE RUSSIAN PEOPLE
E. A. Krumschmidt

THE DOUGHGIRLS
Virginia Field
Arleen Whelan
William J. Kelly

SOMETHING FOR THE
BOYS
Ethel Merman
Bill Johnson

NINE GIRLS
Barbara Bel Geddes

DARK EYES
Eugenie Leontovich
Ludmilla Toretzka
Jay Fassett

THE PATRIOTS
Cecil Humphreys
Raymond Edward
Johnson

COUNTERATTACK
Morris Carnovsky

THIS ROCK
Billie Burke

HARRIET
Helen Hayes
Rhys Williams

KISS AND TELL
Joan Caulfield

OKLAHOMA!
Joseph Buloff

TOMORROW THE
WORLD
Skippy Homeier

THREE'S A FAMILY
William Wadsworth

Index of Plays

Index of Authors and Composers